TANKER WAR IN THE GULF

TANKER WAR IN THE GULF

Operation *Earnest Will*, Diplomacy and Seapower in Practice

TOM DUFFY

CASEMATE

Pennsylvania & Yorkshire

Published in the United States of America and Great Britain in 2026 by
CASEMATE PUBLISHERS
1950 Lawrence Road, Havertown, PA 19083, USA
and
47 Church Street, Barnsley, S70 2AS, UK

Copyright 2026 © Tom Duffy
Tom Duffy has asserted his right to be identified as author of the work

Hardback Edition: ISBN 978-1-63624-556-0
Digital Edition: ISBN 978-1-63624-557-7

A CIP record for this book is available from the British Library

All rights reserved. No part of this book may be reproduced or transmitted in any form or by any means, electronic or mechanical including photocopying, recording or by any information storage and retrieval system, without permission from the publisher in writing.

The opinions and characterizations in this piece are those of the author and do not necessarily represent those of the U.S. government.

Printed and bound in the United Kingdom by CPI Group (UK) Ltd, Croydon, CR0 4YY
Typeset in India by Lapiz Digital Services, Chennai.

For a complete list of Casemate titles, please contact:

CASEMATE PUBLISHERS (US)
Telephone (610) 853-9131
Fax (610) 853-9146
Email: casemate@casematepublishers.com
www.casematepublishers.com

CASEMATE PUBLISHERS (UK)
Telephone (0)1226 734350
Email: casemate@casemateuk.com
www.casemateuk.com

Front cover: The USS *John Young* shells a pair of Iranian command and control platforms in response to a Iranian missile attack on a Kuwaiti tanker, October 19, 1987. (Official U.S. Navy Photograph—USNI Photo Archives)
Back cover: Crewmembers aboard the USS *Raleigh* use their free time to jog on the ship's flight deck while the ship leads the USS *Hawes* (left) and the GAS KING in the Persian Gulf during convoy number 12, October 21, 1987. (Official U.S. Navy Photograph—USNI Photo Archives)

The Publisher's authorised representative in the EU for product safety is Authorised Rep Compliance Ltd., Ground Floor, 71 Lower Baggot Street, Dublin D02 P593, Ireland.
http://www.arccompliance.com

Contents

Prologue vii
Acknowledgements xi
Timeline xv

1	The Return of Classical Strategy	1
2	The Strategic Context of Operation *Earnest Will*	13
3	Into Harm's Way	33
4	The *Earnest Will* Convoys Begin—July to October 1987	53
5	A Series of Retaliatory Events—October 1987 to April 1988	75
6	To End a War—April 1988 to August 1988	99
7	The Other Navies in the Gulf	123
8	The Outcomes of Operation *Earnest Will*	141
9	Why the Tanker War Matters Today	155

Glossary 169
Appendix 1: Text of UNSCR 598 175
Appendix 2: Text of Russian February 1988 Non-Paper on Proposal for a Naval Presence 179
Endnotes 181
Bibliography 219
Index 225

Prologue

The officers in the wardroom of the USS *Cochrane* asked each other versions of the same question as the ship pitched and yawed in the oily swells of the North Arabian Sea in the summer of 1987: "What are we *doing* here?" The ship had deployed to the Persian Gulf before, part of what had become routine deployments to the region after the 1979 Iranian hostage crisis, but this deployment was different.

The wardroom table was long and rectangular, welded to the deck and running athwartships and perpendicular to the rest of the ship. The surgical lights hidden in the overhead attested to the structure's backup function in time of war—this was to be the ship's operating table. *Cochrane* was no stranger to a high operating tempo, and there were daily reminders of potential conflict. Indeed, months prior to this very short-notice deployment, the ship had been operating in the Sea of Okhotsk, getting overflown by Russian aircraft and doing its part for the Maritime Strategy.

But this deployment was different. The ship had four days' notice that it was leaving its Japanese homeport of Yokosuka, bound for the Middle East. The executive officer advised those with apartments ashore to pay ahead for six months and to find a way to extend that if necessary. As the ship backed away from the pier, those onboard were surprised to see a number of their shipmates waving them goodbye—the ship's captain, a decorated veteran of the riverine war in Vietnam, had taken the precaution of "bottom blowing" the short-timers and the less dependable members of the crew and leaving them ashore. As the ship rapidly headed south, the operations officer, another former riverine sailor, took to reminding the younger officers that there were only two things to remember about war: Rule One was that people died in war, and Rule Two was that there was no changing Rule One. The 37 U.S. sailors killed in a missile attack against the USS *Stark* the previous month were an ever-present reminder of the stakes of getting it wrong.

In a sense, the officers knew *what* the ship was doing off the coast of Iran in June 1987—*Cochrane* was tethered to the aircraft carrier USS

Constellation, providing a floating visual reference on a featureless sea to pilots as they landed their aircraft on the carrier's deck. *Cochrane* was also acting as *Constellation*'s close-in protective "shotgun"; with two five-inch, rapid-fire guns and medium-range surface-to-air missile system, *Cochrane* was there to protect the aircraft carrier from any Iranian aircraft or missile attacks that had somehow made it through the battle group's concentric outer lines of defense. The cynics among the crew believed that the relatively elderly *Cochrane*'s role was in fact that of "missile sponge"—surging ahead to take the hit to protect the highly valued carrier.

The ship's officers and crew knew their jobs; they knew what they were doing. Their question was really, "*Why* are we doing this?" But that's not an appropriate topic for the U.S. military, which prides itself on being "apolitical."[1] It was, however, an appropriate question for the newly politically appointed Secretary of the Navy James Webb, a highly decorated Vietnam War combat veteran and the author of a number of books known for addressing difficult questions.

In the aftermath of the attack on the *Stark*, Webb pestered Secretary of Defense Casper Weinberger with a series of difficult questions: "How will we know when we have won? What is victory? Why are we getting involved in the middle of a war in the Persian Gulf?"[2]

In retrospect—and perhaps only in retrospect—we now know the answers to Webb's questions. America in 1987 was becoming involved in the "Tanker War"; an offshoot of the larger Iran–Iraq War, a large-scale conflict dragging on since 1980 that had recently expanded from land battles to increasing attacks on the oil tankers vital to the economies of the region. America's portion of the Tanker War—known as Operation *Earnest Will*—turned out to be a victory at the tactical, operational, and strategic levels of war—the only clear-cut win for the United States in the Middle East over the last 50 years. *Earnest Will* was not intended to end the eight-year-long Iran–Iraq War, but—as a result of the *Vincennes* incident—it ended up providing the excuse that concluded that conflict. The U.S. presence largely saw off the Soviet threat to the Persian Gulf during a time when the Cold War was still a major concern. And, in stark contrast to later land operations in Iraq and Afghanistan, *Earnest Will* unquestionably achieved its policy goals, leaving a political situation favorable to American interests.

The U.S. intervention in the Tanker War is a vivid reminder of the roles that chance and contingency play in war. While some of the countries involved may have had ideological structures with which they viewed the world—the revolutionary Iranians imbued with their view of political Islam, the Reagan administration seeking to contain Communism—the Tanker War itself lurched from event to event rather than unfolding according to any plan. The overall outcome was favorable to the United States, but those results were much more attributable to actions and individuals than they were to any blueprint or ideology.

English military historian Sir Michael Howard, founder of the "war studies" approach to the study of international relations, proposed "three general rules of study" when considering "The Use and Abuse of Military History."[3] Those rules can be applied to Operation *Earnest Will*, which represents a discrete, two-year campaign—one that can be usefully explored "in width, in depth, and in context."

This relatively recent but little-remembered conflict represents a time when America won its wars as well as its battles. It is a reminder of the options that seapower provides to America, an understanding whose importance grows as some contemplate a conflict with the People's Republic of China. And it is evidence that the current American "way of war," hobbled by an Army-derived, land-centric "joint" doctrine that struggles to move beyond the operational level of conflict, is not the only way to fight and think about war.

Acknowledgements

Lord Tennyson captured the operator's dilemma when he wrote of those engaged in the *Charge of the Light Brigade*: "Theirs was not to reason why/ Theirs was but to do and die." Discerning the rationale for such actions often makes most sense in retrospect; hence, books like *The Reason Why*, in which writers afterward seek to comprehend completed events.[1]

I have always found writers such as Cecil Woodham-Smith inspiring and, like her, I am neither a credentialed historian nor do I come from academe. My background is that of practitioner, with decades of service in the U.S. Navy and the U.S. Foreign Service. My interest in the Tanker War comes from being one of the early participants as a naval officer and subsequently serving in the Persian Gulf region as an American diplomat. As a now retired naval officer and diplomat, I need to emphasize that the opinions and characterizations in this book are those of the author and do not necessarily represent those of the U.S. government.

Home on leave from the Navy over the holidays in 1987, after my small part in the operation, I was pinioned by my Uncle George at a family gathering: "But why were you there? What on earth were you thinking?"

Uncle George had more credibility than most to ask such questions. A retired firefighter, he had been an infantryman with the U.S. Army's 10th Mountain Division during its slog up the Italian peninsula in 1944, crediting his survival to the typing skills that kept him out of nightly patrols if not out of living in the front line. In later life, he would write pointed letters to the president in the White House on foreign policy; I always lived in dread of having one of those letters come back to me for a draft response when I was working at the State Department, as he tended to ask a lot of good, hard questions.

In leaving the Navy, having served as USS *Cochrane*'s missile and fire-control officer in the opening phases of Operation *Earnest Will*, I applied to study for the MA in War Studies at King's College London. I recently found my draft application letter to King's—and in it was Uncle George's question: why *were* we in the Persian Gulf in the late 1980s? I wrote my graduating "extended essay" on *Earnest Will* and then left the subject untouched, going on to rejoin the Navy to work on the Maritime Strategy in the Pentagon as part of OP-603, the Navy Staff's "Strategic Concepts Group," and then on to a 32-year career in the United States Foreign Service, where I spent most of my time working either in the Middle East or on United Nations affairs, especially concerning the Security Council.

Toward the end of my Foreign Service career, the State Department assigned me on two separate occasions to teach about national security strategy at the U.S. National War College in Washington, D.C. During my brief foray into academe—where, alas, I encountered all too few military historians—I began to present papers at academic conferences. A call for papers at the 2023 McMullen Naval History Symposium reminded me of my long-shelved *Earnest Will* paper, which I updated and presented at the Naval Academy in Annapolis in September 2023. I then built upon that paper for a presentation at a conference on "NATO's Maritime Strategies and Naval Operations since 1985," cohosted by the Institute for Security Policy at Kiel University (ISPK) and the Bundeswehr Centre of Military History and Social Sciences (ZMSBw) in Laboe, Germany, in March 2024. This book originates from both of those papers. I am grateful to my colleagues from King's in the 1980s, who suggested the topic for my "extended essay," as well as to Captain B. J. Armstrong, U.S. Navy (USN) of the U.S. Naval Academy, Dr. Sebastian Bruns of ISPK, and Commander Dr. Christian Jentzsch of ZMSBw for the opportunities to present. The presentation in Laboe featured Professor Geoffrey Till in the audience, an occasion for some trepidation as he had been the King's College supervisor for my original 1989 work. It strikes me that this book is more War Studies than straight military or naval (or even diplomatic) history, and I owe a debt to Professor Till and to Michael Howard for originating the War Studies approach in the first place.

In particular, the focus at King's College on Clausewitz proved to be very helpful throughout my subsequent career. Back in the 1980s, prior to the introduction of the BA in War Studies and the massive expansion of the MA program, we 40-odd MA students at King's spent the first month reading *On War* cover-to-cover, were quizzed regularly by the entire War Studies faculty, and then returned to Clausewitz in seemingly every subsequent topic. I had Professor Brian Bond as the intimidating convenor of a regular "pastoral supervision" session, in which he tried to further educate nine MA aspirants in the finer points of applied military history. Bond wrote about his overall orientation in his memoirs: "What really stimulated my imagination however were the strategic ideas of Clausewitz and Corbett which really opened up an exciting new way to study military history." This approach was also evident in Professor Till's presentations, and the influence of both historians is evident in the pages of this book.[2]

As a diplomatic practitioner for the next 30 years, I found the King's experience extremely useful. First, while use of history by the military is fairly well-known, it is not as obvious that diplomats make extensive use of history in our everyday work, affecting everything from background memos, to contextualizing reporting cables, to informing negotiating strategies. Second, King's emphasis on Clausewitz helped me to make sense of the war zones I later found myself working in and served as a useful discriminator when it came to future colleagues—if they knew their Clausewitz, they had generally also thought deeply about other aspects of war. By contrast, those who had only superficially studied *On War* or, worse yet, knew nothing beyond the Clausewitz quotes found in other books could be relied upon to be superficial in other aspects as well.

Professor Till emphasized the works of Julian Corbett, and I'd like to thank those behind the recent Corbett 100 project—especially Dr. James W. E. Smith of King's College London and Dr. David Kohnen of the U.S. Naval War College; this book's points on Corbett and limited war come from a paper I delivered at the Corbett 100 session at Naval War College in Newport in 2022. Professor Donald Stoker, formerly of the Naval War College Program at the Naval Postgraduate School and the author of several works on Clausewitz, provided the kernel of the idea that the American concept of limited war as applying to means rather than ends is a significant factor in why the United States has been winning battles but losing wars. My former colleague at the National War College, J. Furman Daniel III, author of a recent volume on Clausewitz, helped to ensure my Clausewitz references met the mark.

While working in OP-603 immediately after graduating from King's, I began studying with the Fleet Seminar extension program of the Naval War College, which—at least at that time—was teaching the same national security studies program to its junior officers as to its senior officers. The timing in all of this was important—when I later taught at the National War College, I was instructing senior officers (colonels and captains)—who were often encountering Clausewitz and strategy for the very first time. I, by contrast, had that exposure very early in my professional career and in my late twenties—indeed, I graduated via correspondence course from the Naval War College during my first Foreign Service tour, dodging car bombs in Bogotá, Colombia. That sequence—Fleet/King's/OP-603/Naval War College/three decades in the diplomatic service—meant that I was testing out in the field what I had learned as a junior officer and diplomat—wondering what on earth was going on, ready to constantly question my superiors and, even more importantly, being subject to acerbic questions from my bosses that had me reviewing and reformulating my strategic studies education from the very start. I could spout theory to my bosses all I wanted, but I was being corrected in real time by regional and subject matter experts whom I greatly respected. In my later teaching at the National War College, I found that the senior officer students were not so greatly favored—it is much easier to recognize you don't have the answers when you are a lieutenant than when you are a colonel or a captain.[3] I hope that an air of informed skepticism is present in the book, in which, to quote Corbett "the aim has been to give in narrative form and free from technicalities an intelligible view not only of the operations themselves but of their mutual connection and meaning, the policy which dictated them, their relation to military and diplomatic action, and the difficulties and cross-currents which in some cases delayed their success and robbed them of the expected results."[4]

Thanks also to the curators and archivists at the U.S. Naval Institute, especially Brendan Reicherter and their colleagues at the Navy Department Library, History and Archives Division, Naval History and Heritage Command, particularly Matt Proietta. All of us owe a debt of gratitude to Declan Ingram for the charts and maps in the book in addition to his creation of the cover, which encapsulated the violence and the quotidian routine of the war.

Thanks finally to my wife Anne and my children Tommy and Elena for their patience as I was putting this together and especially to my mother, Maureen Habel, who as a writer and editor of nursing journals, was merciless in demanding clarity when writing. May this pass her inspection. Any errors in fact or interpretation are solely attributable to me.

Timeline

1979

- January 16: Shah leaves Iran.
- February 1: Ayatollah Khomeini returns to Iran
- March 30–31: Countrywide referendum votes for the establishment of the Islamic Republic of Iran.
- November 4: Iranians seize U.S. Embassy in Tehran and take 52 American diplomatic personnel hostage.
- December 24: Soviet Union invades Afghanistan.

1980

- January 23: American State of the Union Address articulates the Carter Doctrine.
- September 22: Iraq launches a large-scale invasion of Iran.
- October 7: Iraq declares Persian Gulf along the Iranian coast north of 29.03°N, a prohibited war zone, and begins attacks on Iranian ships.

1982

- May 30: Iraqi bombs strike Turkish oil tanker *Atlas I* at Kharg Island; the first tanker to be hit during the Tanker War.
- December 18: Iraqi *Exocet* hits Greek tanker *Scapmount*; the first tanker to be written off.

1983

- October 23: Bombing of U.S. USMC Barracks in Beirut.

1984

- February 7: U.S. Marines begin withdrawal from Beirut.
- February 14: Iraqi *Exocet* hits and sinks Liberian tanker *Neptunia*, becoming the first tanker to sink in the Tanker War.
- May: Iranians begin attacking ships of countries supporting Iraq.

1986

- February 9: Iranians capture the al-Faw peninsula.
- November 2–4: GCC Summit.
- December 10: Kuwait approaches the United States and the Soviet Union about reflagging tankers.

1987

- March 7: United States announces Operation *Earnest Will*.
- May 17: An Iraqi jet hits USS *Stark* with two *Exocet* missiles.
- July 20: UNSCR 598 adopted.
- July 22: First *Earnest Will* mission.
- July 24: *Bridgeton* hits mine off Kuwait Harbor.
- August 10: *Texaco Caribbean* hits mine in the Gulf of Oman.
- August 11: France and the United Kingdom (separately) announce deployment of minesweepers to the Persian Gulf.
- August 15: A mine destroys *Anita* in the Gulf of Oman.
- September 21–22: *Iran Ajr* captured in the act of minelaying.
- October 8: U.S. special operations forces engage Iranians at Middle Shoals.

- October 18: Iranian-fired *Silkworm* missile hits *Sea Isle City* in Kuwait Harbor.
- October 19: U.S. forces destroy Rostam oil platform in response to *Sea Isle City* strike in Operation *Nimble Archer*.

1988

- April 14: USS *Samuel B. Roberts* strikes mine in the Persian Gulf.
- April 18: U.S. forces destroy Sassan and Sirri oil platforms and half of Iran's operational navy in Operation *Praying Mantis*.
- July 3: USS *Vincennes* shoots down Iran Air 655.
- July 18: Iran accepts UNSCR 598.
- August 8: Iran and Iraq agree to a cease-fire.

CHAPTER I

The Return of Classical Strategy

> You just don't in the 21st century behave in 19th-century fashion by invading another country on some completely trumped-up pre-text.
>
> —U.S. SECRETARY OF STATE JOHN KERRY ON THE INITIAL RUSSIAN INVASION OF UKRAINE (2014)

Why bother with the classical strategists? What do these books, written 100 or even 200 years ago, have to do with our modern, 21st-century world?

What if we are *not* living in a modern world, but simply the *world*? What if the immediate post-Cold War world is *not* the pattern for future? A *Financial Times* article reviewing the World Economic Forum (WEF) and its annual, celebrity-strewn forum in Davos, Switzerland observed:

> Many of the assumptions that underpin a Davos view of the world are a product of a very specific period in time. WEF is a triumph of a mindset about the nature of progress that has dominated most western politics since the end of the Cold War. The great philosophical and political questions of human life are settled, it says, and the future will be based on [a] ladder of technology with commerce scaling to better humanity from here on in.[1]

What if those questions are *not* settled, and what if Plato was right when he remarked that "only the dead have seen an end to war?" It is a question as pertinent to Russia's activities in Ukraine as it is to the hundreds of thousands who died in connection with the Iran–Iraq War of the 1980s—of which the Tanker War was, as the U.S. Navy recognized at the time, a "sideshow."[2] How do we make sense of this all?

The Tanker War occurred just before one of those periodic twilights in American maritime strategic thinking. U.S. Chief of Naval Operations Admiral Frank Kelso in his 1990 congressional confirmation testimony, two years after the end of the Tanker War, decried the need for a maritime *strategy*—famously putting it "on the shelf" for the time being—and instead identified the need for broader national *policy*.[3] Admiral Kelso was technically correct—an overarching national post-Cold War policy was required for any implementing strategy to make sense—but he then went on during his four years serving as the Navy's top admiral to champion "Total Quality Leadership" (TQL), an attempt to convert management guru W. Edwards Deming's industrial "Total Quality Management" into how the U.S. Navy did business.[4] Kelso's focus—after all what the admiral finds interesting, the officer corps finds fascinating—redirected the bandwidth for Navy strategic thinking into TQL implementation, with questionable outcomes for future ship procurement and thinking about war.[5] To be fair, Kelso's TQL orientation found a receptive audience in America in the 1990s, which was searching for a post-Cold War "peace dividend." Further, the word strategy itself had been so widened from its initial military meaning as to become little more than shorthand for purposeful planning.

British military historian Sir Michael Howard cautioned that "the term 'strategy' is now generally used to describe the use of available resources to gain any objective, from winning at bridge to selling soap," and felt compelled to stress that he was writing of strategy in the "traditional sense": looking at the role "played by force, or the threat of force, in the international system."[6] Sir Lawrence Freedman, in his magisterial book *Strategy: A History*, differentiated between "strategies of force," "strategy from below," and "strategies from above." In Freedman's telling, the first is associated with classical military usage, the second with domestic political movements, and the third with business elites.[7] Beatrice Heuser wrote of the need to highlight "Strategy with a capital 'S'—the link between political aims and the use of force, or its threat …"[8] Scottish military historian Sir Hew Strachan felt compelled to emphasize "the lost meaning of strategy," arguing that the purpose of strategy "is to make war usable by the state" and that it exists to enable the state to "if need be, use force to fulfill its political objectives."[9]

It may be significant that none of these writers are American. There are different schools of thought about war and strategy—and these differences matter. In the United States, strategy is often associated with business leadership and management. A seminal article on the topic, "What Is Strategy?" published in the *Harvard Business Review*, is noteworthy for its comprehensive review of strategy that includes absolutely no references to either war or violence.[10] That approach makes sense in a business context—Walmart is not generally concerned with a competitor shelling customers in its parking lots—but the principally commercial use of the word serves to broaden the use of the term so widely that it loses important meaning. Similarly, the U.S. government is known for having a "war on poverty," a "war on inflation," and a "war on drugs"; American organizations and companies devise marketing and fundraising strategies. The practice is found in Europe as well: two professors from INSEAD in France are notable for their book *Blue Ocean Strategy*, which focuses neither on navies nor the maritime.[11] While using the words "strategy" and "war" are understandable as motivational rhetorical devices, their indiscriminate use has rendered the words effectively meaningless, and this lack of precision has political consequences.

The Russian 2014 and 2022 invasions of Ukraine remind us there is a separate and recognizable human activity called war, in which organized violence is used to achieve political results. For the American national security establishment, the Cold War abstractions of potential nuclear conflict followed by the attractions of the ahistorical, post-Cold War unipolar moment served to blind many regarding the fundamental meaning of strategy. The consequences over at least the last 50 years have been a string of American tactical and operational victories unconnected to strategic success, and the way we think about and talk about war and strategy are contributing to that unfortunate outcome.

Michael Howard felt compelled to ask—over half a century ago—about the value of studying the "classical strategists" even then, and the answer has become no easier with the passage of time.[12] In a world that now has email, the internet, and an entire intangible "cyber domain" of warfare, what possible use could these old writers have for today's problems? The challenge of new domains is not a new one—Howard was exploring the utility of classical strategists when dealing with an earlier "new" domain: that of nuclear weapons. He was the founder of an overall "war studies" approach to international relations, which he described as "distinguished by our roots in traditional theory and history from the 'behaviorism' and abstraction that characterized American teaching of the subject."[13]

Howard captured the distinctive aspect of pre-nuclear age strategic thinkers:

> It need hardly be said that students of strategy have generally assumed that military force is a necessary element in international affairs. Before World War I, there were few who questioned even whether it was desirable. After 1918, many regretted its necessity and saw their function as being to ensure that it should be used as economically, and as rarely, as possible. After 1945, an even greater proportion devoted themselves to examine, not how wars should be fought, but how they could be prevented, and the study of strategy merged into that of arms control, disarmament and peace-keeping. There the "classical strategists" found themselves working with scholars of a different kind; men who believed that the element of force was not a necessary part of international intercourse, but could be eliminated by an application of the methodology of the social sciences.[14]

In the first part of the 21st century, those later thinkers would appear to have triumphed, and Western leaders find the "element of force" inconceivable in international relations.[15] Actions such as the Russian invasions of Ukraine therefore come as a real shock, and leaders similarly struggle to conceive of how competition with China will play out. As we grapple with a *post*-post-Cold War world, a return to writers who lived in a pre-nuclear world of multipolarity in which force was consciously used as a policy tool has much to recommend it. Howard himself chose to focus on "thinkers who assume that the element of force exists in international relations, that it can and must be intelligently controlled, but that it cannot be totally eliminated."[16]

Two of those thinkers continue to stand out today: Carl von Clausewitz, a Prussian soldier and onetime director of the Kriegsakademie, whose best-known work *On War* was published, incomplete and posthumously, in 1835; and Sir Julian Corbett, a British lawyer and naval war college lecturer, whose best-known work *Some Principles of Maritime Strategy* was published in 1912. One might think that—surely—there are more up to date references and thinkers, but there are at least two reasons to focus on these writers.

Sir Julian Corbett, British maritime strategist who expanded Clausewitz's idea of limited war and then explained why limited wars are available only to seapowers. (From *Some Principles of Maritime Strategy*, 1911, courtesy of D. M. Schurman)

First, it is useful to consider what makes these two thinkers stand out. In working through Clausewitz's long and sometimes dense work—remembering that the entire work was organized, assembled, edited, and published by his familial survivors after his unexpected death at age 51—several themes about war jump out: chance, violence, and, above all, politics. If one reads subsequent writers who tout formulas or weapons systems guaranteed to win wars, propose ways to fight wars in which no people get hurt or killed, or, above all, make statements such as, "We need to get the politics out of war," then one can be reasonably sure they have either never studied Clausewitz or have only done so superficially. He is, after all, famous for being "more quoted than actually read."[17] Someone familiar with Clausewitz would recognize that *all* wars are "wars of choice"; the decision to mount a defense rather than to simply surrender is *always* ultimately a political decision.[18] Additionally, Clausewitz wrote much more about history—*On War* only represents some 20 percent of his overall writings. Someone who has persevered through a study of Clausewitz is likely to have a greater respect for the intersection of history and strategy—for, as he put it, theory "must have been derived from military history, or at least checked against it."[19]

Corbett—another extensive writer on history—stands out because of his focus on the maritime and his grounding in Clausewitz. He is easier to read, having started out as a lawyer and then having moved onto a successful career as a novelist and naval historian. Corbett was writing as a senior advisor to the British Royal Navy as it grappled with maintaining Britain's global leadership, the advent of new technology, and a looming conflict that would metastasize into World War I. Corbett—who came from a maritime power—was also able to think about the role of navies and the sea in a way that eluded Clausewitz, who from start to finish focused on the continent of Europe.

Second, it is helpful to consider the question of whether it is worth the time to read old books. American strategist Bernard Brodie, addressing "The Continuing Relevance of *On War*" in one of the prefatory chapters to the enormously influential 1976 translation of Clausewitz's *On War*, directly confronted this question of the utility of reading old writers. Writing about other classic books, he allowed that not all old books deserve continued attention: "First, however great they were in their own times they are not particularly relevant to ours and second, that whatever wisdom they do contain which is relevant to our own times has no doubt been absorbed and exploited by later writers."[20]

Brodie then drops the hammer: "Clausewitz's work stands out among those very few older books which have presented profound and original insights that have *not* been adequately absorbed in later literature."[21] Michael Howard gets at some of the reasons behind this lack of uptake in his points on the predominance of social scientists in what passes for modern strategic discourse. Brodie complains of a modern "school of thinkers who are allegedly experts in military strategy and who are certainly specialists in military studies but who know virtually nothing of military history ... and who seem not to care about their ignorance."[22]

A review of more recent writings would seem to further demonstrate that Clausewitz has "*not* been adequately absorbed in later literature." One contemporary example is the focus on the "gray zone," a situation in which putative opponents "seek to secure their objectives while minimizing the scope and scale of actual combat."[23] Given the role of the political use of violence in that definition, Clausewitz would likely have simply called it "war." Recondite and abstruse terms such as "the gray zone" and "hybrid warfare" are instead "just another example of the strategic studies community needlessly confusing itself by generating new terminology to replace what is not broken."[24] Hew Strachan argues that even prominent civilian defense writers have been mistaken: "Martin van Creveld, John Keegan and Mary Kaldor, among others, have argued that war traditionally defined, that is, war between states conducted by armed forces, is obsolete."[25] Recalling that Strachan specifically associates strategy with the use of force, he continues:

> The conclusion might be that strategy is dead, that it was a creature of its times, that it carried specific connotations for a couple of centuries, but that the world has now moved on, and has concluded that the concept is no longer useful. That would be a historically illiterate response.[26]

It is therefore worthwhile to seek a more historically literate response and a reconsideration of the Tanker War and what it reveals about strategy—especially maritime strategy—is worth the time and effort.

***

Conflict can be divided into two categories—*limited* and *unlimited* wars—but it matters which aspect of war one is limiting. In the modern world, we generally think of limited vs. unlimited as applying to *ways* and *means*—in other words, an unlimited war is one in which all conceivable and available weapons are widely used, such as mass mobilization, carpet bombing, or nuclear weapons.[27]

Clausewitz defined it differently—when he spoke of different types of war, he focused instead on *ends*—the idea that "war can be of two kinds ... either the objective is to *overthrow the enemy*—to render him politically helpless or militarily impotent ... or *merely to occupy some of his frontier districts* so that we can annex them or use them for bargaining at the peace negotiations."[28] The difference in outlook is significant: a focus on ways and means tops out at the operational level of war; a focus on ends brings in the strategic level of war, the level that revolves around the political rationales for which the war is being fought. The operational level focuses on winning individual battles and larger campaigns; the strategic level focuses on winning wars.

Clausewitz came late to the realization of the importance of differentiated ends in war; his points are contained on two pages in one of the last parts of his final, unfinished, book.²⁹ Corbett consciously built on Clausewitz, coined the terms limited and unlimited wars in order to better illustrate Clausewitz's differentiation, and then made the concept of limited war a critical element in the opening 72 pages of *Some Principles of Maritime Strategy*. Corbett went on to describe how limited wars can only really be fought by seapowers. Professor Kevin McCranie of the U.S. Naval Academy observed that "Corbett's adaptation of Clausewitz's limited war theory is among the most important of his theoretical legacies."³⁰ The Naval War College's Michael Handel credited Corbett with going beyond Clausewitz and articulating "a new concept of limited war."³¹

Corbett specifically argued that:

> Limited war is only permanently possible to island Powers or between Powers which are separated by sea, and then only when the Power desiring limited war is able to command the sea to such a degree as to be able not only to isolate the distant object, but also to render impossible the invasion of his home territory.³²

Corbett emphasized the importance of geography, noting that in cases of "war between contiguous continental states ... we get no real generic difference between limited and unlimited war."³³ and that, in the case of land battles, "there will be no strategical obstacle to [the enemy's] being able to use his whole force."³⁴ While the initial political aim in a land conflict may be limited, the physical proximity and availability of reinforcements can create their own escalatory dynamic, a condition in which—as Corbett phrased it—"it is in the power of either belligerent, as Clausewitz himself saw, to pass to unlimited war."³⁵

Corbett goes so far as to say "the true meaning and highest military value of what we call command of the sea" is the ability to fight limited wars.³⁶ Corbett argues that, in case of "two belligerents hav[ing] a common frontier"—a classic continental conundrum—either or both countries can "pass at will to unlimited war."³⁷ He goes on to emphasize that, in the case of insular or maritime states, "the belligerents had no contiguous frontiers, and this point is vital."³⁸

Corbett was writing in the period just prior to World War I, but his observations apply to later wars—and directly to the Tanker War which, at least for the United States and its participation in that conflict featured a continental power on one side—Iran—and a maritime power on the other—America. While Iran and Iraq are "contiguous continental states," Iran and the United States had "no contiguous frontiers," and this point did indeed turn out to be "vital." *Earnest Will*'s success was not simply due to its limited political objectives. Instead, success was also linked to the ways and means in which the war was fought—at sea.

***

Since the 1980s, the United States has engaged in military operations in the Middle East with both limited *and* unlimited ends. At least three of them resulted in American strategic defeats, and those defeats were intrinsically tied to the unlimited objectives of their wars.

Operation *Desert Storm* in 1991 was unquestionably a tactical and operational success for the United States and allied forces seeking to push Iraq out of Kuwait—but, in retrospect, it was only an opening campaign and not a completed war. Indeed, *Desert Storm* represents a clear case of confusing victory at the operational level of war with victory at the strategic level of war—a bit like a successful team leaving the field before the game is actually over. *Desert Storm* was a conflict that started out as a limited war—expelling Iraq from Kuwait—and turned into an unlimited war—overthrowing Iraqi leader Saddam Hussein. It is a reminder of how war itself can perform as an independent actor that changes the aims and the expectations of the participants once the violence starts. The actual fighting of war, or sometimes even just the preparations, can double back to affect the policies that seek to instrumentalize war in the first place. The mutation of objectives that is often derided as "mission creep" is in fact inherent in any protracted conflict.

The George H. W. Bush administration emphasized in public statements that it did not intend to push all the way to Baghdad in 1991 and overthrow Saddam—in other words, the articulated war aim was that of a limited war focused solely on pushing Iraqi forces from Kuwait. However, it is clear that the first Bush administration was planning from the start for Saddam's removal—in reality, an unlimited political aim. Planning for early airstrikes targeted Saddam's palaces, and the Iraqi leader was seen as a lawful target; he, after all, "wore a military uniform, sported a sidearm, and commanded Iraq's forces with absolute authority."[39] The United States dropped propaganda leaflets before and during the war, urging Iraqi troops to overthrow Saddam.[40] One of the intended messages of the preparatory bombing campaign in Iraq itself was "Hey, your lights will come back on as soon as you get rid of Saddam."[41]

The Bush administration was able to avoid making further, farther-reaching public statements because, in large part, it believed Saddam would fall without the use of any further military means. James Baker, U.S. secretary of state during the 1991 war, later commented, "We did not think—the president nor any of us thought at the time that Saddam would continue in power having suffered such a resounding defeat."[42] President Bush later said that he had "miscalculated" in assuming that "Saddam could not survive a humiliating defeat."[43] The Bush administration and its allies did not drive north to Baghdad in 1991 primarily because it appeared such a risky move would be unnecessary. Whatever the rhetoric at the time, though, it is clear that Saddam's ouster was an unarticulated war aim for the West, even if the George H. W. Bush administration had no effective plan for actually guaranteeing Saddam's downfall.

It also seems clear that Saddam himself recognized *Desert Storm* as a politically unlimited war. As he phrased it in a 1992: "After their experiences with us, which did not achieve its ends regardless of the withdrawal from Kuwait, they might wonder how much force they need to deploy this time to achieve what they failed to do the last time."[44] An exhaustive review of captured Iraqi documents following the 2003 war concluded: "Saddam defined losing in simple and personal terms—being removed from power. Using Saddam's framework of understanding, he did not lose the 1991 confrontation."[45]

The American effort to topple Saddam remained a constant through the 1990s. American intelligence agencies conducted significant covert action programs throughout the decade, promoting an Iraqi coup against Saddam. In 1997, Secretary of State Madeline Albright defended continued sanctions on Iraq, suggesting that only "a change in Iraq's government could lead to a change in U.S. policy."[46] The United States Congress in 1998 passed the Iraq Liberation Act, saying that "it should be the policy of the United States to seek to remove the Saddam Hussein regime from power in Iraq and to replace it with a democratic government."[47]

Operation *Iraqi Freedom* in 2003 explicitly had unlimited political ends—inherent in the name of the operation itself—and a consciously articulated war aim of deposing Iraqi leader Saddam Hussein. The operation morphed from a hunt for Weapons of Mass Destruction to the establishment of democracy to countering terrorism, all the while targeting Saddam and replacing the Ba'ath party. However, in the end, as a comprehensive 2019 U.S. Army War College study of the 2003 U.S. intervention concluded: "an emboldened and expansionist Iran appears to be the only victor."[48]

Operation *Enduring Freedom* in Afghanistan—again, the unlimited end is inherent in the operation's codename—sought not simply the capture of those responsible for the 9/11 attacks but also to replace the Taliban and transform Afghanistan's society. The operation culminated in a humiliating Western withdrawal from the country in 2021, with the Taliban returned to power, after the expenditure of billions of dollars and euros and the death, injury, and displacement of hundreds of thousands of people. The problems were baked into the approach, with some warning against depending on unlimited war in the first place to handle the threat from Afghanistan, but an American tendency to view war in terms of ways and means rather than ends left little other politically realistic choices.[49]

***

Earnest Will, in stark contrast to these other three operations, never explicitly nor implicitly sought the overthrow of the revolutionary Iranian regime, no matter how desirable that goal may have been or how deep the Iranian governmental antipathy toward America. *Earnest Will*'s goal was to stop Iranian attacks on merchant shipping; that's how the United States would know it had won that war.[50] It is worth recalling that the Reagan administration was not averse to overthrowing governments—replacing the Sandinistas in Nicaragua was, after all, the root of the Iran–Contra scandal. However, the administration did not take actions in 1987 and 1988 to overthrow Ayatollah Khomeini, but rather to blunt Iranian efforts.[51]

In looking at U.S. military operations in the Middle East, it can be argued that the only clear-cut victory the United States has enjoyed—victory being defined as sustainable political outcomes on terms favorable to the United States—has been the limited war of *Earnest Will*. In the words of a recent Naval War College Review article: "Participants and historians judge the operation to have been a success."[52] In the words of one contemporary account, "US intervention in the Gulf not only worked, it was directly (though not solely) responsible for the end of the bloodiest and longest conventional war since World War II."[53] The fact that it *was* a limited war, and that it was fought with navies, was key to that success.

Earnest Will represents a compelling example of a classic *maritime* strategy—actions taken at sea intended to influence events on land. There were moves to expand the conflict ashore in Iran—indeed, a U.S. four-star admiral advocating such an approach ended up getting fired as a result—but land operations in connection with *Earnest Will* are counterfactual speculation. In the actual event, the violence occurred on and over the water.

As we digest the lessons of recent failed operations on land—especially in Afghanistan (2001–21) and Iraq (1990–91, 2003–11)—it is worth recalling that there is "something uniquely cost-effective about seapower as compared to landpower."[54] Given pending budget choices and the threat of conflict with the People's Republic of China (PRC), it is an observation worth keeping in mind. It is worth the time to review the Iran–Iraq War, the Tanker War, and Operation *Earnest Will* in detail, as they reveal the often-overlooked options that seapower provides, while at the same time serving as a reminder of the violence and chance that differentiate war from all other human activities.[55]

CHAPTER 2

The Strategic Context of Operation *Earnest Will*

> We would abdicate our role as a naval power, and we would open opportunities for the Soviets to move into this chokepoint of the free world's oil flow. In a word: If we don't do the job, the Soviets will.
> —PRESIDENT RONALD REAGAN, JUNE 15, 1987[1]

No military operation occurs in politics-free isolation—as much as the practitioners might desire it—and Operation *Earnest Will* was no different. The use of American military force in the Persian Gulf in 1987 and 1988 only makes sense in the context of a swirl of political drivers. The question "Why are we here?" touched on political topics not widely—or perhaps even usefully—discussed on U.S. Navy ships and followed an ultimately circular route: the Cold War, to reliance on regional proxies, to the Iranian Revolution, to the Iran–Iraq War, and then back to the Cold War.

The U.S.–Soviet confrontation was global—from an American perspective, NATO and the north Atlantic were always part of a much larger arc of competition. Some of the earliest incidents in the Cold War began in Iran in the 1940s, and a concern over Soviet activities in the Persian Gulf and the Indian Ocean were a long-standing factor in American defense planning. In the words of a four-star U.S. Army general concerned over the Indian Ocean writing in 1970: "The Soviet naval threat is not a 'possibility,' it is a present, real, direct, immediate danger."[2] The December 1979 Soviet invasion of Afghanistan prompted the declaration by U.S. President Jimmy Carter of the Carter Doctrine in his January 1980 State of the Union address:

> Let our position be absolutely clear: An attempt by any outside force to gain control of the Persian Gulf region will be regarded as an assault on the vital interests of the United States of America, and such an assault will be repelled by any means necessary, including military force.[3]

Carter warned in that same speech: "The Soviet effort to dominate Afghanistan has brought Soviet military forces to within 300 miles of the

Indian Ocean and close to the Straits of Hormuz, a waterway through which most of the world's oil must flow." He continued that the situation "demands collective efforts to meet this new threat to security in the Persian Gulf and in Southwest Asia."

Yet, just as the threat from the Soviet Union to the Persian Gulf appeared to be increasing, the collective efforts the United States had been counting upon to maintain security in the region were collapsing. The United Kingdom after World War II, and especially after the failed 1956 Suez intervention, reconsidered all of its previously imperial responsibilities: "What had seemed to the late Victorians romantically splendid seemed to mid-century Britons perfectly nonsensical."[4] The British announcement of the pullback of their military forces "east of Suez"—announced in 1968 and completed by 1971—began the 1970s by withdrawing an important stabilizing element from the Gulf and ended up enabling Imperial Iran.[5]

American policy in response to the British pullback—compelled after the debacle in Vietnam to avoid deploying large numbers of American forces to areas other than Europe—was to look for friendly countries to shoulder the security burden. The idea—known as the Nixon Doctrine—was to outsource security requirements, believing that cooperative regional powers could act as proxies to help ensure the security of areas of interest to the United States. The British came to a similar conclusion regarding the Persian Gulf, encouraging the unification of what became the United Arab Emirates (UAE) as well as a balance of power to be maintained between Iran and Saudi Arabia.[6] Even then, the British chose to look the other way when the Shah's forces took over Abu Musa and the Greater and Lesser Tunb islands from what would become the UAE the day before the British protectorate agreement expired.[7] The capture of those islands in 1971 not only sent an early signal of Iranian interests in replacing Britain as the Gulf's protecting power as well as de facto international acquiescence—those three islands were later to play key roles in the Tanker War.[8]

The manifestation of the Nixon Doctrine for the Persian Gulf was known as the "Twin Pillars" policy. The two pillars were Saudi Arabia and Iran, as the Soviet-oriented Iraqis did not fit the political equation for either the Americans or the British. Despite the suggestion of equality in the word "pillars," the emphasis from the start was on supporting Iran. President Nixon in particular personally favored Iran, and the American national security bureaucracy received clear direction to approve whatever military hardware the Shah requested.[9] As a measure of that support, the United States throughout the 1970s provided Iran with previously unimaginable sales of state-of-the-art equipment quite comparable to that used by the U.S. military, some of which—including F-4 *Phantom II* fighter bombers, F-14 *Tomcat* fighters, and *Harpoon* missiles—would end up being turned on their American providers.[10] By the time of the Iranian Revolution in 1979, Iran had purchased 330 American high-performance military aircraft, grouped into 22 squadrons around the country.[11]

The change in the Iranian government prompted by the Iranian Revolution illustrated an important drawback of depending upon proxy forces: fundamental divergences in individual national political interests and outlooks. As a Ukrainian general later phrased it regarding American cooperation with his country in reaction to Russia's 2022 invasion: "We are allies, but we have different goals. We protect our country, and you protect your phantom fears from the Cold War."[12] The American relationship with Imperial Iran transformed from close cooperation in 1978—when thousands of U.S. Department of Defense-associated personnel were enabling a massive military train-and-equip effort, alongside some 30,000 Americans working in the country—into a confrontation with revolutionary Iran holding 52 American officials hostage in 1979.[13] It became clear that one of the pillars supporting regional security had collapsed. American and Imperial Iranian interests had mainly coincided in containing the Soviets and supporting the Shah's regime; by contrast, Iranian desires to expel non-regional forces from the Persian Gulf have been a constant, no matter what regime was running the country.

Iran's views on how the Persian Gulf should be controlled and by whom have a long pedigree—this is not an issue that somehow originated with the 1979 Islamic Revolution. As the Shah of Iran phrased it in the early 1970s, "Well, you know that we declared long ago that we should not like to see a foreign power in the Persian Gulf. Whether that power be Britain, the United States, the Soviet Union or China our policy has not changed."[14] In negotiations surrounding the Law of the Sea Treaty in the 1980s, revolutionary Iran's position remained the same—as one international legal text put it: "Iran's position in the Third UN Conference on the Law of the Sea (UNCLOS III) that produced the 1982 LOS Convention 'remained faithful to monarchical Iran's worldview.'"[15] These Iranian views have continued into the 21st century. In 2023, Iranian Revolutionary Guard Corps Commodore Alireza Tangsiri was quoted as saying, "The United States should not be present in our region. The security of the Persian Gulf is provided by Iran and the countries of the region, and there is no need for you or any other country to be present."[16]

British maritime historian Geoffrey Till described how different countries view the sea differently: "To the great maritime powers, the sea stands for opportunity and freedom … The competing view to this is characteristic of national states of a 'continental' persuasion who tend to think of the sea in rather the same way they think of land … the sea may sometimes be … [a source] of danger and strategic vulnerability."[17] These two competing views were to become very clear as the maritime United States and the continentalist Iran contested control over the Persian Gulf in 1987 and 1988 and continue to this day.

***

The abrupt, 180-degree transformation of the American–Iranian relationship from an informal alliance with the Shah to open hostility with revolutionary Iran provided the political backdrop for future interactions. This shift was exemplified by Gary Sick, the principal White House aide for Iran during the Iranian Revolution and the hostage crisis, who titled his book on U.S.–Iranian relations *All Fall Down*. American historian David Crist aptly described the resulting state of affairs as *The Twilight War*.

A recurrent theme for the military capacity of revolutionary Iran, especially throughout the 1980s, was a lack of spare parts and technical assistance for the sophisticated American weapons systems purchased by the Shah. A U.S. arms embargo was imposed in 1979 when the hostages were seized. Iran tried to return systems such as the F-14 and its associated AIM-54 *Phoenix* missile system shortly after the revolution, reckoning with the cost and complexity of keeping such a weapons system operational.[18] Even after the U.S. hostages were released in 1981, there was still an understandable feeling of antipathy toward the Ayatollah, and American companies were in no hurry to do business in Iran, even though the scale of the Iran–Iraq War began to trigger strong demand for American weapons, ammunition, and spare parts. That antipathy was sufficient for the United States to begin to crack down on other countries supplying Iran from their national stocks of American weapons or other sophisticated systems in an economic campaign known as Operation *Staunch* and—while smuggling of U.S. weapons systems continued—it was estimated that only about 10 percent of Iran's weapons needs were being met in its desperate fight against Iraq.[19] A key talking point in *Staunch*—which was, in many ways, effective in restricting arms flows to Iran—was Iran's support for Hezbollah and its actions in Lebanon.

Activities in Lebanon in the early 1980s turned out to be a major factor regarding later American intervention in the Persian Gulf, which might otherwise have been considered an unrelated theater. Repeated clashes between Israel and the Palestinian Liberation Organization (PLO), which was operating essentially as a state-within-a-state from southern Lebanon, resulted in a massive Israeli invasion of Lebanon in 1982, optimistically codenamed Operation *Peace for Galilee*. The Israeli war aims were to end PLO attacks—a limited war aim—as well as to destroy the PLO and install a pro-Israel government in Beirut—unlimited war aims. Not for the last time did the Israelis score tactical successes but arguably strategic failures. The operation and subsequent Israeli occupation of southern Lebanon resulted in the movement of PLO headquarters from Lebanon to Tunisia but also sparked a domestic Lebanese reciprocal reaction in the creation of Hezbollah, backed by Iran.[20]

The PLO withdrawal was overseen by an interpositional multinational peacekeeping force—intended to form a barrier between the PLO and the Israelis—and which included an American contingent of U.S. Marines. From the start, there were those in the U.S. Department of Defense who expressed concern about the involvement of American forces in the peacekeeping operation on the ground in Lebanon.[21] While the initial deployment of the Multinational Force—comprising American, French, and Italian troops—was successful in securing the exit of the PLO, their continued presence inevitably became intertwined with domestic Lebanese politics.

In the words of the official U.S. government report on the 1983 bombing of the U.S. Marine Corps barracks in Beirut—an attack which killed 241 American servicemen, including 220 Marines, losses which constituted the largest single-day death toll for the Marines since Iwo Jima in World War II, as well as the deadliest day for the U.S. military since the Tet Offensive in Vietnam—"The mission of the U.S. contingent of the Multinational Force (USMNF) was to establish an environment that would facilitate the withdrawal of foreign military forces from Lebanon and to assist the Lebanese Government and the Lebanese Armed Forces (LAF) in establishing sovereignty and authority over the Beirut area."[22]

That mission, originally intended to be of short duration, entailed not just the enhancement of the Lebanese Armed Forces, but also the provision of Naval Gunfire Support from U.S. Navy ships off the coast of Lebanon in support of the LAF in their fight against militias. While these actions made sense in the context of trying to restore an internationally recognized, legitimate government in Lebanon, they also meant that the Marines were no longer seen as neutral peacekeepers but rather as having taken a side, becoming belligerents and, therefore, targets.[23] The relatively benign environment in which the Marines had landed in August 1982 had become much more confrontational by the time of the barracks bombing in October 1983. While recent scholarship has challenged the idea that the American decision to withdraw the Marines from Lebanon on February 7, 1984, was immediately linked to the October 23, 1983 bombing, it seems clear that—within the Middle East—the two actions were seen as connected.[24]

Lebanese actors associated with Iran stepped up their efforts to take American hostages in Beirut to help guard against possible American military retaliation.[25] Efforts to secure the release of those hostages, as well as hopes of keeping revolutionary Iran away from the Soviets, led directly to the Iran–Contra scandal, in which the United States sought to provide arms to Iran—in direct contravention of Operation *Staunch*—in return for Iran using its influence to release American hostages in Lebanon.[26] It came as a real surprise to the international community when the Iran–Contra scandal publicly revealed that the United States itself was supplying U.S. TOW anti-tank and HAWK anti-air missiles to Iran, albeit as a way to get American hostages held in Lebanon released rather than as some carefully calibrated effort to affect the Iran–Iraq war.[27] Iran–Contra set up a considerable "say/do" gap for the United States, which had been publicly strident on not compensating hostage takers while, at the same time, secretly providing weapons to the country widely seen as directing the hostage takers.[28]

The wholesale U.S. military withdrawal from Beirut proved an enticement to revolutionary Iran to attempt the same outcome closer to home. The difference between American rhetoric and American practice meant that Gulf nations would focus on deeds rather than words; the subsequent dispatch of American forces to the region and their reactions to adversity would therefore receive careful attention. U.S. Defense Secretary Weinberger would later write, with considerable understatement, "My staff and I were well aware of the negative image we had in the region as a result of past history."[29] Weinberger went on to say that he saw the eventual tanker escort mission for the U.S. Navy "not as a problem but as an opportunity."[30]

The Iran–Iraq War

Revolutionary Iran, led by a radical Shia government, not only posed a military threat to the shipment of (non-Iranian) oil through the Strait of Hormuz, but also a separate ideological and local threat to the Sunni countries of the region.

The same Iranian political threat to the southern Gulf states that would lead to their financial support for Iraq throughout the 1980s also applied to Iraq itself—the Islamic Republic of Iran had ideological motivations to overthrow the secular Ba'athist regime and replace it with an "Islamic Republic of *Iraq*," overseen by Shia clergy faithful to Ayatollah Khomeini's vision of the proper relationship between government and religion.

Friction between Ba'athist Iraq and revolutionary Iran started almost immediately, with small-scale military clashes starting as early as June 1979.[31] The two countries severed diplomatic relations in June 1980, and Iranian radio began to denounce Saddam Hussein and call for the overthrow of the Ba'ath regime. Border clashes continued throughout the summer of 1980, and both Iran and Iraq would later point to fighting at the beginning of September near Qasr-e-Shirin, a historic Iranian border town hundreds of miles inland from the Persian Gulf as the beginning of the Iran–Iraq War, in what would become the largest conflict in the world in the last quarter of the 20th century.[32]

By September 1980, Saddam Hussein had evidently been convinced by Iranian exiles that Ayatollah Khomeini led "a weak fundamentalist regime that would collapse if given a push."[33] A successful attack on Iran would also allow for a revision of the 1975 Algiers Accord governing the Shatt al-Arab waterway separating the countries; Iraq's goal was for the restoration of complete control. Saddam's opportunistic, large-scale invasion utilizing many divisions along a front measuring hundreds of miles encompassed the limited war aim of territorial acquisition but also the unlimited aim of overthrowing Khomeini's regime. In attacking the Islamic Republic of Iran, Saddam, however, neglected the old saw of "never make war on a revolution"; not only did the initial attack have a unifying effect on the Iranian population but "like its revolutionary predecessors in France, Russia, and China, [Iran] had succeeded in bringing up younger talent that was committed to the revolution, thereby defeating what appeared to be a superior military force."[34] From the Iranian perspective, the fight was a Clausewitzian/Corbettian unlimited war from the start, with the overthrow of Saddam Hussein a clearly articulated war aim for most of the conflict. Domestically, the mobilization and focus required for the war helped Khomeini to see off recurring coup attempts and other internal political challenges to his regime.

An Iraqi operation that was intended to be a quick and easy land grab that would somehow topple the neighboring government instead devolved into an eight-year slog, reminiscent of the worst features of World War I, featuring trench warfare, large-scale human-wave infantry assaults, and the extensive use of chemical weapons. The political goals for the belligerents were different and, on the Iranian side, laid the foundations for a long war. The Iranians consistently sought Saddam's removal, an admission of Iraqi war guilt for starting the conflict, and monetary reparations. The Iraqis, by contrast and evidently coming to the conclusion that Ayatollah Khomeini would remain in power, pushed instead for the more limited aims of an end to Iranian political subversion within Iraq and control over the entire Shatt al-Arab—conditions which allowed them to consistently advocate for a cease-fire as the decade wore on.

Regionally, the Iranian Revolution triggered reciprocal reactions in neighboring states, who faced a delicate balancing act. As a 1988 (and therefore pre-*Desert Storm*) account put it: "Until the Iranian Revolution the Gulf monarchies had felt threatened by subversive activities of revolutionary Iraq. If Iraq was to win the war, that threat, it was feared, would return with a vengeance … if Iran was to win the war, the Gulf Cooperation Council (GCC)[35] states feared, then Iran would turn on them."[36]

That 1988 account of GCC meetings went on to note, however, that:

> The Gulf Arab monarchs and Saddam Hussein shared the common perception that revolutionary Iran was a threat to their regimes. This perception was shared particularly by Saudi Arabia, Kuwait, Bahrain, and Oman. But only the first two of these states were in any position to aid Iraq when the [Iran–Iraq] war broke out. They wished to help Iraq because they believed that it invaded Iran at least in part for the purpose of containing the contagion of the Iranian Revolution. They shared this Iraqi objective without approving the war as an appropriate means to that end, but they felt they had little choice other than to help Iraq. Short of committing their troops, Saudi Arabia and Kuwait aided the Iraqi war efforts both financially and logistically. As the principal paymasters of Iraq, they spent anywhere between $20 to $40 billion on Saddam Hussein's war machine. Logistically, Kuwait was the lifeline for Iraq, a distinction for which the Kuwaitis paid dearly in the form of Iranian "accidental" air raids on Kuwait … Saudi Arabia quietly made three Red Sea ports available for the transshipment of military equipment to Iraq …[37]

These ongoing support efforts by Kuwait and Saudi Arabia triggered increasing levels of attacks by the Iranians; those Iranian attacks, in turn, were instrumental in bringing in the naval forces of outside powers.

The Iran–Iraq War itself featured air battles, ballistic missile strikes, and naval warfare, but the key aspect throughout the eight-year stalemated fight was the largely static land battle of attrition along their shared border and nearly 700-mile front. Iraq's offensive in September 1980 had been checked by November and was quickly followed by Iran's recovery of its lost territory throughout 1981. In the following years, the Iraqi Army followed a generally deadlocked approach reminiscent of the Western Front in World War I, favoring mass artillery bombardments and siege rather than actions associated with maneuver warfare. By 1982, Iran had shifted to the offensive, often depending on costly human-wave attacks, and invaded Iraq in an attempt to militarily overthrow Saddam's regime. Succeeding years saw a continued war of attrition and a series of inconclusive "final offensives" by the Iranians, as well as initial attacks on merchant shipping, including tankers. It was not until 1988 that Iraqi military reorganization and fresh supplies of Soviet-produced weaponry enabled Iraqi forces to conduct effective combined arms and maneuver warfare, leading to a series of major Iraqi victories and the effective collapse of front-line Iranian military forces.

While U.S. arms sales to Iran (other than Iran–Contra) ceased with the taking of U.S. hostages, the Iranians did use their remaining stocks throughout the war, along with whatever could be obtained on the black market. The high-tech inventory inherited from the Shah meant that Iran turned out to be the only time the AIM-54 *Phoenix* missile—the very-long range air-to-air missile paired with the F-14—was ever successfully used in combat. The "beyond visual range" aspect of the *Phoenix*, intended for long-range protection of American carrier battle groups, meant that U.S. rules of engagement (ROE), which required U.S. pilots to visually identify their targets, militated against actual American use of the missile. Iranian pilots had no such restrictions, and one *Phoenix* missile used in early 1981 was reportedly able to destroy three Iraqi warplanes that were flying tightly bunched together.[38] In the late 1990s, U.S. Navy F-14s operating as part of Operation *Southern Watch* over Iraq in two engagements fired three *Phoenix* missiles, but none reached their intended targets.[39] By contrast, Iranian F-14 pilots are credited with approximately 78 air-to-air victories over the course of the eight-year Iran–Iraq War, despite the disruptions to the military caused by the Iranian Revolution.[40]

As the war dragged on, Iran had greater oil export earnings as well as a larger population—which fit with an approach to war that depended largely on lightly trained and equipped infantry, and a revolutionary and religious mindset that translated into a greater willingness to take casualties. Iran's superior resources and unlimited war aims served as motivation to continue to find different ways to prosecute the war.

The Tanker War

The stalemate on land and maximalist Iranian political demands prompted the Iraqis to target Iran's economy—in particular, the transportation of oil by tankers, which was critical to funding Iranian arms purchases as well as assuring food security for the Iranian population. From the beginning of the war, the Iranians were able to effectively blockade Iraqi ports, forcing Iraq to rely on land-based pipelines through Turkey, Syria, and Saudi Arabia to export oil and on non-Iraqi ports to receive military supplies. While these land-based options brought with them their own set of political complications—the Syrians, for example, would restrict Iraqi oil flow amount for political and financial gains—they also deprived the Iranians of any at-sea targets operating under Iraqi colors. By contrast, as a history of the naval war between Iran and Iraq observed, "The geographic isolation of Iran from the oil markets and the lack of an oil pipeline exporting system … meant that the country was over-reliant on its loading terminals and the security of sea lanes in the Persian Gulf for exporting its oil."[41]

The difference in oil-exporting dynamics between the two countries meant that there was a disparity in targets afloat—while virtually no ships flew the Iraqi flag, there were plenty of ships flying the Iranian flag—especially oil tankers.[42] Thus the Iraqis began targeting Iranian oil tankers as well as foreign ships carrying supplies for the Iranians, initiating "the Tanker War" which would eventually bring in Western navies. Iranian retaliation for those shipping attacks targeted tankers servicing Kuwait and Saudi Arabia, both of which were providing financial support for the Iraqi war effort. The Tanker War—even though a strategic sideshow to the overall Iran–Iraq War—represented "the largest loss of merchant ships and mariners' lives since the Second World War … By the end of the 1987, write-off losses in the Gulf War stood at nearly half the tonnage of merchant shipping sent to the bottom in World War II."[43]

Between 1980 and 1988, 411 merchant ships were attacked by the Iraqis and the Iranians.[44] While the conflict is called the Tanker War, tankers themselves made up only 61 percent of the targets—the rest were freighters and bulk carriers transporting supplies as well as smaller support vessels. The attacks in practice affected only a very small proportion of the high maritime traffic area of the Persian Gulf—every month, there were some 900–1000 major ship movements and only about 1 percent of the ships were actually attacked.[45] Over the course of the Tanker War, 432 sailors lost their lives—as it happens, the single largest loss of life occurred with the strike against a U.S. Navy warship.

Iraq began attacking ships bound to or from Iranian ports at the extreme northern end of the Gulf at the outset of the war in 1981. Reflecting just how politically isolated the Iranians were, President Reagan commented early in the conflict that "I think we have always recognized that in a time of war, the enemy's commerce and trade is a fair target, if you can hurt them economically. So, in that sense, Iraq has not gone beyond bounds, as Iran has done."[46] As the war went on, the United States would shift that argument toward one instead focused on freedom of navigation for all countries. However, throughout the Tanker War, the United States was never effective in politically influencing Iraqi attacks on shipping, even though those attacks are what triggered Iranian retaliation and eventual Western naval involvement.

By 1983—enabled by the provision of French aircraft and *Exocet* anti-ship missiles—the Iraqis declared an exclusion zone over the entire upper Persian Gulf, including the area around Kharg Island, the principal northern oil-transshipment point for Iran.[47] In practice, despite extensive Iraqi targeting of Kharg Island and its tankers, Iranian oil exports actually rose in 1984 and 1985, due to the challenge of effectively targeting oil infrastructure and Iranian battle damage repair capacity.[48] The Iranians sold oil originating from Kharg at a discount to those foreign ships willing to risk the journey.[49] The Iranians additionally developed a shuttle tanker service, allowing their own ships to onload at Kharg Island and then transfer their cargoes to foreign ships much further down the Gulf at Larak Island, where they were safer from Iraqi attacks. All these factors helped to persuade foreign flagged-tankers to continue their export of Iranian oil, and Iraqi attacks on those smaller, bottom-of-the-market foreign ships never attracted the same notoriety attached to similar Iranian attacks on larger tankers sailing to the ports of the southern Persian Gulf.

The Iraqis benefited from two asymmetries in the war: first, their lack of maritime assets deprived the Iranians of like targets, prompting them to attack international shipping and, second, the two countries had different war aims. Iraq, having failed to topple the Iranian Revolutionary government, could settle for the limited war aims of the restoration of the geographical status quo that existed prior to the Iraqi invasion and perhaps gain more control over the navigation of the Shatt al-Arab waterway dividing the countries. Iran, by contrast, continued with its unlimited war aim of deposing Saddam Hussein until just before the end of the war. The unlimited Iranian war aim meant they were playing for much higher stakes and a continual search for new and "decisive" ways forward.

Iranian rhetorical threats to close the Strait of Hormuz were backed by an increased Iranian military presence on the islands around the Strait. It was these Iranian threats—ultimately counterproductive, given Iran's longstanding desires to keep foreign forces out of the Persian Gulf—that would bring in Western navies. The Iranians also began a sea-based visit/board/search/seizure program aimed at vessels bringing in war supplies to benefit Iraq. The Iranians were well within their legal rights in inspecting and confiscating war materials headed to their enemy. That said, inconsistencies in the way the Iranians exercised this legal right—particularly their strafing of crew quarters on merchant ships—provided a basis for later U.S. military action. A subsequent American legal case, quoting reports made by the UN Secretary General, described 140 attacks by Iran on "innocent merchant shipping," noted the UN reports listed only 35 incidents where the Iranians did carry out visits and searches ("none of which is reported to have been attacked subsequently by Iran"), and charged that there was "no indication that Iran made a prior effort to stop and search the vessels it did attack, as required by the laws and customs of war." The United States went on to comment: "This is not surprising given Iran's attitude that merchant ships could be legitimate military targets simply because the vessels involved, or their cargoes, belonged to states that allegedly supported Iraq in the war."[50] The concept that Iran was indiscriminately using force would later serve as an important talking point for the increase of U.S. military forces in the region.

Iraq began to aggressively enforce the declared exclusion zone in 1984, using *Exocet* missiles and newly arrived *Super Étendard* aircraft to strike ships supporting Iran. A practice had been established of Iraq firing *Exocets* at fairly long ranges without bothering to positively identify their individual target. The Iranians also benefited from new weapons purchases—deliveries of *Silkworm* surface-to-surface missiles from China. The new weapons enabled a new, naval role for the Iranian Revolutionary Guard Corps, which joined in the

Iranian *Saam*-class frigate after attacking the crew quarters of the Romanian-flagged oil tanker *Dacia*. (Norbert Schiller)

overall Iranian effort to deter Iraq from further attacks on Iranian ships and pressure the southern Gulf states to reduce their political and financial support for Saddam Hussein's Iraq. By the end of 1984, 71 merchant ships had been attacked, compared to the 43 merchant ships in total that had been attacked during the first three years of the war. Indeed, during those first three years, all the attacks on merchant ships had been at the hands of the Iraqis—it was not until 1984 that the Iranians began responding at sea.[51]

The initial Iranian strikes against ships came by air and targeted Kuwaiti and Saudi tankers in May 1984. The next month, a Saudi F-15 shot down an Iranian fighter over Saudi waters, and the Iranians began to shift their approach away from their steadily degrading air force and toward more sustainable efforts by sea. Iranian boarding and searching of foreign vessels attracted the attention of foreign navies, and a French warship in 1985 blocked an Iranian naval vessel from inspecting a French cargo ship.[52] By early 1986, the Iranians continued to expand their visit/board/search policy, inspecting a West German ship on January 9, an American ship on January 12, and a British ship on January 13.[53]

On land in February 1986—in one of the biggest developments on land to happen in years—Iranian forces captured Iraq's al-Faw peninsula, upon which it would station *Silkworm* missiles capable of striking ships in Kuwaiti harbors. While the capture of al-Faw, by itself, would not accomplish Iran's war aim of toppling Saddam Hussein, the trend and momentum were sufficiently alarming to the southern Gulf states that they called a special session of Arab foreign ministers.[54] The Iranian offensive, along with the prospect that Iran

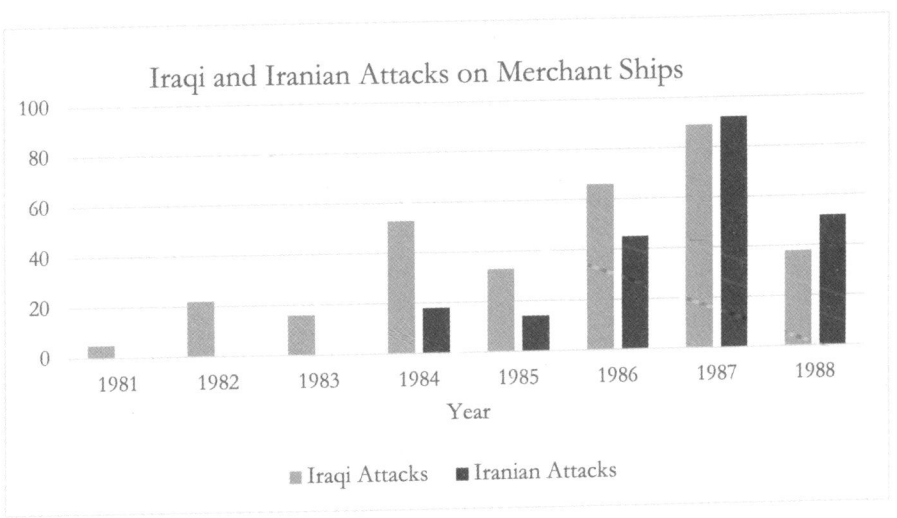

could maintain its efforts and conceivably win the war, likely encouraged the southern Gulf states to seek ways to internationalize the conflict, bring in the superpowers to rebalance the odds, and hopefully find a way to end the war.

One of those ways to further internationalize the Iran–Iraq War would be moves by the Kuwaitis by the end of 1986 to reflag their oil tankers under American and Soviet colors.⁵⁵ Up to that point, the five permanent members of the UN Security Council (the United States, the United Kingdom, the People's Republic of China, France, and the Soviet Union—the "P5" or "Perm 5") had reacted to the Iran–Iraq War in a variety of ways, including the passage of United Nations Security Council Resolutions (UNSCRs) focused on abstract concepts such as freedom of navigation. Country-by-country, however, several P5 members were financially profiting from the war. After an initial stoppage of arms shipments in September 1980 in reaction to the Iraqi invasion, both France and the Soviet Union resumed shipments to Iraq in May 1981—in the interim, the Chinese signed contracts for *Silkworm* missile deliveries.⁵⁶

Chinese-made *Silkworm* missile being launched. "The Chinese-version of the *Styx* anti-ship missile, known as CSS-N-1 Scrubbrush by U.S. Intelligence, being launched from ashore in a coastal defense role." (USNI, Chinese Navy)

It was, after all, the arrival of French *Super Étendards, Mirages,* and *Exocet* missiles that enabled the Iraqis to operationalize their threats against Iranian shipping. Some 40 percent of French arms exports in 1982 went to Iraq, including the *Mirage* fighter jets and *Exocet* missiles that would eventually be used by Iraq to attack the USS *Stark*.[57] The Chinese *Silkworm* missiles would end up becoming a major threat to Western ships in the final years of the war. Russian weapons remained a mainstay for Iraqi forces throughout the entire war and well through the 1990s.

The overall Iran–Iraq War—unusually for a Cold War conflict—had up to 1986 largely avoided the political support or intervention of the two Cold War superpowers, the United States and the Soviet Union. As Canadian military historian Gwynne Dyer once memorably put it:

> The war between Iran and Iraq that began in 1980 involved two regimes so unappetizing that, as a member of the State Department put it, his only regret was that both sides couldn't lose. The Soviet attitude was not greatly different in practice, and both superpowers ended up offering limited support to the Iraq regime, which they regarded as slightly the lesser evil.[58]

While the United States and the Soviet Union had been content to stay on the political sidelines of the Iran–Iraq War, the December 10, 1986, reflagging request by the government of Kuwait forced the superpowers to take a more active interest.[59] The Kuwaiti strategy was that, at a minimum, the Iranians would think twice about attacking an oil tanker flying an American or Soviet flag as well as a hope that superpower involvement could bring an end to the Iran–Iraq war.[60] A Western diplomat serving in Kuwait was even more direct regarding the Kuwaiti reflagging request: "I don't think it has anything to do with shipping. The goal is to get the superpowers involved."[61]

The initial American reaction was one of caution, taking refuge in the bureaucratic complications that would come with shifting a foreign ship to sail under American colors—examples would include sailing under a U.S. master and the ship meeting U.S. Coast Guard inspection standards.[62] On the face of it, almost any ship anywhere could sail under American colors if it met all the requirements; the wrinkle in the Kuwaiti request was the need to relax some of the regulatory standards if the reflagging were to be done immediately.

The Kuwaiti request prompted a number of American interagency meetings, with Defense Secretary Caspar Weinberger and National Security Advisor Frank Carlucci arguing in favor but with Secretary of State George Shultz arguing against, concerned about American ability to see the operation through to the end.[63] President Reagan made the final decision in early March, influenced by news of Soviet agreement to escort the tankers, underscoring the Cold War dimension to the matter. Kuwait, prior to its liberation by American-led forces in 1991, had played a careful balancing game between the superpowers; the Kuwaiti 1980s approach to both superpowers reflected both an—at-least-to-that-point—attempt by Kuwait to avoid security dependence on either superpower, as well as an inkling that a clear Soviet response would likely provoke an American reaction. That unequivocal Soviet "yes" broke the American bureaucratic log-jam—it also meant that the U.S. government had a unified position guided by a clear Presidential decision prior to the *Stark* incident in April.

The official American response agreed to the Kuwaiti reflagging request and conditioned the assistance on the Kuwaitis dropping their parallel request to the Soviets. Secretary of Defense Weinberger was clear in his memoirs about the Cold War aspect of the Operation *Earnest Will*: "Many claimed later that we were played against the Soviets by the Kuwaitis, and somehow we were taken in. That ignores some basic facts." Weinberger emphasized the importance of energy resources to the West and what he described as a longstanding desire by the Soviet Union "to move into an area so vital to us." He noted the Soviets' relative self-sufficiency in oil, cited Russia's earlier acceptance of a Kuwaiti request for assistance, and warned that "the Gulf states, already concerned about American reliability for a number of reasons, would not be able to deny basing and port facilities to their new protectors. Then we would indeed see a large Soviet Naval presence in the Gulf."[64]

In his communications with Congress, Weinberger emphasized the Cold War context of U.S. decision-making: "The United States seeks to minimize Soviet political and military inroads in the region and does not want to legitimize Soviet naval presence in the Gulf." However, when it came to the larger political context, Weinberger signaled a willingness to work with the Russians: "We are not averse to working with the USSR in multilateral efforts to end the war. Ending the threat of conflict will benefit both countries, as well as the wider region."[65]

In the end, it was not the land war, use of chemical weapons, or attacks on civilian populations—all of which would be cited as justifications for subsequent wars in the region—that brought in Western forces. Instead, it was the threat to the world's oil supply that motivated the military intervention of outside powers, undergirded by continuing Cold War suspicion regarding the Soviet Union. Even then, the attacks on merchant ships had gone on for six years before the West did much beyond pass fairly general UNSCRs. Looming over everything was the Cold War—and the desire to forestall Soviet intervention—that ended up internationalizing the Iran–Iraq War.

Also significant was an American focus on limited war aims from the very start. As the White House press spokesman highlighted the month before the UN Security Council passed UN Security Council Resolution 598, a document that would later play a major role in ending the conflict, the American vision for the larger Iran–Iraq War was "the earliest possible negotiated end, leaving no victor and no vanquished."[66] The spokesman clearly laid out objectives for U.S. policy, which were to remain consistent throughout the duration of what would become Operation *Earnest Will*:

> The administration's overriding goals in the Persian Gulf today are to help our moderate Arab friends defend themselves, to improve the chances for peace by helping demonstrate that Iran's policy of intimidation will not work, to bring about a just settlement of the Iran–Iraq war that will preserve the sovereignty and territorial integrity of both parties, to curtail the expansion of Soviet presence and influence in this strategic area, and to deter an interruption of the flow of oil.[67]

***

From the start, there was an assumption that conventional deterrence would make any actual fighting by Americans unnecessary. The sight of the American flag on formerly Kuwaiti ships, accompanied by U.S. Navy warships, would provide protection along the lines of the dynamic protecting a cop on the beat—protection provided not so much from the police officer's individual firepower as it was by the knowledge that any attack would bring down the full fury of the entire police department. MIDEASTFOR Commander Rear Admiral Harold "Hal" Bernsen was very clear in his oral history: "We always thought the deterrent US military power would prevent the Iranians from carrying out a purposeful attack on our forces."[68]

Those assumptions, perhaps implicitly, were part of the planning for what became Operation *Earnest Will*, the U.S. Navy escort of reflagged Kuwaiti tankers through the Persian Gulf. Originally designated Operation *Private Jewels*—the presumably random computer-generated operational codename was changed once someone considered the optics—the overall plan was that of a classic convoy escort operation, with naval assets protecting merchantmen as they transited through dangerous areas. In the case of *Earnest Will*, the simple and robust plan was for the merchant ships to gather in the Gulf of Oman, prior to running the gauntlet of the Strait of Hormuz. They would be escorted by several U.S. Navy surface combatants, protected by carrier and land-based aircraft, guarding against potential air and surface attack from the Iranians as they transited the length of the Gulf and arrived in the territorial waters of Kuwait, whereupon the protection of the tankers would then become the responsibility of the Kuwaitis. When the tankers were ready to leave Kuwait, the process would work in reverse.

In setting up the U.S. escort operation, there was an understandable expectation that the Iraqis—whom the United States were tacitly supporting—would not attack an American ship. When such an attack *did* occur, the *New York Times* caught the feeling of surprise: "The hit on the Stark by an Exocet missile resulted in part from the Navy's assumption that an Iraqi warplane, which was watched by Awacs early warning aircraft as it flew south from Iraq toward Bahrain, was unlikely to attack."[69]

Ultimately, as naval historian Mike Palmer observed in his comprehensive history detailing America's expanding role in the Gulf over the 19th and 20th centuries:

> The Reagan Administration's decision to reflag the Kuwaiti tankers marked a critical turning point in the history of U.S. involvement in the Persian Gulf. De facto intervention in the Iran–Iraq War demonstrated that Americans took seriously their interests—commercial, strategic, and geo-economic—in the Gulf, and as the Carter Administration had pledged, would fight to protect them. Reagan demonstrated that the Carter pronouncements and policies that many critics, both foreign and domestic, had dismissed as bluster and rhetoric were, in fact, earnest statements of American intent.[70]

American domestic political factors played a major role throughout the operation. A generally bipartisan approach concerning the Soviet Union reflected concerns felt by the American people, even if there were wide divergences about the best way to deal with the USSR. A perceived naivety on the part of Jimmy Carter regarding the Soviets—the comment attributed to him, "I've learned more about Russia in the last two months than I knew about them my whole life," after the surprise Soviet invasion of Afghanistan in 1979, has entered the American political lexicon as shorthand for underestimating adversaries. This perception helped to bolster aggressive moves by the Reagan Administration, as well as the political support to fund and build a "600-ship Navy."[71]

By the time of *Earnest Will*, the Reagan administration was entering its second term and having to deal with actions taken during its first term. The intervention in Beirut in 1983, and the rapid withdrawal of the U.S. military after the bombings of the U.S. Embassy and the USMC barracks, contributed to international doubts about U.S. judgement and staying power. The use of U.S. forces fueled discussions of the War Powers Act, a piece of legislation that the Reagan administration had to keep in mind throughout the decade. The approach of subsequent administrations toward going to war—President George H. W. Bush took the risk of calling for a congressional vote prior to launching *Desert Storm* and President George W. Bush had the wide-reaching, post-9/11 "Authorization for the Use of Military Force" behind him—have obscured how much of a limiting factor the War Powers Act was during the 1980s.

Additionally, Iran–Contra Congressional hearings were occurring at the exact time of the opening stages of Operation *Earnest Will*, keeping Iran on the front pages of U.S. newspapers and encouraging congressional freelancing, such as the June 8, 1987, letter to the *New York Times* in which Congressman Thomas Downey (D-NY), citing the passage of UNSCR 552 in 1984 as evidence of P5 consensus on the Iran–Iraq War, proposed that the United States request the UN Security Council create a UN task force to protect merchant shipping in the Gulf.[72] Downey's idea would later be taken up by two former U.S. cabinet secretaries and, ultimately, the Soviet Union. And, as demonstrated by the leading questions from Navy Secretary James Webb, there were also internal concerns about the wisdom and feasibility of the operation.

All in all, the Reagan administration faced considerable friction in pushing forward on a controversial policy in the Persian Gulf.

CHAPTER 3

Into Harm's Way

> I don't know if we were ever in any danger, but we were certainly in a place that is dangerous.[1]
>
> —COMMANDING OFFICER, USS CARNEY, MAY 2024, AFTER UNEXPECTEDLY FIGHTING OFF THE HOUTHIS IN THE RED SEA.

Sending a ship "into harm's way" has become something of a throwaway line for speakers—automatically placed into speeches without a great deal of thought—but American history is replete with examples of ships being attacked or otherwise coming to grief without America consciously being in a war. The phrase itself comes from American Revolutionary War hero Captain John Paul Jones, who famously declared: "I wish to have no connection with any ship that does not sail fast; for I intend to go in harm's way." Less remembered are the circumstances of the quote and the fate of the ship being referred to: Jones wrote the lines after converting a former French East India merchantman into the USS *Bon Homme Richard*, a ship later lost with half its crew in a victorious battle against the British frigate HMS *Serapis*.[2] While the loss of the ship occurred in a context in which all sides knew they were at war, it also set a standard from the earliest days of the U.S. Navy that warships could be placed in very risky situations.

The explosion aboard the USS *Maine* in 1898 in Havana Harbor—the ship was there on what might now be called a presence mission, observing the Cuban War for independence—killed 261 Americans and helped to precipitate the Spanish–American War. The strafing of the USS *Panay* by Japanese aircraft in 1937, with the loss of three lives, likely reminded many Americans that they had a Yangtze River patrol in China.[3] The torpedoing of the USS *Reuben James* by a German U-boat in October 1941—weeks prior to America's entry into World War II—cost the lives of 115 sailors.[4]

The attack in the Persian Gulf on the USS *Stark* in May 1987 was therefore not the first time something like this had happened in American history nor, indeed, was it the last—the attack on the USS *Cole* in Aden in October 2000, with the loss of 17 sailors, was another reminder that operating ships is a dangerous business in both peacetime and war. U.S. Navy ships are funded, built, crewed, and deployed for a reason, and there were solid policy rationales for *Stark* to be in the Persian Gulf when she was attacked.

Stark's presence in the Gulf predated the official beginning of Operation *Earnest Will* by several months—the U.S. Navy's escort of reflagged tankers through the Persian Gulf did not officially start until July 24. *Stark* was there as the latest in a long line of U.S. combatants being deployed to the Gulf. USS *Ticonderoga*—a *Lackawanna*-class screw sloop of war built in 1863, whose name was later associated with a class of cruisers to include an early namesake of the USS *Vincennes*—was the first U.S. warship to sail through the Gulf in 1879.[5] Later, U.S. naval forces increased their presence in region, especially with tankers moving Middle Eastern oil in support of World War II operations.

The U.S. Navy began a permanent, sea-based presence in the Persian Gulf in 1949. In the words of a report from the Office of the Chief of Naval Operations assessing the Navy's later performance in Operation *Desert Storm*:

> Navy presence was embodied in the "little white fleet" of USS *Duxbury Bay* (AVP 38), USS *Greenwich Bay* (AVP 41) and USS *Valcour* (AVP 55)—former seaplane tenders—which rotated duties as flagship for Commander Middle East Force and his staff. All three ships were painted white to counter the region's extreme heat … Accompanied by one or two other rotationally deployed warships, the Middle East Force (MIDEASTFOR) provided the initial U.S. military response to any crisis in the region, as well as humanitarian and emergency assistance. For the next 30 years, three or four ships at a time were assigned to MIDEASTFOR—generally a command ship and two or three small combatants such as destroyers or frigates. Because temperatures in the Arabian Gulf, Red Sea and Indian Ocean reached as high as 130 degrees, the non-air-conditioned ships rotated every few months …[6]

American presence—both military and diplomatic—could be relatively limited in the Gulf immediately after World War II because the primary security duties were the responsibility of another country. In terms reminiscent of what the British themselves would one day use to describe their three-ship Armilla Patrol, which began in 1980, "American policy-makers decided to put forth a visible symbol of American interest in the stability of the Persian Gulf by introducing [in 1949] a low-profile naval force of three small ships … our officials believed that the British Fleet, still dominant in the area at the time, could deal with any combat situation that might

USS *Duxbury Bay*, Middle East Force flagship, in the Shatt al-Arab between Iraq and Iran in December 1961—part of MIDEASTFOR's "Little White Fleet." (U.S. Naval History and Heritage Command Photograph, NH 102678)

arise."[7] The traditional Royal Navy presence in the region served to diminish the need for a large U.S. Navy showing, allowing the Americans to play the role, as American naval historian Michael Palmer once phrased it, of "No. 2 Englishmen in the Gulf."[8]

The initial British post-World War II presence—a combination of naval deployments and deep political relationships, coupled with the oil-funded rising defense capacities of Iran and Saudi Arabia—served to keep threats in check, particularly from the Soviet Union. After a British strategic realignment in 1968 to withdraw from security commitments "east of Suez," America's pivot toward the "Twin Pillars" approach of supporting and cooperating with the Shah's Iran and the Kingdom of Saudi Arabia to maintain security in the region seemed a good way to minimize U.S. force requirements. Britain's post-1968 downsizing in Bahrain allowed the U.S. Navy to take over British piers and port facilities for shore-based support. In 1972, the U.S. Navy stationed a permanent MIDEASTFOR flagship—the USS *La Salle*, a relatively spacious amphibious ship specially converted for the weather conditions of the

Gulf. Continuing the white paint scheme, the *La Salle*—known to sailors as "the galloping ghost of the Persian coast"—engaged in presence missions in the region, supplemented by rotating "grey-hulled" combatants doing regular deployments to the Gulf.

In response to the 1979 Soviet invasion of Afghanistan and the Iranian hostage crisis, the U.S. Navy's presence in the region increased to nearly 30 ships, including an aircraft carrier battle group operating in the North Arabian Sea. In April 1980, USS *Nimitz* and its battlegroup served as the base for Operation *Eagle Claw*—the ultimately failed attempt to rescue 52 Americans held hostage in Tehran that cost the lives of eight U.S. servicemen. The lessons learned from *Eagle Claw* contributed to the establishment of the Joint Rapid Deployment Force, which later evolved into U.S. Central Command, established in 1983.

By 1987, the Iran–Iraq War had devolved into a pattern of land operations and attacks on merchant ships, but there had been no attacks on U.S.-flagged vessels, either military or civilian. The number of U.S. flagged merchant ships had generally been quite low; the Kuwaiti reflagging effort greatly increased that number. Further, despite the appalling attacks on merchant ships to date, the vast majority of merchant traffic continued.

By the time *Stark* entered the Persian Gulf in March 1987, the U.S. warship presence in the Gulf had normalized to a command ship along with visiting combatants; *Stark* was one of those rotating combatants, scheduled to spend several months in the Gulf before returning to its homeport of Mayport, Florida. This initial approach to the Kuwaiti reflagging request was to be taken mainly "out of hide" as the U.S. Navy would term it—an additional duty to be taken on without the provision of significant additional sources.

Stark was an FFG-7, an *Oliver Hazard Perry*-class frigate (designated with the hull classification symbol "FF") that also featured a sophisticated guided-missile system ("G")—hence, the class-wide designation of "FFG." Warships can be thought of as "high-mix"—battleships, aircraft carriers, cruisers—or "low mix"—destroyer escorts, corvettes, frigates. As an official training module for future FFG-7 engineering officers put it: "The Navy of the mid-seventies was being designed to consist of a limited number of very expensive, very capable warships (high mix) and many less capable warships (low mix), fully capable of performing certain tasks. This was known as the 'High mix—Low mix concept.' The FFG-7 class represents the low mix end of the spectrum."[9]

Warships are built to high damage control standards—it is those standards, crew sizes, and weapons systems that effectively distinguish them from merchant ships. Warships are designed with watertight subdivisions, as well as separation and redundancy for vital systems such as steering and firefighting. However, there are differentiations between classes of warships themselves, and the FFG-7s were intended from the start to be relatively inexpensive, lower-end ships—making up in high numbers for the relatively lower combat capability of individual ships. Designed from the start to be sea-going escort vessels for merchant ships, the FFG-7s featured the anti-submarine and anti-air war capabilities deemed necessary to handle the long-range Soviet threat to convoys crossing the Atlantic Ocean. It is worth noting that the FFG-7s were low mix in the context of U.S. Navy ships; they are, in a global context, relatively large, well-armed ships and some later served as the flagships for several foreign navies.

A key design feature for the FFGs was weight reduction on the upper part of the ship, which led to the extensive use of aluminum in the ships' construction. Concerns were raised even during the design phase about the possibility of the aluminum superstructure cracking in response to wave motion. A lesson learned from the loss of British ships to Argentine bomb and missiles strikes during the 1982 Falklands War was aluminum's susceptibility to fire damage. As one report noted: "Extra 'survivability features' were added during construction [of FFG-7s], including Kevlar and aluminum fragmentation armor, and Halon firefighting systems. However, the vulnerability of the aluminum superstructure could only be mitigated, not eliminated."[10] Subsequent combatant construction, such as those of the *Arleigh Burke*-class of U.S. destroyers, has instead shifted to all-steel construction.

Stark was no stranger to the dangers of attacks against ships in the Gulf. During an earlier deployment in 1984, the crew had witnessed an Iranian attack against a civilian diving-support ship and had rescued the ship's crew.[11] In 1987, *Stark* left her homeport of Mayport, Florida, on February 5 for a routine, scheduled six-month deployment.[12] However, this deployment was to end up anything but routine.

Departing Bahrain early in the morning of Sunday, May 17, *Stark* steamed into the middle of the Gulf, getting ready for an engineering training assistance visit scheduled for two days later, on May 19. The ship was preparing for an Operational Plant Propulsion Examination (OPPE), a high-intensity, highly consequential exam that demanded a lot of dedicated, focused preparation on the part of *Stark*'s leadership.[13] The ship took up a patrol area west of the Iranian-declared exclusion zone and engaged in a series of communication exercises throughout that Sunday with the command ship *La Salle* and a

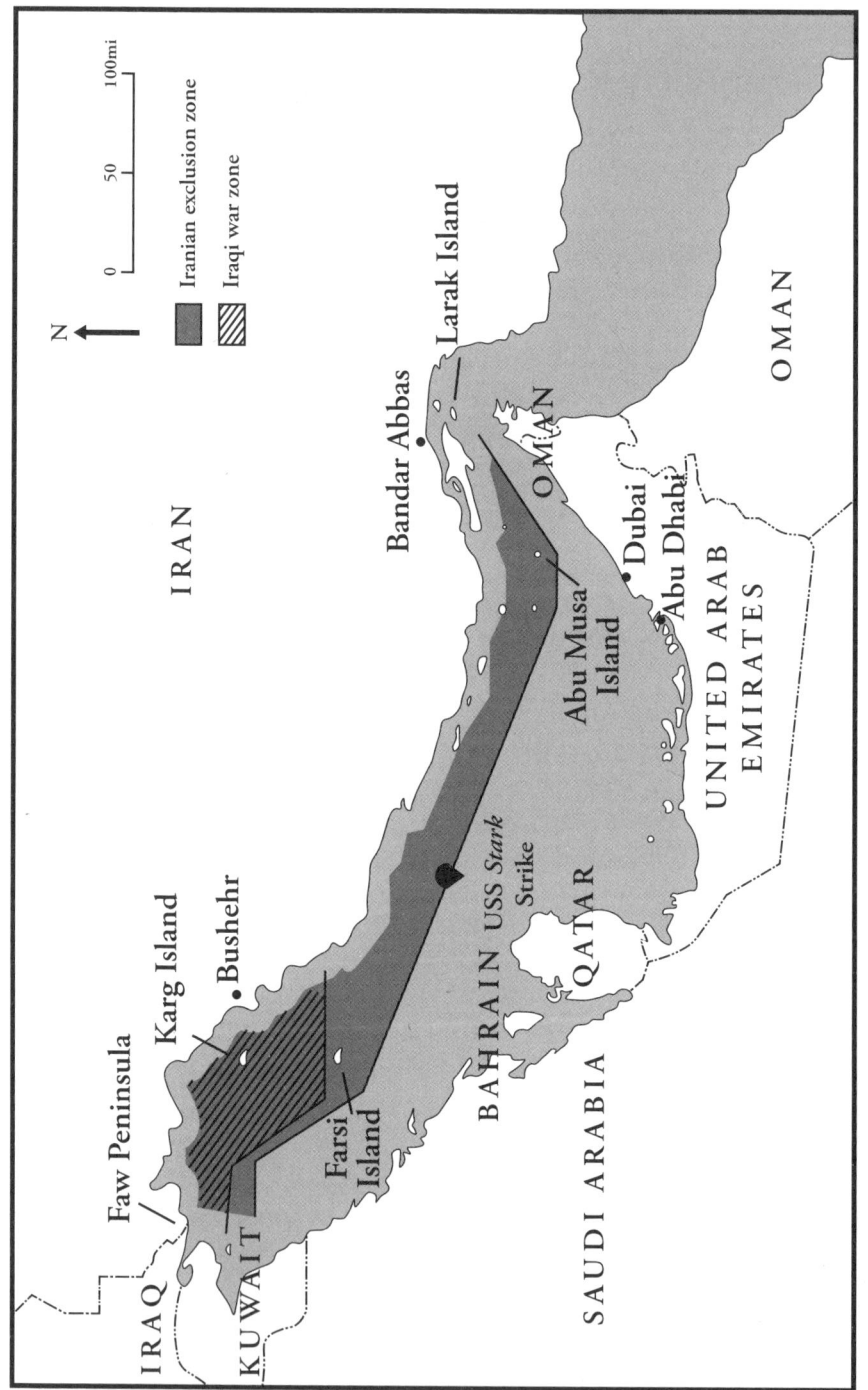

Location of the strike against USS *Stark*, outside of the Iranian and Iraqi exclusion zones.

destroyer, the USS *Coontz*—both pierside in Bahrain, as well as with a U.S. Air Force E-3 AWACS aircraft overhead. Early in the evening, *Coontz* and the AWACS picked up an unknown aircraft heading toward *Stark*; *Stark* picked up the aircraft shortly, thereafter, heading in from the west—from the direction of Iraq. The relatively primitive tactical data systems shared by the U.S. Navy, the U.S. Air Force, and the Royal Saudi Air Force had symbols designating contacts as friendly, hostile, or unknown—this particular aircraft was designated "friendly."[14] In the meantime, as *Stark* continued OPPE preparations, the ship surged to full power, making maximum speed through the Gulf and putting a premium on watchstanders to look out ahead for possible collision risks from surface contacts. The ship throttled back to a normal speed just before 9:00 pm.

The plane was being flown by the Iraqi Air Force, loaded with two *Exocet* anti-ship missiles, both of which were then launched at *Stark*.[15] British journalist Robert Fisk later interviewed former Iraqi *Mirage* pilots knowledgeable of the incident:

> It was a routine flight over the Gulf to hunt for Iranian ships. There was a "forbidden zone" from which we had excluded all ships and the *Stark* was in that zone. The pilot didn't know the Americans were there. He knew he had to destroy any shipping in the area—that's all. He saw a big ship on his radar screen and he fired his two missiles at it. He assumed it was Iranian. He never saw the actual target. We never make visual contact—that's how the system worked. Then he turned to come home.[16]

While the Iraqi pilots may have assured themselves that *Stark* had been in an exclusion zone, the location of the ship at the time of attack—26–47N/051–55E—placed the ship well outside both the Iraqi and the Iranian declared war zones. The Iraqis told Fisk that, contrary to rumors at the time, the Iraqi pilot had not been subsequently executed—"I saw him a few months ago [in 2003] … he obeyed all our rules. We were fighting a cruel enemy. It was a mistake. We weren't going to get rid of one of our senior pilots for the Americans."[17]

Reports have subsequently emerged that suggest the attacking Iraqi aircraft was not a *Mirage* but rather a *Falcon* business jet modified to carry two *Exocet* missiles.[18] While those types of reports may call into question some of the details provided by Fisk's Iraqi pilots, Fisk nonetheless captured the war-weary "these kind of accidents happen" mindset. What is indisputable is two missiles from an Iraqi aircraft hit the USS *Stark*.

In the words of the subsequent official U.S. Navy investigation, *Stark*'s "Tactical Action Officer [TAO] and other watchstanders assumed the aircraft would fly benignly by."[19] The investigation continued: "The Tactical Action Officer gave little or no credence to the possibility that the Iraqi fighter would indiscriminately attack STARK ..."[20] As further evidence of the initially routine nature of the encounter, the investigation recounts:

> The Executive Officer [the ship's second-ranking officer] entered CIC [Combat Information Center] on routine business approximately five minutes before the attack occurred; and he remained in CIC near the TAO station before the first missile hit. He did not inform himself of the tactical situation; and, therefore, did not feel there was anything remiss in the way the watch was responding to the Iraqi fighter.[21]

Key positions in *Stark*'s CIC were unmanned. The Weapons Control Officer was not in his chair by the time the *Exocets* reached their terminal phase, inbound toward *Stark*. The crewman responsible for the ship's fire-control radars—necessary for engaging *Stark*'s SM-1 air-to-air missiles and 76 mm gun—was away in one of the ship's heads. That position also controlled the ship's Close-In Weapons System (CIWS—pronounced "sea-whiz"), the R2D2-looking Gatling gun that served as the ship's last line of defense against a missile attack. When the missiles hit, the CIWS was still in standby mode, never having been armed. The ship's Super Rapid Blooming Offboard Chaff (SRBOC) system—a mortar-launched canister of radar-reflective strips designed to "bloom" away from the ship and distract the seeker heads of incoming missiles—was not armed until just before the first missile hit.[22] The Navy investigation concluded: "STARK never fired a weapon nor employed a countermeasure, either in self-defense or in retaliation. Thirty-seven members of STARK's crew died as a result of the attack."[23]

The first indication that *Stark*'s crew realized they were under attack appears to have come from the ship's forward lookout, a junior seaman equipped with, at most, a pair of binoculars. At 9:07 pm, he saw a bright light off the port bow—which turned out to be the exhaust flames of the *Exocets* heading toward the ship. The light was initially identified as a surface contact. Back in CIC, the watch noticed that the Iraqi aircraft had changed course; crewmembers began to broadcast warning notices over the radio to the aircraft but—by that point—the Iraqi missiles were already past the point of no return.

A minute later, a lookout yelled over the "JL"—the ship's venerable sound-powered phone circuit linking the ship's lookouts to the bridge—the warning "MISSILE INBOUND, MISSILE INBOUND." At this point, the junior officer of the deck on the ship's bridge could also see the missiles homing in on *Stark*. The first missile hit the ship just as the team on the bridge began to sound the ship's General Quarters alarm, meaning that few of the crew were at their battle or damage-control stations when the first missile impacted.

Indeed—given the 9:09 pm time of the attack on a Sunday evening—many of the crew were in their racks recovering from an early start to the day or getting a last bit of rest prior to relieving the watch at midnight or the busy workweek ahead.

The results were catastrophic. In the words of the Naval History and Heritage Center's official history of the USS *Stark*:

> The frigate sounded General Quarters and locked her fire control onto the jet, but mere seconds later the first missile slammed into the port side nearly 13 feet above the waterline, under the port bridge wing and at about Frame 100, on the second deck. The *Exocet* did not detonate but tore into the ship, severing the firefighting water lines to the forward part of the ship, and breaking apart and spilling volatile fuel. About 25 seconds later the second missile hit a few feet aft of but nearly in the same location and exploded in Crew Compartment 2-100-0-L, the fuel from the first missile feeding its fiery detonation. The shock of the hits tore fixtures from bulkheads and wrecked equipment. The heat from the fires and the acrid and blinding smoke impeded damage control efforts, and flames melted aluminum superstructure and decks. Men off watch asleep in their racks awoke to an inferno and screamed as they died.[24]

Both *Exocets* had struck *Stark* in the forward half of the ship. These types of *Exocets* had a maximum range of 38 nautical miles but were fired from only 22 miles out. Their relatively short flight time made for a lot of unexpended fuel, and they came to rest still spewing ignited propellant within the forward berthing compartments of the ship, which at that time of night were full of sailors. While the warhead of the first failed to explode, the second warhead detonated as designed, magnifying the damage. The lethality of the attack is reflected in the casualty numbers: while 37 sailors died, 21 were otherwise injured.[25] U.S. Navy sailors at the time trained to fight fires reaching 1,800 degrees Fahrenheit; the fires aboard *Stark* were estimated to have reached in excess of 3,000 degrees.[26]

The locations of the missile hits destroyed berthing compartments, and the resulting fires melted much of the aluminum superstructure, driving sailors out of CIC and ultimately off the bridge, but the ship's engineering spaces remained intact. While the main fire water conduit was severed—including, potentially critically, to the forward part of the ship containing *Stark*'s SM-1 and *Harpoon* missiles, all of which contained the kinds of warheads and propellant that had made the *Exocets* so lethal—the ship's keel remained intact and the officers and crew reverted to the damage-control training so prioritized by the U.S. Navy. The men of *Stark* formed firefighting parties fore and aft and fought the fire in the middle of the ship. Additional Navy ships and aircraft provided supplementary damage-control material and specialized

Iconic photo of USS *Stark* the morning after being hit by two Iraqi *Exocet* missiles. The crew's damage-control efforts saved the ship, and it was eventually able to steam back to the United States under its own power. (National Archives)

medical personnel, and a civilian salvage tug came alongside and helped with the firefighting. While the ship retained propulsion and was able to steer from an emergency station back aft in place of the unusable bridge, *Stark* was soon towed back into harbor in Bahrain.

In contrast to the widespread criticism of *Stark*'s unpreparedness for battle, the officers and crew were commended for their damage-control efforts. Despite extensive damage, the ship did not sink, and *Stark* was later able to steam back to the United States under its own power for comprehensive repair work and eventually returned to serve in the fleet. In the words of the otherwise extremely critical official report of the incident: "The fact that USS Stark suffered no deaths or serious injuries in connection with their damage control efforts is directly attributable to the clear thinking, exceptional courage, and extraordinary heroism displayed by many of its officers and crewmembers."[27] The Chief of Naval Operations, in his comments forwarding the official incident report up to the Secretary of Defense, concluded by personally recognizing "the exceptional individual valor and competence exhibited by the surviving STARK crewmembers involved in her damage control effort.

USS *Stark* after the Iraqi missile strike, showing extensive fire damage on the ship's port side. *Stark* is moored in Manama, Bahrain next to USS *La Salle*, the MIDEASTFOR command ship painted in Persian Gulf white, which is flying the union jack at half-mast in memory of *Stark*'s dead. (National Archives)

Their action was in keeping with the highest Navy traditions and probably saved the ship."[28] The executive officer and tactical action officer, who helped to lead the damage control efforts, were both decorated shortly after the attack with the Navy and Marine Corps Medal, the "senior peacetime award for heroism … awarded to individuals who … distinguish themselves by heroism not involving actual conflict with the enemy."[29] The non-combat nature of the awards is evidence that the United States did not yet see itself as being at war. The story goes that the TAO had to interrupt the testimony that would determine whether he was to be court-martialed in order to go up on deck to receive his award.

The story of what happens next to *Stark*'s officers is as traditional as the sending of *Stark* into harm's way in the first place. When the USS *Pueblo* was captured by the North Koreans in 1969, the counsel to the Navy's court of inquiry laid out the stakes: "This is a matter of accountability. When a sophisticated piece of equipment is lost, someone must give an accounting for this loss. People must be held accountable or we would have no way of control."[30] One of the admirals on the *Pueblo* court of inquiry summed up

Officers and crew decorated for heroism for saving USS *Stark*. Two of the officers pictured would also have their Navy careers ended due to their roles in the circumstances of the original attack. (Official U.S. Navy Photograph via PHC C. Hinkle and PH2 J. Jones)

the general Navy feeling on these kinds of incidents: "If only he had fired one shot. It would have made all the difference."³¹

Rear Admiral Grant A. Sharp, commander of Cruiser-Destroyer Command TWO based in Norfolk—and, as it happens, a son of Admiral Grant Sharp, Jr. who, as CINPAC, had been in *Pueblo*'s chain of command in the months before that ship was captured—convened an investigation in Bahrain shortly after the incident.³² That investigation produced a report, dated June 12, 1987, recommending that *Stark*'s commanding officer, Captain Eric Brindel, and the tactical action officer at the time of the attack, Lieutenant Basil Moncrief, face a court-martial on charges of dereliction of duty and that the executive officer, Lieutenant Commander Ray Gajan, be referred to admiral's mast on similar charges.³³ Upon completion of the report, all three men were "detached for cause" and removed from their positions. From the start, however, there was a sense *Stark* had not been sent on an obviously wartime deployment. In the immediate aftermath, one

Navy officer was quoted as saying, "Does this say the Navy is vulnerable? The answer is yes—in a peacetime environment. In a war, these ships can defend themselves."[34]

Admiral Frank Kelso, the four-star admiral in charge of the Atlantic Fleet and future Chief of Naval Operations—who would have been the convening authority for the court-martials—downgraded the punitive actions from court-martial to admiral's mast because of the "extraordinary and heroic" efforts by Brindel and Moncrief to save the ship and the crew after the attack. Kelso went on to explain "the degree of culpability is mitigated by the unique circumstances of the incident and its aftermath."[35] In letters to Admiral Kelso, both officers "admitted and accepted accountability for the lack of readiness and inadequacy of measures taken to protect the Stark."[36] Brindel and Montcrief received letters of reprimand and immediately ended their naval careers. Brindel retired at a lower rank; Montcrief resigned his commission. Gajan received a letter of admonition, which in effect blocked him from further promotion and he retired several years later. In a story describing the next steps for Captain Brindel, one top admiral was quoted as saying: "His Navy career is ended. What more do you need to do to the guy? Is he accountable? Yes. Do we need a court-martial to prove that? Hell, no. I think he will live with this for the rest of his life."[37]

The consequences for *Stark*'s officers echo classic books about the U.S. Navy. At the end of *A Matter of Accountability,* USS *Pueblo* Commanding Officer Lloyd Bucher avoided a court-martial, in part because "during his internment [in North Korea], Commander Bucher upheld morale in a superior manner ... provided leadership ... and contributed to the ability of the crew to hold together and withstand the trials of detention."[38] At the conclusion of *The Caine Mutiny*—a Pulitzer Prize winner for fiction—the 25-year-old protagonist opens a bag of mail one day on the ship to find two letters—a Bronze Star medal citation for saving the ship after a kamikaze attack and a career-ending letter of reprimand resulting from his court-martial for mutiny. Placing both documents in a folder to close out his career, "He carefully inserted the citation and the letter of reprimand side by side, and sealed them in, thinking as he did so that his great grand-children could puzzle out the inconsistency at their leisure."[39]

***

Accountability for ships' officers is one thing; accountability for national decision-makers and countries is quite another. One of the remarkable twists of the Tanker War story is that—while the Iranians had nothing directly to do whatsoever with the *Stark* incident—the Islamic Republic of Iran ended up taking the blame.

Operational accountability went no farther than the officers of the *Stark*, despite initial defensive efforts by Captain Brindel to implicate his supervisory commands.[40] In 1969, congressional testimony on the chain of events that had led to the USS *Pueblo* being captured, then-Chief of Naval Operations Admiral Tom Moorer testified that "no single individual made the decision"; Congressional House Armed Services Committee Chairman Otis Pike concluded, "There's blame enough for everyone here."[41] For the *Stark* incident, political accountability shifted rapidly toward the Iranians—Iraqi actions were widely and immediately seen as an accident. The *Washington Post* quoted President Reagan saying two days after the *Stark* attack: "Iran 'was the real villain in the piece' because it had refused to negotiate an end to the 6 ½-year gulf war."[42] Above all, in what turned out to be one of the closing acts of the Cold War, concern about the Soviet Union continued to loom over strategic choices.

Less than two weeks after the attack on *Stark*, President Reagan clearly articulated U.S. policy in the Persian Gulf, reaffirming that the United States had "vital interests" in the area:

> Mark this point well: The use of the vital sealanes of the Persian Gulf will not be dictated by the Iranians. These lanes will not be allowed to come under the control of the Soviet Union. The Persian Gulf will remain open to navigation by the nations of the world ... Freedom of navigation is not an empty cliché of international law. It is essential to the health and safety of America and the strength of our alliance.[43]

The president went on to say, "Until peace is restored and there's no longer a risk to shipping in the region, particularly shipping under American protection, we must maintain an adequate presence to deter and, if necessary, to defend ourselves against any accidental attack or against any intentional attack."[44] President Reagan's May 29, 1987, announcement was an unusually clear articulation of American strategic goals for a conflict. It also turned out to be prescient in forecasting what would terminate the U.S. intervention: the end of the Iran–Iraq War and a cessation of attacks on ships.

While Reagan's articulation of policy goals was clear, it needed to get past a couple of inconsistencies. First, U.S. military operations in the Gulf, by temporarily shutting down ship movements, in and of themselves interfered with freedom of navigation. Second, and more seriously, the statement said nothing about *Iraqi* attacks on merchant ships. It was the Iraqis who had first attacked merchant ships, dating from the start of the Iran–Iraq War and, during the two years of American convoy operations, continued to attack Iranian merchant ships, albeit at lower numbers than the Iranians. Iraqi attacks on Iranian tankers generally provoked Iranian retaliatory attacks on neutral merchant ships—meaning, ultimately, it was the Iraqis who were the drivers of a chain of events that led to *Earnest Will*. It is a reminder of just how destabilizing Saddam Hussein was while in power—in between invading Iran in 1980 and invading Kuwait in 1990, his attacks on shipping in between ended up precipitating an international maritime response in the Persian Gulf. The United States attempted to persuade Saddam's Iraq to cease its attacks on Iranian shipping and infrastructure, but those diplomatic efforts rarely resulted in lasting effects.

Those critiques aside, there were two clear war aims for the United States—two measures to assess whether America was winning this limited war. The United States by itself could not end the Iran–Iraq War, but there were at least two, related results that it *could* directly impact: (1) swatting down Iranian air and surface attacks and (2) demonstrating American resolve.

Stopping Iranian attacks on merchant shipping was a binary metric that measured progress; one would know if you were winning the war if those attacks declined or stopped altogether. As Deputy Secretary of State Richard Armitage once phrased it with respect to a later conflict: "There are only two metrics that really matter in war: number of violent incidents and, within that figure, the number of violent incidents initiated by the enemy."[45]

The United States also had the opportunity to demonstrate resolve by continuing the mission after the deaths suffered aboard USS *Stark*. It is easy to caricature arguments appealing to national reputation, but "fear, honor, and interest" date back to Thucydides as reasons that countries engage in war. Further, observers in the Middle East were watching closely to see how the United States responded in the wake of *Stark*. Iraqi leader Saddam Hussein, while publicly apologetic and quickly proffering $27 million in compensation, was privately incredulous, remaking to his senior aides, "If someone had attacked my ship, I would have bombed the airfield the airplane came from."[46] Iranian Revolutionary Guard Commander Major General Mohsen Rezai told his colleagues in Tehran: "The Americans cannot take casualties. Vietnam and Beirut showed that … Any losses and the Americans will flee the Gulf."[47] Osama bin Ladin, observing in the following decade after the Americans rapidly withdrew from Somalia in the wake of the "Blackhawk Down" incident, made lack of American resolve a key pillar in his 1996 fatwa targeting the United

States: "God has dishonored you when you withdrew and it clearly showed your weakness and powerlessness."[48]

American strategic discourse generally limits itself to permutations of deterrence, signaling, and containment, but only one side in a conflict has to actually use violence for those discussions to appear superficial and superseded—as heavyweight boxer Mike Tyson once pithily phrased it: "Everybody has a plan until they get punched in the face." Clausewitz got at this reality in a chapter he titled *The Use of Battle*: "The character of battle is slaughter and its price is blood."[49] He was writing in response to Napoleon's effective use of violence after an extended, relatively tranquil international period marked by armies maneuvering rather than fighting. Steeled by the defeat of the Prussians by the revolutionary French, he was scathing: "Laurels were to be reserved for those generals who knew how to conduct a war without bloodshed … recent history has scattered such nonsense to the wind."[50]

Continuing on that theme, Clausewitz went on to write:

> We are not interested in generals who win victories without bloodshed. The fact that slaughter is a horrifying spectacle must make us take war more seriously, but not provide an excuse for gradually blunting our swords in the name of humanity. Sooner or later someone will come along with a sharp sword and hack off our arms.[51]

American decision-makers in 1987 were not peppering their speeches with Clausewitz quotes, but their actions demonstrated these essential truths about war. Their subsequent increases of forces into the theater demonstrated that—rather than withdrawing such as was the case after the 1983 USMC barracks bombing in Beirut—the United States intended to stay, even if there were to be casualties. It is worth recalling the purpose of all this violence—this, again, was a limited war. The goal was not to overthrow the Iranian regime; rather, the goal was to cease Iranian attacks on shipping and, in President Reagan's words, to avoid showing "weakness, a lack of resolve and strength."[52] Those turned out to be achievable goals.

The *Stark* incident put the Kuwaiti reflagging effort on the front pages of American newspapers and prompted Congressional hearings. Within the U.S. government itself, however, the fierce debates had been held earlier in the year, and the decision had been made—the focus became how to continue with the mission and avoid future *Stark*-like incidents. Discussions in Washington and at CENTCOM headquarters in Tampa focused on the rules of engagement—particularly regarding the point where a U.S. Navy ship's captain was authorized to launch weapons. While such authorization was clarified, in a larger sense the captains and crews on the scene already knew the circumstances had changed.⁵³ Noted naval analyst Mike Vlahos wrote shortly thereafter: "Before 17 May … shooting down a (friendly) Iraqi aircraft on the assumption it had hostile intent—was to be avoided."⁵⁴ After the *Stark* incident, reacting the way the ship did became almost unimaginable, with an almost instinctive, fleet-wide understanding that U.S. Navy ships were not to take the first hit and that ships' captains and crews would not be second-guessed for what previously might have been viewed as aggressive behavior.⁵⁵

It is worth recalling that *Stark* was not attacked as part of a Kuwaiti tanker escort mission—those convoys would not start until late July. However, the May attack prompted a revisualization of how the mission would now be conducted, given the reminder of the deadly stakes. Initial planning had been to add two additional warships to the six already present with MIDEASTFOR and then marshal the Kuwaiti tankers, two or three at a time, to make the 600-mile passage under escort. It was not a particularly efficient way to move the tankers, but it made effective use of MIDEASTFOR's relatively limited resources.

Those plans shifted in the immediate aftermath of the *Stark* attack and the United States significantly increased its presence in the region. In the years leading up to the 1979 Iranian Revolution, the average number of U.S. Navy combatants assigned to Middle East Force in the Persian Gulf had stood at five ships. In 1980, in response to the hostage crisis, that number increased to seven ships, in addition to aircraft carriers and ships outside the Gulf in the North Arabian Sea and Gulf of Oman, which increased significantly for that year—a region that might see a carrier a couple of months a year suddenly hosted over two complete carrier battle groups.⁵⁶ From 1981 to 1986, combatants within the Gulf dropped back to five with aircraft carrier numbers stabilizing at an average of one carrier battle group on station in the North Arabian Sea throughout the entire year—a loading known as a "1.0 carrier presence."

In 1987, in response to *Stark*, the number of U.S. Navy surface combatants in the Gulf spiked to 13 ships, rising to 17 in 1988.⁵⁷ The types of ships deployed within the Gulf also changed—as a lesson-learned from *Stark*, all deployers were required to have a CIWS installed, which relegated a number of older ships to operations outside the Gulf, where they escorted what continued to be a 1.0 aircraft carrier presence. It would not be until Operation *Desert Storm* in 1991 that the U.S. Navy felt comfortable deploying aircraft carriers within the Persian Gulf itself.

For the *Earnest Will* missions themselves, the post-*Stark* revised planning featured the same marshalling pattern of escorting several tankers along

600-mile, two-day routes along the Southern Gulf, but now with more escorts. Additional ships were on standby, stationed on either side of the Strait of Hormuz, outside the range of Iranian *Silkworm* missiles. Plans were developed to use aircraft from the carrier to attack key Iranian military installations ashore, reinforced by USAF aircraft, if necessary, to retaliate against Iranian attacks.

Between the *Stark* attack in May and the first *Earnest Will* convoy in July, the Reagan administration faced detailed questioning. In June testimony before the Senate Armed Services Committee, Undersecretary of State for Political Affairs Michael Armacost emphasized the reliance on deterrence that undergirded the entire operation:

> Iran has not attacked any U.S. naval vessel. It has consistently avoided carrying out attacks on commercial ships when U.S. naval vessels have been in the vicinity. In its recent actions, it has displayed no interest in provoking incidents at sea with the United States. Of course, it would be foolhardy for them to attack an American flag vessel. Those ships would have American masters—that is, the reflagged [Kuwaiti] vessels. They will carry no contraband. They pose no danger to Iran. They will be defended if attacked.[58]

Armacost's belief that the Iranians would be deterred from attacking American ships had a long pedigree in the United States government; as a Top Secret CIA analysis of robust Iranian mine warfare capabilities assessed in 1984: "To avoid an incident that might give the United States an excuse to intervene in the Gulf, Iran probably would not mine areas patrolled regularly by U.S. Navy vessels."[59] However, if the goal of deterrence is "to persuade an adversary, through the threat of military retaliation, that the costs of using military force to resolve political conflict will outweigh the benefits," then it is not clear the Iranians were effectively deterred at *any* stage of the conflict. American communications and preparations had focused on the threat posed by aircraft, small boats, and *Silkworm* missiles with little effective attention on what turned out to be the actual initial threat—mines.[60]

A factor complicating American assessments was that there were *two* separate Iranian navies to deal with—the first was the regular, Islamic Republic of Iran Navy (IRIN), and the second was the Iranian Revolutionary Guard Corps Navy (IRGCN). The IRIN—particularly during the Tanker War—were mainly professional military personnel, many of whom had trained in the United States during the time of the Shah. They were familiar with Western naval procedures and the amount of destructive capacity represented by the U.S. Navy but were also the object of political and religious suspicion by the revolutionary government. Their counterparts in the IRGCN had impeccable revolutionary credentials but lacked experience in seamanship and maritime culture, to say nothing of knowing little of how major navies actually operated. However, it was this second navy—and its constant competitive influence on the first navy—that drove the naval war in the Gulf. An example of this influence could be found in the person of Lieutenant Commander Abdollah Manavi, IRIN, commanding officer of the IRIN frigate *Sabalan*, which grew infamous for its attacks on the bridges and crew spaces of targeted merchant ships, earning Manavi the callsign "Captain Nasty."

Second, the way the Iranian navies fought was unexpected. An American proclivity to underestimate mine threats is a recurring feature of the American way of war. During the Korean War, having driven the North Korean Navy from the sea, the U.S. Navy found its further efforts thwarted by North Korean mines. In the words of Rear Admiral Allan "Hoke" Smith, the U.S. commander of the UN Blockading and Escort Force off Wonsan in 1950: "We have lost control of the seas to a nation without a Navy, using a pre–World War I weapon, laid by vessels that were utilized at the time of the birth of Christ."[61] As it happens, some of the minesweeping assets constructed in the 1950s to deal with that Korean War threat would find themselves put to use in the Persian Gulf nearly 40 years later, sweeping mines designed by the Russians

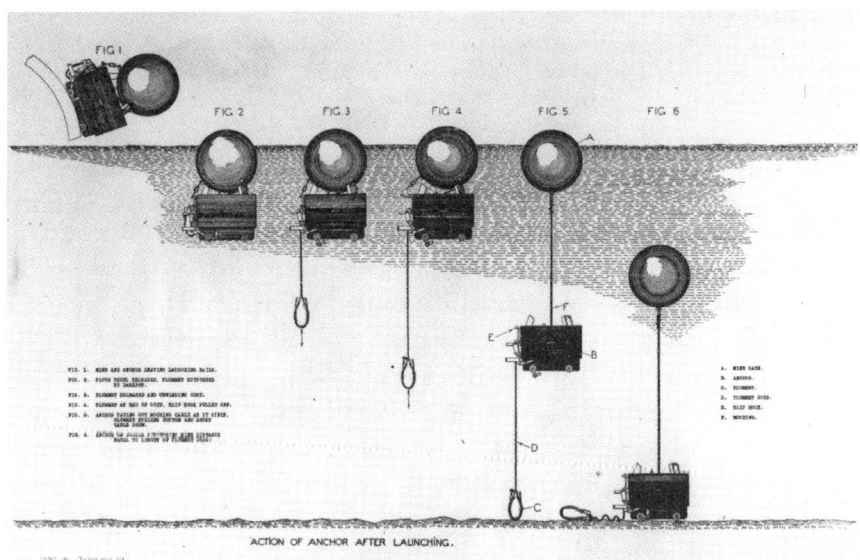

Process of laying WWI-era mines such as the Iranian SADAF-01 (Myam) and SADAF-02 (M-08) North Sea Mine Barrage. Diagram shows the action of the mine's anchor after launching from a mine-laying ship. (NHHC Photograph Collection, NH 61113)

in 1908 and then reverse engineered by the Iranians from those provided by their future partner in the "Axis of Evil," the North Koreans.

The Iranians had learned from Libyan use of mines in the Red Sea in 1984, particularly their ease of deployment, plausible deniability, and disproportionate psychological effects.[62] Unless minelaying was caught in the act, it could be difficult to determine who was laying the mines—an aspect particularly appealing to the Iranian Revolutionary Guard; Tehran would attempt to attribute later mine incidents to divine intervention—the "invisible hand of God."[63] The covert aspect also appealed to Iran's ultimate decision-maker—Ayatollah Khomeini—who approved the secret use of mines against convoys but did not approve open attacks on U.S. warships.[64]

Coincidentally, on the same day as the *Stark* incident, a Soviet tanker hit an Iranian mine as the ship entered Kuwait's harbor; three more mine strikes occurred nearby in the next month and nine more were later discovered and destroyed. The Iranians had not been targeting the Soviets; they had hoped to dissuade the Kuwaitis from proceeding with the reflagging mission. As historian David Crist summed up the thinking before the first official *Earnest Will* convoy in late July:

> Remarkably, when faced with an obvious Iranian military attack against Kuwait using naval mines, no one in either Tampa or Washington bothered to change the assumptions guiding the American convoy operations. [American military leaders] continued to believe that Iran would never dare to take such an overt action against the United States. Faith in the deterrent effect of the carrier and American firepower clouded every level of American decision making.[65]

As the United States prepared for the first *Earnest Will* convoy on July 22, 1987, the U.S. Navy task force was prepared for airstrikes such as those which had damaged the *Stark*, as well as surface-to-surface missile attacks from Chinese-manufactured *Silkworm* missiles or even small-boat attacks. The Iranians, perhaps recognizing this, chose to respond with mines, a reminder of the reciprocal nature of war when dealing with a thinking enemy.[66]

Clausewitz is associated with the term "fog of war," but he did not actually use that phrase. Instead, he wrote, "War is the realm of uncertainty; three quarters of the factors in which action at war are wrapped in a fog of greater or lesser uncertainty."[67] He continued: "War is the realm of chance. No other human activity gives it greater scope; no other has such incessant and varied dealings with this intruder."[68]

Uncertainty, chance, and mines were what awaited the U.S. Navy as it started its Persian Gulf escort missions.

CHAPTER 4

The *Earnest Will* Convoys Begin—July to October 1987

> Everything in war is very simple, but the simplest thing is difficult.
> —CLAUSEWITZ[1]

Maritime strategy often focuses on "choke points." While ships at sea have an infinite range of courses to get from point A to point B, they are channelized by geography at key approach points. British Admiral Sir John "Jackie" Fisher—the Royal Navy patron of Sir Julian Corbett—summed up the concept in 1904: "Five keys lock up the world! Singapore, the Cape, Alexandria, Gibraltar, Dover. These five keys belong to England."[2] Given the importance of oil to the world economy and the amount of tanker traffic originating from the Gulf, the Strait of Hormuz is such a choke point.

The Strait is relatively deep and subject to strong currents, making it difficult to plant mines. In terms of preparing for any Iranian attacks, it therefore made more sense for the Americans to focus on possible threats on or above the water, and the first *Earnest Will* convoy was accordingly oriented to seeing off those kinds of attacks. Of particular concern were the Chinese-provided *Silkworm* missiles—large, relatively unsophisticated anti-ship cruise missiles with a large warhead, fired from land-based launchers. *Silkworms* were based on technology from the 1950s but could do real damage if they managed to lock on and hit a ship. Firing the liquid propellant-fueled *Silkworm* required a great deal of preparatory work, observable to a watching foe. The United States therefore had the option to strike *Silkworm* launch sites during their extended preparation phase, rather than having to destroy them preemptively. Fixed *Silkworm* land-based sites also provided potential targets for retributive strikes.

The first *Earnest Will* convoy mission—two tankers and three U.S. Navy warships—departed the Gulf of Oman, outside the Persian Gulf, the morning of July 22. The tankers were the *Bridgeton* (401,000 tons, formerly the Kuwaiti *al-Rekkah*), and the *Gas Prince* (48,233 tons, formerly the Kuwaiti

Earnest Will convoy number 12, October 1987. The ships in the convoy include the frigate USS *Hawes* (FFG-53), the flagged Kuwaiti tanker *Gas King* (originally *Gas al-Burgan*), the cruiser USS *William H. Standley* (CG-32), and the amphibious assault ship USS *Guadalcanal* (LPH-7). Other than the mine strike on the first convoy, no *Earnest Will* convoy ended up being attacked by the Iranians. (Official U.S. Navy Photograph via PH2 J. Elliott)

Gas al-Minagish). Ship sizes are frequently indicated by their tonnage, an application of Archimedes' principle of the amount of water displaced by the weight of the ship and a useful approximation of a ship's overall size. The escorts were the cruiser USS *Fox* (7,900 tons); the destroyer USS *Kidd* (9,700 tons); and the frigate USS *Crommelin* (4,200 tons), a sister ship to the *Stark*. The *Bridgeton*, the sixth-largest tanker in the world at the time, was in fact significantly larger than the largest ships in the U.S. Navy inventory—a nuclear-powered aircraft carrier such as the USS *Nimitz* normally displaces around 97,000 tons.

Overhead, jets from the carrier USS *Constellation* in the North Arabian Sea flew patrols over the convoy as it began its transit through the Strait of Hormuz, the first 50 miles of their eventual 600-mile journey through the Persian Gulf. Normal ship traffic through the usually bustling Strait halted as civilian mariners awaited the outcome. Three Iranian F-4E fighter/bombers—American-built aircraft, sold to Iran during the time of the Shah—took off from their base at Bandar Abbas, flying patterns over Iranian territory, and then feinting toward the convoy. The *Fox* issued radio warnings and then

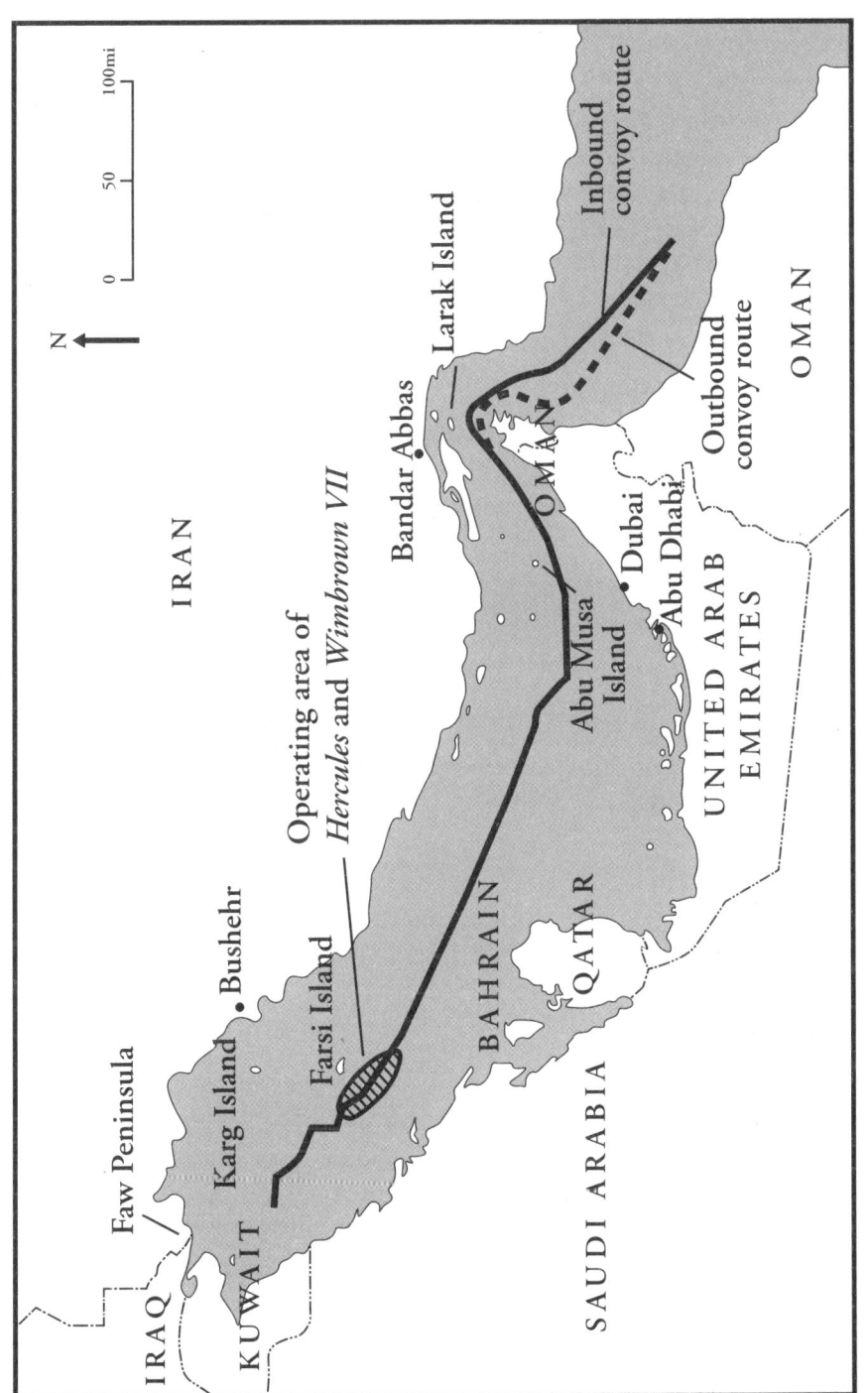

Earnest Will convoy routes.

locked its fire-control radars onto the Iranian planes. *Fox* was an older ship, armed with SM-2 surface-to-air missiles that featured a longer range than the SM-1s carried by the FFG-7s; accordingly, its AN/SPG-55 fire-control radar—a big, old-fashioned, drum-shaped radar with a dome-like bulge at the business end—put out a lot of radiation, immediately getting the attention of the Iranian pilots. Unlike the more efficient, combined radars carried by newer ships, there was no mistaking the signal received from a dedicated fire-control radar: they exist not for navigation, but instead only to put ordnance on target. The Iranian F-4Es, with the radar warning receivers likely blaring in their cockpits that their planes were specifically being targeted, broke off their approach and returned to base.

The ships of the convoy were also on the lookout for land-based Iranian fire-control radars associated with *Silkworm* missile targeting and launches. The Americans were ready to shoot down Iranian air threats, but there had to be threats in the first place—the mere existence of an Iranian weapon was not evidence of hostile intent. The Iranians, under orders from Ayatollah Khomeini to avoid direct confrontations—no matter the views of individual Iranian Revolutionary Guard commanders—avoided giving the American ships any pretext for attacks. Indeed, for the first eight months of *Earnest Will*, the Iranians avoided using their *Silkworms* against any U.S. Navy ships, but there was no way the Americans could have predicted that Iranian forbearance.

The convoy steamed through the Strait of Hormuz, eventually out of the range envelopes of the *Silkworms*, and continued up the Gulf. The convoy's course—dictated by the shallow geography of the Gulf and the deep draft of the tankers—took the ships past Iranian-occupied Abu Musa Island, the base of armed Iranian speedboats such as *Boghammars* and *Boston Whalers*. The *Boghammars* were known for their fast, swarming attacks on merchantmen; the course mandated by the depth required by the tankers took the convoy closer to Abu Musa than the U.S. Navy normally operated, and the sea lanes were now crowded with small fishing boats and dhows, making it difficult to distinguish between peaceful small craft and fast-attack craft. The Americans did not know of Khomeini's orders to avoid direct attacks and were at a high state of stressful readiness during the passage.

Moving farther north into the Gulf brought possible Iraqi airstrikes into consideration. The *Stark* incident was universally regarded as an accident, and the United States had arranged for deconfliction procedures with the Iraqis, but there was still the recognition that Iraqi pilots simply fired at large targets and that further accidents could happen. In the late evening of Thursday, July 23, and the early morning of Friday, July 24, the United States began picking up indications of large numbers of armed Iranian small craft in the vicinity of Farsi Island in the middle of the Gulf. Radio Tehran had announced on July 23 that the tankers carried "prohibited goods," and the convoy made preparations to repel a nighttime swarming attack by small boats.

Friday's dawn revealed a horizon clear of Iranian threats and the convoy; its crews, breathing a sigh of relief, turned to the last leg of courses that would take them into Kuwait's harbor and the transfer of protection duties to Kuwaiti authorities. Aboard the *Bridgeton*, breakfast trays were being carried to crewmembers on watch; witnesses report then hearing a loud metallic clank, feeling the shock wave of a massive explosion, and seeing trays of bacon and eggs flying into the air, and the lines holding the mast snap—the sixth largest tanker in the world had hit a mine on the way to Kuwait's harbor.

The damage to *Bridgeton* was negligible—even a 50-square-meter hole is manageable for a 400,000-ton ship and its 31 crewmembers, and the ship's unloaded state meant there was no risk of a massive oil leak. The threat to smaller ships, such as the 7,900-ton *Fox* and its 418 crewmembers, was of a different magnitude; a mine hit to an American small combatant could easily sink the ship and kill hundreds of American sailors. *Fox* and the other two U.S. warships quickly took station behind the *Bridgeton* as the massive tanker gradually slowed from 16 down to three knots, forming a kind of conga line that took the entire convoy through what, for all anyone knew, could have been an extensive minefield. If any ship could absorb further mine hits, it was the *Bridgeton* and coming to a complete stop would have taken the gigantic ship half an hour.

Admiral Bernsen, the MIDEASTFOR commander, captured the stakes of the Iranian mining attack:

> The Iranians had absolutely no idea what ship they were going to get with a mine. It could just as well have been the *Kidd* as it was the *Bridgeton*. And, in fact, more likely, because the escort was ahead. It was absolutely only by the grace of God that they didn't hit a U.S. warship ... And my bet is that they really put the mines in there to get a U.S. warship and that really they were disappointed when they hit the *Bridgeton*.[3]

The mine that struck the *Bridgeton* had been surreptitiously laid the previous night by what was subsequently determined to be the Iranian vessel *Sirjan*, one of a chain of nine contact mines. The mines were extremely basic, based on a 1908 Russian design; they could do serious damage if they made contact with a ship's hull, but they could only be used in shallower water—such as the waters in the northern Gulf off Kuwait.[4] The Iranians had managed to lay two lines of mines but, fortunately, the convoy did not make contact with the second line and made it to Kuwaiti waters seven hours later without further incident.

The first *Earnest Will* convoy was already a matter of considerable publicity, with international media awaiting its arrival; the sight of U.S. warships straggling into Kuwait Harbor being protected by the ships they were supposed to be escorting did not have the makings of a foreign policy success. American officials scrambled to put a positive spin on the story, saying the incident underscored the dangers of the Gulf and the need for international involvement.

Internally, the mining incident provoked significant responses. First, it was clear that the United States was not deterring the Iranians from attacking; it was simply channeling Iranian violent responses into ways and means for which the Iranians might have a greater chance of success. American leaders are much more comfortable talking in terms of deterrence than they are in terms of fighting—as Michael Howard had observed, international relations in the nuclear age were dominated by those "who believed that the element of force was not a necessary part of international intercourse, but could be eliminated by an application of the methodology of the social sciences." The actual application of force, which would appear to be an admission that deterrence had "failed" in the parlance, accordingly, could set up future disputes between those who believe that deterrence had to be "reestablished" vs those who instead saw force as a tool to achieve discrete foreign policy goals.

Second, it was clear that additional assets would need to be sent to the Gulf. The most obvious of those assets were platforms dedicated to mine countermeasures (MCM), such as minesweeping ships and helicopters. Assets were available, but they would need to be surged to the area and supported once there. While the number and capability of surface combatants had increased after the *Stark* incident, there was a notable omission in the types of platforms deployed—there were little-to-no assets specialized in dealing with mines. Part of this was a reflection of American naval force structure, which during the Cold War prioritized open-water conflict with the Soviet Union. The United States did have its own mine countermeasure forces, but they were oriented toward the protection of domestic American ports in the event of global war and therefore a mission directed toward the Navy Reserve rather than the active-duty Navy, with older, smaller platforms and part-time training.[5]

From an American force-planning standpoint, it is unclear whether there was a formal U.S. post–World War II decision that minesweeping would be the NATO naval contribution to burden-sharing or whether a traditionally perfunctory U.S. Navy attitude toward mine warfare meant that the Americans simply assumed that other countries would take up the slack or that the U.S. Navy would find a way to muddle through. Since the early days of NATO, the Soviet mine threat to western European ports had motivated European specialization in mine countermeasures. Indeed, of 159 American-made smaller coastal minesweepers constructed in the 1950s, "all but twenty were transferred to foreign navies under the Military Defense Assistance Program; most went to European NATO allies, who were assigned primary responsibility for Atlantic minesweeping."[6] Another factor was a post-Vietnam force-structure decision that prioritized helicopter-based minesweeping, which effectively curtailed further focus on surface-based mine countermeasure assets.[7]

The relatively casual attitude toward mine warfare by the U.S. Navy could be puzzling, given that—as naval historian Scott Truver observed—"Since the end of World War II, mines have severely damaged or sunk four times more U.S. Navy ships than all other means of attack."[8] The area itself was also an attractive target for mining; as one mine warfare expert put it—"From a strategic point of view, the Persian Gulf is an ideal mining target. It has favorable water depths and the bottom is soft all along its 500-mile length. Its sea routes are regularly traversed by some of the largest ships afloat."[9] The history of U.S. mine countermeasures is arguably one of belated recognition of the problem of mines, and *Earnest Will* continued this trend. As a comprehensive U.S. Naval Historical Center study observed in the period up to the Korean War: "For more than 140 years the officers and men assigned to MCM had successfully countered mine threats by jury-rigging equipment and by taking measured risks. So successful were their efforts as perceived by the Navy that little funding, prestige, or interest had been given to countering the mine threat, either in war or in peace."[10]

In the context of the 1980s and the Maritime Strategy, mines weren't ignored so much as they were seen a less-pressing concern when compared to the other challenges presented by the Soviet Union, and a task best not only handled locally but—where possible—by allies. The 1984 version of the Maritime Strategy reveals two foundational points of orientation on the part of the U.S. Navy when it came to dealing with mines: (1) such actions should occur as far forward as possible, ideally against the minelayers before they could get their mines in the water, and (2) an expectation that allies would "bear the lion's share of the task" when it came to actual minesweeping.[11] In Phase I of the execution of the Maritime Strategy, the American focus was clearly on protecting American waters: "Reserve Minesweepers prepare for mine countermeasures in U.S. ports, harbors and coastal areas."[12] In Phase II, "The allies would secure their own inshore waters."[13] While burden-sharing made sense from an accounting and budgetary standpoint, the actual usage of weapons was a political decision, and the politics of the Gulf were different from the politics of NATO defending Europe.

Once mines were determined to be a significant threat in the Gulf, requests to the Europeans to deploy those NATO mine-clearing assets to the Gulf were rebuffed by individual member states, arguing that a Middle Eastern deployment was "out of area" for NATO. It may seem odd now, after extensive post–Cold War NATO deployments in Afghanistan and in combating pirates off the coast of Somalia, but during the Cold War NATO still had Western Europe as its area of primary focus. The out-of-area response also tracked with the views of individual European governments who, at least initially, did not want to get involved in either the Iran–Iraq War or what was shaping up to be a U.S. conflict with Iran.

Clearing mines once laid, however, was only one approach to the problem. Preventing mines from being placed in the first place was an even surer way of keeping sea lanes open, and the United States had a number of assets that could be used to conduct surveillance and strike surface craft before they plant mines. The American response to the *Bridgeton* incident therefore comprised a range of related responses.

The most immediate response was that of flying in counter-mine assets: the U.S. Navy maintained several squadrons of large helicopters specially equipped to sweep mines; one of those squadrons was on standby in the United States even before the first *Earnest Will* mission. Those helicopters could be flown to the Gulf and operate from the USS *Guadalcanal*, a large amphibious ship that at first glance resembled a World War II aircraft carrier, once that ship had left Kenyan waters where it was currently supporting an exercise. The airborne mine-countermeasures (AMCM) could be deployed rapidly, but they could only do so much, such as detecting mines in advance of convoy sailings.

A more thorough response would require the other two parts of the MCM "triad": minesweeping ships and Explosive Ordnance Disposal (EOD) personnel. The initial European demurrals resulted in the Americans turning toward what remained in the U.S. inventory: minesweepers dating from the 1950s. While their technology was dated, they were being employed against contact mines derived from even older, pre–World War I designs, and the vintage minesweepers were effective—once they arrived on station.[14]

Most American minesweepers were Naval Reserve assets and would need to transit to the Gulf from their homeports on the Atlantic and Pacific coasts of the United States. While the helicopters could be on station relatively rapidly, the minesweeping ships would take weeks to months to arrive.[15] In the meantime, the U.S. Navy was able to jury-rig two civilian ocean-going tugs with a cable stretched between them to at least theoretically sweep a channel wide enough to get a tanker through.

A naval cultural value is that it is better to address the source rather than the effects, rather like going after the nest instead of swatting individual hornets. In the days of sail, this meant blockading enemy ships before they could get loose on the open ocean; in the case of mines, this meant ensuring that mines did not get into the water in the first place. Accordingly, the Navy turned toward bringing in surveillance assets to detect Iranian minelayers, attack assets to destroy those minelayers caught in the act or, in the best of all worlds, assets that could both surveil and attack.

For those surveillance and interdiction missions, MIDEASTFOR turned to the Navy's Special Boat Units—Special Operations Force (SOF) assets optimized for using relatively small patrol boats for inshore and shallow water operations based around 65-foot Mk III patrol boats, modified all-aluminum commercial boats used to support drilling platforms in the American Gulf of Mexico. The boats were known for their powerful engines, low radar observability, low silhouettes, and quiet engines. The boats were equipped with search radars and armed with guns fore and aft; in theory, they could run five-day, unsupported missions. The boats were under orders to be discreet—crewmembers sometimes dismounted their weapons, wore civilian clothes, and displayed commercial signage.[16]

Additional SOF assets included U.S. Army Special Operations assets such as AH-6 attack helicopters and MH-6 observation helicopters—both known as "*Little Birds*" for their relatively diminutive proportions. These Special Operations Forces activities were subsumed under a secret plan that ran in parallel to *Earnest Will*, known as Operation *Prime Chance*. Much like the activities of Britain's Special Operations Executive in World War II, the activities associated with *Prime Chance* are the sources of many tales of derring-do. In the context of the Tanker War, U.S. Special Operations forces end up prompting a couple of turning points in the war.

Like the minesweeping ships, the boats and helicopters required advanced basing support. American requests to operate from bases in Saudi Arabia or Kuwait were turned down—both countries, at this point, were seeking to limit their political liability in any coming conflict.[17] It is worth recalling that all these events occurred before Operation *Desert Storm* several years later and what later became the almost routine presence of U.S. forces in Kuwait and Saudi Arabia. The United States eventually settled on stationing two large barges—the *Hercules* and the *Wimbrown VII*—in the northern Persian Gulf as mobile sea bases. Politically, the stationing of U.S. forces aboard barges at sea rather than bases on shore illustrates one of the political benefits offered by seapower. Stationing American forces in Kuwait or Saudi Arabia would have tied those countries to U.S. military actions. The two Arab countries therefore would be acquiring the political costs of basing foreign military forces but with little-to-no control over what those military forces actually did—a condition of almost unlimited political liability. Basing the foreign military forces at sea, however—even if both countries financially supported the barges—helped to provide military capability while minimizing political liability.

Given that these smaller operational assets measured their mission time in hours and days, vice the weeks and months associated with large ships, it would be helpful for those barges to be relatively near the sites of potential action, which meant that the barges themselves were also vulnerable to attack. This threat geometry made for much intra-U.S. government discussion, as all were aware that suffering large numbers of American casualties was one of the largest threats to the overall Tanker War mission itself. The United States could demonstrate resolve by taking hits and still continuing with the mission, but it would be much better to avoid such casualties in the first place.

The introduction of U.S. Army assets into the mission intersected with larger organizational and legal moves regarding the U.S. military. The passage by the United States Congress of the Goldwater–Nichols Department of Defense Reorganization Act in 1986—popularly known as "Goldwater–Nichols" and prompted, in part, by a lack of effective interservice coordination in operations such as *Urgent Fury* in Grenada in 1983—created the expectation for joint rather than single-service approaches to warfare. In September, a new command was accordingly formed for the region: Joint Task Force Middle East (JTFME)—the first of what was to become a slew of JTFs in the following decades—commanded by a two-star U.S. Navy admiral, with a staff drawn from across the services and reporting to the four-star U.S. Marine general commanding U.S. Central Command in Tampa rather than the four-star U.S. Navy admiral in Hawaii.

Earnest Will therefore took place during an organizational transition time for the U.S. military. Prior to Goldwater–Nichols, a sea-based fight in the Persian Gulf would have been overseen by the U.S. Navy. More specifically, it would have received its overall direction from the four-star U.S. Navy admiral commanding the U.S. Pacific Fleet, one Admiral James "Ace" Lyons, U.S. Navy. The reporting chain question was not simply a matter of bureaucratic infighting for Lyons, a Navy maritime strategist with an aggressive reputation. Lyons, instead, favored taking advantage of a temporary bump in U.S. presence in the region in August 1987—due to the overlap that occurs when a battlegroup is relieved on station—to take the war to the Iranian mainland.

Lyons's U.S. Navy-centric plan would have attacked Iranian military and economic targets along the Iranian coast, using the two aircraft carrier battlegroups turning over in the region, along with the battleship USS *Missouri* and its associated battlegroup.[18] His operation *Window of Opportunity* was not about restoring deterrence; its focus was on decimating the Iranian military and economy to the point where it could not fight, and perhaps even bring down the regime in the bargain.[19] Lyons's plan included having the U.S. Marines conduct an amphibious operation to take the island of Abu Musa—held by the Iranians but claimed by the United Arab Emirates—and opened with the words: "Our response [to Iranian mining] needs to be vigorous and decisive. Half measures and gradualism will not do if we are to ever get their attention."[20] In advocating his plan to Secretary of Defense Weinberger, Lyons argued: "The objective of these strikes is to facilitate freedom of navigation and apply pressure to Iran to enter into serious negotiations to end the Iran–Iraq War."[21]

Lyons's plan never stood a chance—the Reagan administration was not looking for a large-scale war with Iran; it had the limited war aims of ceasing Iranian attacks on merchant ships and keeping the Soviets out of the Gulf, not the unlimited aim of overthrowing the Iranian regime. Lyons's idea and approach—which ended up getting him fired—provide the basis for fascinating counterfactual speculation. Had the United States actually followed through on *Window of Opportunity*, thereby effectively coming into the Iran–Iraq War on the side of Iraq, it is hard to imagine Iraq then turning around in 1991 and invading Kuwait. Neither *Desert Storm* nor *Iraqi Freedom* may have then ever occurred, and second-order effects such as the energization of al-Qaeda or the creation of ISIS might never have happened. On the other hand, it is impossible to predict what would have happened the day after *Window of Opportunity* with regard to the Iranians. In fact, however, three U.S. Navy battlegroups did *not* attack the Iranian mainland in a Navy-only fight in August 1987, leaving the remarkable outcome that although the Tanker War and *Earnest Will* ended up being fought completely at sea, that fight ended up being conducted with a joint force.

While the United States grappled with getting minesweepers to the Gulf, there was still a demand signal from the oil shippers to keep the tankers moving; the undamaged *Gas Prince* was now fully loaded in Kuwait Harbor and had contractual obligations for delivery outside the Gulf. The U.S. Navy reluctantly escorted the *Gas Prince* out of the Gulf on August 2. The ship sailed along the Saudi coastline, with the Saudis providing air cover. The Iranians surged eight of their warships during the convoy's passage through the Gulf, and the USS *Kidd* picked up a signal correlating to a *Silkworm* targeting radar, but the Iranians launched no actual attacks.

As these ship movements were taking place in the Gulf, the annual Hajj was being held on the other side of the Arabian Peninsula in and around Mecca. The Iranians, seeking leverage against the Saudis in response to Saudi support for the United States and Iraq, infiltrated Revolutionary Guardsmen into the regular Iranian allotments of Hajj pilgrims with orders to disrupt the Hajj. Saudi security, tipped off to the plan, opened fire on August 1, killing 275 pilgrims—both Guardsmen and civilians.[22] It had been only eight years since the 1979 seizure of the Grand Mosque in Mecca by Sunni extremists, and the Saudis were not taking any chances in losing control of the holiest places in Islam, above all during Hajj. Several days later, the Iranians in the Gulf began a multiday naval exercise codenamed Operation *Martyrdom*. Iranian television broadcast the "Martyrdom Maneuvers, a fairly extensive, dramatically staged (and musically scored) extravaganza depicting mock attacks by Iranian patrol boats and commandos—obviously directed at the United States."[23]

In the midst of all these events, American intelligence—now focused on the mine threat—began picking up signs of new Iranian mining efforts, although it was still unclear as to where the mines would be placed. The Strait of Hormuz itself remained inhospitable to the types of mines the Iranians were using, but those mines could be placed in various areas in the Gulf, as well as marshalling areas that tankers used outside the Gulf. In retrospect, it appears that the Iranian resupply ship *Charak* left Bandar Abbas in the midst of the naval exercise hoopla and laid a string of M-08 mines off the Emirati port of Khor Fakkan, outside the Persian Gulf and just south of the Strait, on August 8 or 9.

While the Khor Fakkan mining was a technical and operational success for the Iranians—their ship was able to lay the mines and not be detected while doing so—it backfired at the strategic level. The Iranian leadership could claim that the mine strikes occurring in the region were the "hand of God," but there was never any real doubt as to which country was seeding the area with mines. The task then became to catch the Iranians in the act of laying mines, which is exactly what the increased U.S. surveillance was later able to do.

In the meantime, the indiscriminate nature of the Iranian mining attacks started to affect other countries. Modern mines can target individual classes of ships, but the Iranian M-08s—based on that 1908 Russian design—were simple contact mines and would explode no matter the class or nationality of the ship that hit them. As early as May—coincidentally on the same day as the *Stark* incident—the Soviet tanker *Marshal Chuykov* struck an Iranian mine coming into Kuwait Harbor. The August Khor Fakkan mine attacks in August were to have more significant political repercussions.

On August 10, the tanker *Texaco Caribbean*—ironically loaded with Iranian crude oil—struck one of the Khor Fakkan mines, spilling 2.5 million barrels of oil. The Emiratis declared an exclusion zone, found several mines, and prematurely declared the area mine-free.[24] On August 15, the 156-foot service vessel *Anita*, operating from the UAE with a British skipper, struck an undetected Iranian M-08, blew up and sank, killing the master and four other crewmembers. The sinking and death toll were a reminder of what even simple mines could do to small ships, and journalists flying over the area afterward reported seeing two additional mines. This expansion of the mine laying—and, by extension, the Iran–Iraq War—to the Gulf of Oman initiated a series of international reactions.

A late-July American request to European allies for minesweeping assets after the *Bridgeton* incident had been denied; after Khor Fakkan in August, the United Kingdom, France, Italy, Belgium, and the Netherlands reassessed the situation and decided to send mine-clearance assets to the Gulf. These moves were not explicitly tied to an anti-Iranian political coalition. Instead, rather like the Combined Maritime Force operation set up in the region after 9/11, these navies instead depended on informal cooperation mechanisms geared to the minesweeping job at hand. While the European governments made public statements emphasizing that their operations were independent of U.S. activities, there are reports that France privately offered to join in air strikes on Iran if the mining continued.[25]

It is worth emphasizing that the Iranians were operating with an arguably sound strategic concept by using mines. If Iran could trigger a mass casualty event such as that seen with *Anita*, only this time killing 300 American sailors rather than five foreign nationals, and if they could make it occur several times against a foe that was not believed to have any staying power, then they could accomplish their objectives of getting the Americans to leave the Gulf. Neither the Iranian air force nor their army were likely to have the capacity for producing such mass casualty events, but mines conceivably could. The Iranians clearly looked at the Americans through the prism of Vietnam and Beirut—both modern, recent conflicts in which American casualty aversion was seen as a decisive aspect.[26]

The revolutionary Iranian perspective—that the willingness to suffer casualties is a mark of national seriousness—was reminiscent of pre-modern views of conflict that had last been mainstream for the West prior to World

War I. As the chapter in *Makers of Modern Strategy* examining the pre-war European "Doctrine of the Offensive" observed regarding the willingness to accept high casualty figures:

> The armies and nations of Europe thus went to war in 1914 expecting that there would be heavy losses. The spirit in which their young men were indoctrinated was not simply to fight for their country, but to die for it. The concept of "sacrifice," above all "the supreme sacrifice," was to dominate the literature, speeches, sermons, and journalism of the belligerent societies during the early years of the war. And the casualty lists that a later generation was to find so horrifying were considered by contemporaries not an indication of military incompetence, but a measure of national resolve, of fitness to rank as a Great Power.[27]

British Middle East journalist Robert Fisk caught this connection in making a battlefield tour with the Iranians in 1987: "Nor was the First World War a cliché here. With at least a million dead, the battle of Fish Lake was the Somme and Passchendaele rolled into one …"[28] He continued: "I returned from the battle of Fish Lake with a sense of despair. That small boy holding the Koran to his chest *believed*—believed in a way that few Westerners, and I include myself could any longer understand."[29] Navy Secretary Webb's questions of why the United States would want to get anywhere near this war were well grounded. The Iranians, still early in the throes of a religiously based revolution stemming from an approach to political Islam that prioritized the afterlife, may well have been correct in their assessment of relative staying power. The challenge for the United States was to avoid falling into Iranian mass casualty-producing kill zones.

A week after the Khor Fakkan incidents, the United States ran another *Earnest Will* convoy westward into the Gulf; the departure had been delayed even before the incidents because of intelligence warnings about potential Iranian mine action. The convoy departing on August 19 made it to Kuwait without incident. An eastbound convoy was then able to safely escort the *Bridgeton*—temporarily repaired and partially loaded—along with the *Gas King*, *Ocean City*, and a ship that would later be the source of another major incident, the *Sea Isle City*.[30]

The Iranians were not inactive while all this was happening. The Iranian Revolutionary Guard developed a plan to mine the main approaches into Bahrain, including the route being used by the U.S. Navy.[31] The Guard commandeered an Iranian Navy resupply vessel—the 176-foot-long *Iran Ajr*—and loaded it with M-08 mines. What the Iranians did not realize was—with the U.S. Navy now on high alert for any activities involving mines—that the *Iran Ajr* was being tracked and under surveillance.

Aerial port view of the captured Iranian mine-laying ship *Iran Ajr*. Mines are clearly visible on deck. The capture of the ship—the day before Iranian leader Ali Khamenei's address to the UN General Assembly in New York City—could not have occurred at a worse time for the Iranians. (NAID)

On the night of September 21, three U.S. Army AH-6 and MH-6 *Little Bird* helicopters, operated by the U.S. Army's 160th Special Operations Aviation Regiment and flying off yet another FFG-7, the USS *Jarrett*, hovered 200 yards from the *Iran Ajr* and observed as the crewmembers removed tarps and began to roll "mine-like objects" off the stern. This deployment of U.S. Army helicopters from a U.S. Navy ship was a consequence of a more joint approach to warfare. MIDEASTFOR commander Rear Admiral Hal Bernsen was listening to the reports in real time aboard his command ship *La Salle*; when he heard the description of "mine-like objects," he directed the *Little Birds* to attack. The Iranians were completely caught by surprise and were strafed by the helicopters, leaving the *Iran Ajr* on fire and dead in the water. The helicopters returned to the *Jarrett* to rearm; when they returned to the Iranian ship, they were surprised to see it back underway and continuing to lay mines. The American helicopters reattacked and the Iranians this time abandoned ship.[32]

The Americans were now in a position to take the *Iran Ajr* as a prize of war, a situation the U.S. Navy had not faced in many years. U.S. ships converged on the Iranian position. Real-time communications stretched all the way back to Washington, and the decision went to Secretary of Defense Weinberger in the Pentagon, who authorized the ship's seizure. The decision troubled the National Security Advisor, Frank Carlucci, and his deputy, Colin Powell. Powell, in a communication with Weinberger that demonstrated American casualty sensitivity and foreshadowed later Chairman of the Joint Chiefs of Staff (CJCS) Powell's advice to President George H. W. Bush to stop Operation *Desert Storm* at the 100-hour mark, told the defense secretary that "the President has been informed" but "we do not want to risk American lives by seizing the ship. We want to keep it contained and get them to surrender."[33] Carlucci subsequently told Weinberger the president had approved seizing the ship but that—somewhat gratuitously—the military should avoid unnecessary risks to U.S. personnel.[34]

At daybreak, the operation began to seize the ship, complicated by the presence of deployed mines in the water and possible survivors still aboard the *Iran Ajr*. The USS *Guadalcanal*—now deployed in the Gulf to support helicopter minesweeping operations—also hosted U.S. Navy SEALs and EOD teams. Those groups flew to *La Salle* via helicopter, then approached the *Iran Ajr* via LCM-8 "Mike" boats, shallow draft landing craft resembling their World War II D-Day forebearers that would be able to steer around any mines.[35]

The only Iranians left aboard the *Iran Ajr* were dead crewmembers, along with nine undeployed M-08 mines still left on deck. As a sign of how confused and rapidly developing the whole situation was—after all, the encounter had only begun less than 10 hours previously—several U.S. Navy Special Boat Unit Mk IIIs nearly engaged in a friendly-fire incident. Sortieing separately from Bahrain in dense morning fog, two Mk IIIs were proceeding on directions to find an Iranian landing craft at a certain part of the map, board, and seize it; the third Mk III with the secure communications had run aground and been left behind.[36] As one account put: "Incredibly, [Special Boat Unit Commander] Evancoe had been told nothing about the TF-160 attack on the boat. Nor about the fact that it had been abandoned and nor that it had now been boarded by the SEALs."[37] It was a mix of Clausewitz's reminders of the danger, fear, and confusion that differentiate war from all other human activities as well as the gallows humor of John F. Kennedy, a former war-time Navy PT boat commander, when he learned that a U-2 had blundered into Soviet airspace at a bad time during the Cuban Missile Crisis: "There's always some son of a bitch who doesn't get the message."[38]

The Mark IIIs approached the Iranian ship completely unaware of other U.S. forces in the area, the U.S. forces in the area had no idea the Mark IIIs were in the vicinity, and both groups thought the others could well be Iranian reinforcements. Further, as a legacy of the Shah's arms buildup, the Iranians had Mark IIIs of their own.[39] As one of the SEALs aboard *Iran Ajr* put it: "There was absolutely no deconfliction whatsoever and no communications."[40] Despite the fear and tension associated with the first experience of combat for most of the American participants, the U.S. forces discerned their mutual national identity and did not open fire on one another. In another indication of the previously close relationship between the United States and pre-revolutionary Iran, one of the American rescuers of the *Iran Ajr* crew now floating in life rafts was surprised to find that the severely wounded captain spoke fluent English. When queried on his language skills, the captain revealed "I am a graduate of the United States Merchant Marine Academy."[41]

One of the LCMs towed the *Iran Ajr* out of its self-created minefield and the USS *Jarrett* towed the ship—now flying U.S. colors—to international waters just north of Bahrain. USS *Guadalcanal* coordinated search and rescue activities that recovered the surviving Iranian sailors, who were eventually repatriated to Iran via the Sultanate of Oman. Iranian ships that sortied to salvage the *Iran Ajr* were warned off. Further U.S. searches of the ship revealed a chart showing where mines had been planted and documents that included overall mining plans.[42]

The capture could not have come at a worse time for the Iranians—it was "High-Level Week" at the United Nations in New York City, the period of maximum attention in the UN General Assembly, featuring world leaders making highly visible national speeches at the elaborate UN podium. Iranian President Ali Khamenei was due to give his high-profile national address at the UN General Assembly the day following the *Iran Ajr*'s capture. Khamenei's credibility in claiming *Iran Ajr* was a merchant ship carrying supplies was undercut by the photos of the Iranian ship with its deck full of mines.[43] President Reagan, speaking on the opening day of High-Level Week, had called for the acceptance of UNSCR 598 and its call for a cease-fire. Khamenei—speaking the next day as the highest level Iranian official to visit the UN since 1980—instead condemned the capture and, as contemporary accounts reported, he gave an 80-minute speech, "reading from a text that had been printed in advance as a hard-covered book, complete with gold-inked borders and intricate Islamic designs on each page," that accused the Security Council of being "a paper factory for issuing worthless and ineffective orders."[44]

Mines on deck of captured *Iran Ajr*. (Official U.S. Navy Photograph via PH3 Henry Cleveland)

Given the intelligence trove now being exploited by the Americans, as well as the worldwide condemnation and embarrassment at being caught in the act, the Iranians put their mining operations on an extensive pause. However, the strategic dilemma for the Iranians remained: the Iran–Iraq War continued, Iraq continued to get economic support from southern Gulf states exporting oil, and the detested American naval presence in the

THE *EARNEST WILL* CONVOYS BEGIN—JULY TO OCTOBER 1987 • 71

Gulf had grown rather than shrank. The Iranians accordingly turned to other ways to prosecute the war.

First the Iranians, still smarting from their abortive effort to disrupt the Hajj back in July, decided to strike another way—by attacking Saudi and Kuwaiti oil production facilities rather than the ships carrying the oil. The Iranian Navy and the Revolutionary Guard Navy planned to work together in a combined flotilla, in a major attack ashore along the northern border of Saudi Arabia with Kuwait, targeting production facilities, pumping stations, and perhaps even a desalination plant—crucial for the water supply of the Saudi capital, Riyadh, 260 miles to the southwest.[45]

American intelligence picked up indications of the impending attack and worked with the Saudis on a coordinated response, but operational miscues on the part of the Iranians and a delay in the start of their operation gave rise to doubts about the veracity of the information.[46] In the meantime, work continued on the floating American base in the northern Persian Gulf—the former oil barge *Hercules*—that serviced *Prime Chance* patrol boats and helicopters monitoring the Iranians. The American special operators on the barge, operating from a tradition of aggressive patrolling rather than defensively reacting to attacks, on October 8 sought to deploy the maritime version of a floating listening post with Farsi speakers aboard near the Middle Shoals buoy west of Farsi Island. The Americans on the barge had not been read into the highly classified intercepted Iranian attack plan on Saudi Arabia; the American Middle Shoals listening post had unwittingly been directed into a marshalling area for the rescheduled Iranian attack.[47]

The American patrol boats headed at night toward Middle Shoals buoy were preceded by a flight of *Little Bird* helicopters; there, the American helicopters found three small unknown boats tied up to the buoy. When those boats—which turned out to be an Iranian *Boghammar* and two smaller craft—heard the rotors, they fired at the noise, prompting a fierce counterattack by the SOF helicopters. The exchange of fire could be seen from the *Hercules*, eight miles away, and additional helicopters were deployed to join the American patrol boats accelerating toward the fight.[48] As the American forces took control over the area and began recovering Iranian sailors from their now-destroyed boats, there were surprised to find evidence of American-made *Stinger* missiles, originally supplied to the Afghan mujahideen and smuggled into Iran.[49]

Word of the clash at Middle Shoals buoy passed through the Iranian and American chains of command. MIDEASTFOR in Bahrain received reports of an Iranian missile fired at an American helicopter from the Rostam oil platform. Aboard the *Hercules*, the surface-search radars picked up 40 radar surface contacts apparently charging toward the barge; the patrol boats at Middle Shoals were ordered to engage the contacts. The USS *Thach*, another FFG-7 with its *Seahawk* helicopter already in the air helping to provide guidance to the *Little Birds*, opened the throttles on the two DC-8 jet engines that powered the frigate and sped to join the American patrol boats.

Iranian commandos had already landed on the beach in Saudi Arabia when word of the engagement at Middle Shoals reached them. Realizing that American forces were present in strength and on high alert in the vicinity, cognizant of the imbalance in casualties, and mindful that the operational plan may have been betrayed, the Iranians canceled the operation and returned their forces to Iran.[50] Several months later, a U.S. salvage team working at Middle Shoals buoy was able to recover the *Boghammar* and found aboard it more evidence of *Stinger* missiles as well as night-vision goggles—also something surprising to find in the Iranian inventory. There were subsequent reports of the *Boghammar* being restored to service and operating in San Diego Harbor, near the West Coast headquarters of the Navy SEALs.

With mining operations at a standstill and force-on-force engagements resulting in disproportionately high—indeed exclusively *Iranian* casualties—the Islamic Republic then turned to other ways and means to disrupt outside support for Iraq. On October 17, the reflagged tanker *Sea Isle City* (ex-Kuwaiti *Umm al-Maradex*) steered into Kuwait, after having successfully been escorted using an *Earnest Will* convoy along with three other tankers. The operation's concept of operations had always been predicated on the escort of tankers in international waters and around choke points; once the tankers reached Kuwaiti territorial waters, they became the responsibility of the Government of Kuwait.

The launch of an Iranian *Silkworm* missile from the captured al-Faw peninsula toward Kuwait harbor exposed a policy seam line. Iran had fired *Silkworms* at Kuwait before; indeed, a *Silkworm* had struck the Liberian-flagged tanker *Sungari* in Kuwaiti waters the previous day. There is no indication that Iranians knew they would hit a U.S. flagged tanker when they launched their missiles on October 17—this was simply a matter of chance, and the *Silkworm* missiles themselves had been captured from the Iraqis.[51] Kuwaiti defense forces attempted to destroy the missiles in flight but failed. The *Silkworm*'s onboard radar locked onto the bridge of the *Sea Isle City* and exploded, severely damaging the unloaded ship and injuring 18 crewmembers. The wounded included the now-blinded American captain, present aboard the ship as a consequence of operating the ship under the U.S. flag.

Reflagged tanker *Sea Isle City* being escorted by USS *Jarrett* in August 1987. A *Silkworm* missile hit on the tanker's bridge in October—after the ship had entered Kuwaiti waters—prompted Operation *Nimble Archer*. (National Archives)

Technically speaking, the response to the *Sea Isle City* was up to the Kuwaitis, and the American policy to date had been to protect the convoys and only act in self-defense of U.S. warships—all actions to be performed in real-time, as operations were underway. Initial American statements reflected these complexities. State Department spokeswoman Phyillis Oakley characterized the incident as "an attack on Kuwait," differentiating between activities in "international waters" and stressing "in Kuwaiti territorial waters, Kuwait has responsibility."[52] White House spokesman Marlin Fitzwater announced the location of the strike reflected a "somewhat unique situation" and observed that "although it was a U.S.-flagged ship, it did not involve U.S. military personnel in any way or U.S. Navy ships."[53] Any subsequent American response to the strike on the *Sea Isle City* would therefore be one of retaliation—both a widening of the rules of engagement, as well as an action of uncertain legality.

Observers on the scene captured the stakes: "The Americans have got no option right now across the board. And if they fail to respond, the people who want a wholesale withdrawal from the area are going to get it, and then we've got a real mess out here."[54] The Iranians, for their part, appeared to be enjoying the difficult situation the American administration found itself in. President Khamenei, back from his visit to New York City, announced at a Friday prayer service in Tehran that "I can tell you a missile has hit an oil tanker over which the American flag was flying. Where the missile came from, the Almighty knows best," and, in an interview the next day observed the U.S. government "is in a very difficult situation now and it is not clear if it has the necessary elements for a violent action."[55]

Initial American considerations of striking the al-Faw *Silkworm* missile launch site ran into a number of operational concerns. First, the missiles were on mobile launchers, which by their nature can be difficult to find and successfully destroy. Second, the strikes would require the use of carrier-based air; in 1987, U.S. aircraft carriers did not operate in the Persian Gulf, necessitating a long, observable trip for the attack aircraft requiring in-air refueling up and down the Gulf from carriers operating out in the Gulf of Oman. Third, al-Faw was a principal war zone for Iran and Iraq, and the region bristled with anti-air defenses, with significant risk to American personnel; the downing of two American aircraft by Syrian air defenses in late 1983 had, after all, been a contributing factor to the withdrawal of American forces from Lebanon in 1984.[56] Attacks farther south against the *Silkworm* sites around the Strait of Hormuz came with many of the same risks and those assets had not been involved in the *Sea Isle City* attack.

That all said, the Reagan administration quickly decided on the need for a "proportional and measured" response, aimed only at military targets. The stage was set for what would become Operation *Nimble Archer*—an attack using sea-based assets to destroy the Iranian Rashadat oil platform—a modest enough target. In a policy context, however, a line was being crossed—beyond relatively simple convoy escort and actions taken only in self-defense, potential U.S. activities were now widened to include retaliatory acts that broadened the scope for possible follow-on actions. This change in policy and orientation would result in significant acts in the coming six months.

CHAPTER 5

A Series of Retaliatory Events—October 1987 to April 1988

> Proportional response is very stupid. Especially when the best thing that can happen to your opponent is that he becomes a martyr.
> —AMERICAN STRIKE PLANNER IN THE PERSIAN GULF, 1988[1]

The next six months for the Americans in the Tanker War were bookended by two major retaliatory events: Operation *Nimble Archer* on October 19, 1987, and Operation *Praying Mantis* on April 18, 1988. Both operations were in response to Iranian acts and—in their timing and targets—they occurred after Iranian acts rather than spontaneously; moreover, they struck targets only tangentially related to the Iranian acts that prompted the retaliation. As it happens, the record appears to indicate that Iran itself was attacking ships directly following Iraqi attacks on *Iranian* ships; it would therefore appear the Iranians were pursuing a retaliatory strategy of their own.[2] The overall widening of the scope of U.S. military operations was not so much "mission creep"—the overall mission of the U.S. Navy did not change; the goal was still to stop Iranian attacks on merchant shipping—as much as it was a consequence of war's tendency to broaden, especially over time.

As Iranian President Khamenei hinted at—when alluding to policy dilemmas for the United States after the Iranian *Silkworm* missile strike on the *Sea Isle City*, which occurred while the ship was under the protection of the Kuwaitis—the way forward for the U.S. Navy was not clear. American considerations in the immediate wake of the attack were specifically expressed in terms of retaliation for the attack.[3] In a subsequent case before the International Court of Justice (ICJ)—the United States was sued by Iran for damages suffered during the Tanker War—the American argument, however, was of self-defense rather than retaliation. It also seems clear that, from an American perspective, there was an expectation that further Iranian attacks would occur if the United States military did not respond in some way. The

ICJ eventually ruled against the United States, saying that actions against oil platforms were not legally justifiable as self-defense; they did not address the retaliation question.[4] However, the court also ruled that such operations did not violate the 1955 U.S. Iranian "Treaty of Amity, Economic Relations, and Consular Rights," and rejected Iran's claims for damages.[5]

For the United States, the goal was not retaliation for the sake of retaliation or fighting for the sake of fighting—rather, the goal was to deter the Iranians from further attacks by manifesting a forceful response in addition to private communications and strong public statements. In the days immediately following the attack on the *Sea Isle City*, the Reagan National Security Council met and developed an array of six options. President Reagan chose only one of them—an attack on an oil platform—and then personally added a requirement for a 20-minute warning before the United States opened fire in order for Iranians to be able to escape.[6] The targets—reflecting an American desire to limit casualties—presented minimal risk to personnel on both sides.

In explanations later provided in support of the ICJ case, CENTCOM Commander General George Crist explained that the targets—the Rashadat platforms in the Rostam oil fields—were selected because they "were unambiguously offshore—not Iranian land territory" and that they were being used to surveil U.S. military activities in the Gulf: "I believed the best way of undermining Iran's ability to attack U.S. forces was to degrade their ability to observe our forces—in effect, put out their eyes."[7] MIDEASTOR Commander Bernsen described the challenge as "what kind of way do we demonstrate our displeasure," and, reflecting on the decision-making process that approved *Nimble Archer*, gave further evidence of American ultimately limited war aims in the Tanker War:

> A great many things were debated ... we'll take out the town of Bandar Abbas or we'll drop bombs on the Iranian naval base at Bandar Abbas, or we will take out some sort of headquarters or we'll do whatever on the mainland of Iran ... Those rather radical solutions were—except for in some quarters—dismissed pretty much out of hand. No one in Washington in retrospect really was interested in an all-out attack on Iran."[8]

The "prudent yet restrained response" taken by the Reagan administration reflected a continued desire to deter Iranian actions rather than to destroy Iranian capabilities, let alone overthrow the government.[9] There is, however, a missing part to the reciprocal actions that would actually characterize effective deterrence—Iranian perceptions and reactions. It is unclear even in retrospect how the Iranians interpreted any of this; the United States had, after all, lost its embassy in Tehran in 1979, and the documentary record shows a range of largely unsuccessful U.S. efforts to attempt to create some sort of two-way communication channel.[10] Reduced to sending one-way demarches through third-party channels, there was no effective way to measure or assess Iranian reactions. Talking of deterrence may make sense in conference rooms when engaged in budget battles or calming domestic critics, but the record is far from clear that deterrence actually works in affecting the behavior of adversaries—particularly adversaries who are essentially a black box when it comes to determining their decision-making process or even their key decision-makers. As Bernsen later remarked concerning American insights into Iranian decision-making: "I'm not sure that anyone had that kind of detail, quite frankly. I never saw any report, and certainly no report to be authoritative anyway."[11] Effective deterrence as a practical matter would need to be a reciprocal process; a lack of the ability to measure or accurately assess an adversary's responses and calibrate one's own actions would therefore seem to call the entire concept of deterrence as an actual war-fighting concept into question.

In the event, the oil platform selected as a retaliatory target presented a number of technical challenges. The lattices that made up the platform were more air than metal and getting a solid radar lock-on for the fire-control radars could be tricky. The ships selected for the mission carried bigger guns than those found on the seemingly ubiquitous FFG-7, which carried a 76-millimeter (three-inch) gun. Instead, the four ships selected for the *Nimble Archer* mission were a mix of old and new destroyers. USS *Leftwich* and USS *John Young* were large *Spruance*-class destroyers, powered by gas turbine engines and each armed with two five-inch guns capable of firing a range of different kinds of shells. The *Spruances* were designed to be high-mix ships, originally built with a lot of unused space that would be hopefully filled out by later advanced weapons systems—additions that never came to pass because of budgetary restrictions.

USS *Kidd* was an oddity, a modified *Spruance* class that also carried surface-to-air missiles and had been specially constructed to operate in the Persian Gulf. Originally ordered by the Shah of Iran, the transfer was blocked as a consequence of the Iranian Revolution, and the highly capable ship instead entered U.S. Navy service. Within the fleet, the four *Kidd*-class ships were more informally known as the "Ayatollah class."[12] Rounding out the task force was the USS *Hoel*, a steam-powered destroyer from an earlier generation of warships. *Hoel*'s assignment was problematic—it lacked the CIWS, last-ditch anti-missile system that was now required for U.S. Navy ships deploying in the

Gulf after the attack on *Stark*, but this older ship boasted a correspondingly older fire-control system—the Mk 68—that featured both a radar and—in contrast to the more modern destroyers—an old-fashioned combined manned optical and radar gun-directing system. *Hoel*'s manual optical sights, which included a stereoscopic range finder—a lens-based feature closer to pre-World War I dreadnoughts than to modern, radar-guided data-linked systems—could peer through the spray of bewildering radar returns produced by the supporting gridwork of an oil island.

Only *Kidd* was in the Gulf when planning started for *Nimble Archer*; the other three destroyers redeployed from their stations in the North Arabian Sea, using deceptive lighting schemes to get through the Strait of Hormuz.[13] The United States brought overwhelming force to deal with the relatively simple target—in addition to the four-destroyer strike force, the cruisers *Long Beach* and *William H. Standly*—both armed with powerful radars and anti-aircraft missiles systems—along with American F-14 fighters and E-2C airborne radar surveillance aircraft provided protection against any possible Iranian response from the air. All told, *Nimble Archer*—focused on the comparatively straightforward task of blowing up some oil platforms—would be the largest U.S. military operation in the Gulf to date.

On the morning of October 19, *Nimble Archer* commenced. This was not a surprise operation—Washington had been signaling for days that the United States would need to respond to the *Sea Isle City* attack. The attack occurred in broad daylight with clear weather, and there could have been little doubt as to the intentions of the four-ship column steaming toward the oil platform. In accordance with President Reagan's direction that the Iranians on the platform be given a chance to depart before action commenced, the USS *Thach* broadcast warnings—in English and in Farsi, on three separate channels (the bridge-to-bridge "channel 16" monitored by all ships as well as the military air distress and international air distress frequencies monitored by all aircraft)—that firing on the platforms would commence at 2:00 pm local time and that those on the platforms had 20 minutes to depart.

As it happens, there were a number of different platforms in the area and some confusion as to which platform was actually being targeted; this pending operation was, after all, an extreme version of one-way communication. The U.S. warning went out to Rashadat, also known as Rostam. The platforms in the vicinity comprised three separate but connected structures, each on its own pilings. The middle platform had been destroyed by the Iraqis earlier in the war—the fact that the entire series of platforms had ceased to extract oil and was now being used as a surveillance and command-and-control base was a factor in its targeting.[14] There was yet another Iranian platform located some

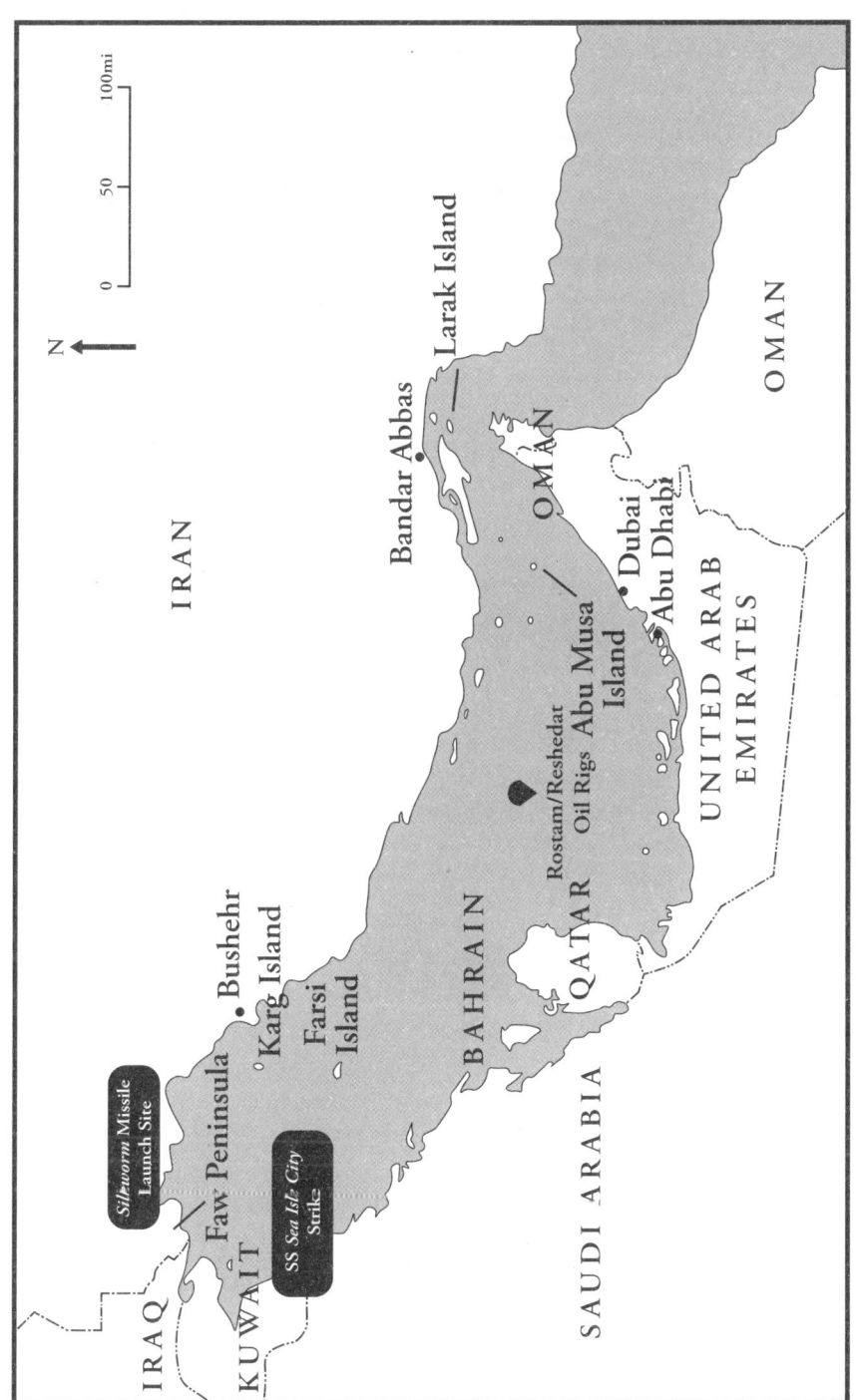

Operation *Nimble Archer* locations. While the missile attack occurred in the northern Persian Gulf, the response was in the middle of the Gulf.

two miles to the north. The Iranians heard the warnings but were confused as to which oil platforms were the subject of the broadcasts.

An Iranian supply boat tied up to the Rashadat platform came up on the bridge-to-bridge radio, claiming to have engine problems and asking for a delay. The U.S. Navy repeated the warning, after which the boat was able to restart its engines, and figures from the platforms evacuated into the vessel. Separately, an Iranian tugboat began collecting personnel from the non-targeted platform.

As promised, the U.S. destroyers began their bombardment at 2:00 pm, using their five-inch guns. The *Hoel*'s older, manned, visual gun director (for the direction)—and the associated radar (for range)—was able to score several direct hits. The newer ships also reported effective hits as well—a complication was trying to destroy a latticed support structure using high-explosive, fragmentary warheads. Participants compared the task to trying to shoot bullets at an antenna or a chain-link fence.[15] Similar to the problems artillery faced in World War I in trying to knock down barbed wire, it took a lot of shells to have any effect on the platforms—the final tally was 1,065 five-inch high-explosive and armor-piercing rounds. One highly visible effect was to destroy a safety valve on the capped wells on the northern platform, which resulted in the wells venting directly to the atmosphere and pillars of flame that could be seen for miles.

After the naval bombardment was complete, SEALs and an EOD team helicoptered to the platforms from the USS *Thach*. The northern platform—thanks to the well fires—was now too hot to approach, and efforts turned to the southern platform. The SEALs were to search for possible Iranian prisoners and any intelligence to gather, but the destruction had been so thorough that there was nothing left to exploit. They then assisted the EOD teams in emplacing destructive charges to completely bring down the southern platform.

U.S. forces on the scene decided to take advantage of the now-evacuated, non-targeted adjacent platform. SEALs boarded that platform, found no Iranians, gathered anything that appeared to be of intelligence value, and destroyed the radar and communication equipment that had been used to spot and report U.S. movements. Charges used to destroy some of the electronic equipment ignited some other interior structures, and the SEAL team left this platform in flames as well.

Reactions to *Nimble Archer* were fairly muted. American media focused on the large number of shells used to inflict damage, but the day's unrelated 23 percent plunge of the U.S. stock market—October 19's "Black Monday" on Wall Street—instead became the major international focus of attention. The Iranians had not specifically targeted the *Sea Isle City* and did not make any further immediate military responses to the shelling of the Rashadat oil platform—in strong contrast to their response after another U.S. retaliatory attack six months later. Instead, the Iranians launched another *Silkworm* missile at Kuwait's oil terminal on October 22 and continued to attack non-escorted merchant ships.

In the meantime, *Earnest Will* convoys began to settle down into a routine, with five convoys moving 16 ships in November and three convoys moving 11 ships in December. The U.S. Navy was proving effective in protecting ships in convoy against Iranian attacks, and neutral merchant ships would tag along with the convoys, even though the U.S. Navy ships—at this point—were under no obligation to protect non-U.S. flagged ships.

Incidents involving attacks on non-escorted, non-U.S. flagged merchantmen, however, continued to occur along with threats to the U.S. mobile sea bases in the norther Persian Gulf. Helicopters from U.S. ships helped to medevac crewmembers from several neutral tankers after attacks made by Iranian speedboats. As a reminder that an Iraqi air threat still existed to U.S. ships, the USS *Richmond K. Turner* nearly shot down two approaching Iraqi aircraft on November 26—Thanksgiving Day. On February 12, 1988, an Iraqi aircraft fired two missiles within eight miles of the USS *Chandler*—participating in an *Earnest Will* convoy.[16]

The near-miss with respect to the *Chandler* prompted a strong subsequent U.S. political response, with the Iraqis suspending attacks on Iranian shipping; given that Iranian attacks had frequently been in retaliation for Iraqi attacks, the Gulf entered a relatively quiet period, with seven *Earnest Will* convoys moving 16 ships in January, 7 convoys moving 18 ships in February, and 6 convoys moving 10 ships in March. Apart from the *Bridgeton* incident on the very first *Earnest Will* convoy, no further reflagged merchantmen had been attacked while being convoyed. In terms of ceasing Iranian attacks on formerly Kuwait/now U.S. flagged tankers, Operation *Earnest Will* was proving very successful in achieving its articulated war aims. However, it was an open question for the Americans as to just how long this mission would last.

The challenge was that the larger strategic issues that drove the Tanker War in the first place continued with no immediate end in sight. By 1988, the Iraqis were demonstrating a fair degree of momentum on land—in February, long-ranged missile attacks on cities resumed, with the Iraqis launching nearly 150 SCUD surface-to-surface missiles at Tehran over the next several months. The *Anfal* campaign began in the north, targeting Kurds along the Iranian–Iraqi border and featuring attacks using mustard gas and nerve agents. On April 18, the Iraqis, again using gas warfare, recaptured the al-Faw peninsula, from which the Iranians had fired the captured *Silkworm* missile that hit the *Sea Isle City* back in October.

At sea, the longstanding Iranian goal of expelling foreign navies from the Persian Gulf not only stagnated; it was getting worse in terms of non-regional navies now operating in and around the Gulf area. It is not clear what prompted the Iranians to restart their mining operations, but the results cannot have been what the Iranians had in mind—a reminder that, in war, at least half of the participants do not get the outcome they expected.[17] It is worth recalling, however, the Iranians were not taking these acts out of some peculiar Persian malevolence—as Canadian military historian Gwynne Dyer once summed it up: "The great majority of wars are fought because the government on at least one side has concluded, after rational calculation, that accepting the consequences of not fighting the war would be worse."[18]

On April 14, the USS *Samuel B. Roberts* had just successfully completed the 25th *Earnest Will* mission, escorting the reflagged *Gas King* and *Rover* to Kuwait. *Roberts* was a relatively new FFG, with many of the same capabilities and vulnerabilities as its sister ship *Stark* and a commanding officer—Paul Xavier Rinn—who had started his naval career under fire along the rivers of Cambodia in the waning days of the Vietnam War. Rinn and *Roberts* had been operating in the Gulf since February, where the ship had gained a reputation for confronting Iranian naval ships targeting neutral merchantmen. The standing U.S. rules of engagement did not allow for use of force to protect neutrals, but there was nothing prohibiting aggressive maneuvering. Rinn, in particular, was known for tangling with the Iranian Navy ships *Sabalan* and *Sahand* while they attacked non-U.S. flagged merchants.[19] Both ships—known as the *Saam* class—had been delivered by the British before the Revolution and were—with the "Ayatollah-class" modified *Spruances* safely retained in American hands—the largest and most sophisticated warships in the Iranian Navy. *Sabalan*'s captain, Abdollah Manavi, had become infamous for his deliberate targeting of crew's quarters following innocuous bridge-to-bridge radio conversations and had acquired the Gulf-wide callsign of "Captain Nasty."

It is not clear whether the Iranians were deliberately targeting the *Roberts*; instead, it would appear that they discerned a seamline in American surveillance coverage in the Gulf and, along that seam, sent the support ship *Charak*—the same ship that had laid Khor Fakkan minefield the previous summer—to sow a circle of mines into a channel that tankers were compelled to use because of nearby shoals. Over the next couple of days, the Iranians proceeded to lay another minefield 60 miles to the southeast, along a route that *Earnest Will* convoys had used in the past.[20]

Roberts headed out to the middle of the Gulf to refuel prior to escorting another *Earnest Will* convoy—and ran smack into the surveillance seam line and *Charak*'s newly laid minefield. While all ships were keeping a routine mine-watch, no actual mines had been encountered for months and none were expected—until *Roberts*'s forward lookout saw something suspicious in the ship's path. Several Iranian mines had broken free and were now bobbing on the surface. *Roberts*'s commanding officer was skeptical about mines, until he picked up binoculars and clearly saw them for himself.

Rinn quickly ascertained that *Roberts* was now in a minefield; he brought the warship to a rapid stop, advised the crew over the ship's public address system, and had crewmembers move away from spaces below the waterline, where a mine could be expected to do the most damage. The crew of *Roberts* had spotted mines ahead; it was a logical assumption that the path the ship had taken up to this point was mine-free, and that reversing along that path was the way to safety. FFG-7s were "single-screw" ships—meaning that they had one propeller and that propeller tended to "walk" the ship perpendicular to its intended course, especially at slow speeds, and especially going backward. The FFG-7s, in addition to their main engines, had auxiliary propulsion unit pods mounted near the bridge wing—a kind of moveable side thruster like those seen on commercial ships. By lowering the auxiliary pods, *Roberts* could mitigate the walking effect of the single screw and back out the same way she came in.

Charak had laid the minefield in a circular pattern. So, while *Roberts* had detected the floating mines up ahead, unbeknownst to its crew there were still moored mines in place behind the ship, and *Roberts* ran into one of the horns of those moored mines, detonating its 250-pound warhead. *Roberts* was backing at the time, and the mine strike occurred on the after part of the ship, just under the ship's port engine, causing extensive damage to the ship and opening a 20-foot hole on the ship's port side. While no one had been killed, many crewmembers were injured, both engines had been knocked off their mounts and were now inoperable, and fuel-fed flames were shooting up through the smokestack. Though unknown at the time of the mine strike, the ship's keel had been broken, and the only thing keeping the two halves of the ship together was the main deck, which had not been designed to take that kind of strain.

Crewmembers were able to restart the ship's diesel power generator—located in the forward part of the ship, and also initially knocked offline—restoring electricity throughout the ship. Captain Rinn informed Navy leadership in Bahrain of the extent of the ship's damage and JTFME Commander Admiral Anthony A. Less asked whether Rinn was considering having the crew abandon ship. Rinn declined, signing off with the phrase "No Higher Honor," the motto his ship had inherited from its famous World War II namesake—a similarly small ship, sunk with guns ablaze while battling a Japanese battleship and cruiser at the Battle of Leyte Gulf in 1944.

Efforts to send other U.S. Navy ships to assist the *Roberts* were hampered by the unknown extent of Iranian mining. Rinn instead decided to use the electrically driven auxiliary power units—which could propel the ship at several knots—to move *Roberts* out of the mine danger area and hopefully avoid hitting other mines in the process. The ship had hit the mine at approximately 5:00 pm on April 14; with the auxiliary power units (APUs) chugging along and its crew somehow keeping the ship afloat, in one piece, and knocking back fires throughout the night. *Roberts* was able to get out of the danger area by the next morning. It rendezvoused with USS *San Jose*—the ship she had originally been scheduled to refuel from—and was taken under tow by commercial tug to Dubai—in significant danger of sinking all the way.

Later simulations of the *Roberts* strike indicated that the ship should not have been able to survive a mine strike of that magnitude at the point where it had hit the ship. Not only did the simulations show the ship sinking within minutes; they showed the ship jackknifing and plunging straight down into

USS *Samuel B. Roberts* (FFG-58) being towed after the April 14, 1988 mine strike. Just below the tow line are the subdued ship numbers used in the Gulf; water is being pumped out of the port side and the ship's stern rests deeply in the water. (National Archives)

the water, taking most of the crew with it.[21] Had the incident proceeded in accordance with the modeling projections, the Iranians may well have had the mass-casualty incident they were presumably seeking.

Rinn was the commissioning commanding officer of the *Roberts*; about 70 percent of the crew were known as "pre-com," top-notch sailors selected as the pre-commissioning team for a new ship. The first-rate quality of the ship's officers and crew, along with an extensive focus on damage control prior to the mine strike, paid off in saving the ship. The officers and crew of *Roberts* were decorated with 10 Bronze Star Medals, 14 Navy Commendation Medals, and multiple Purple Hearts. It is worth noting that Bronze Stars and Purple Hearts are combat awards—the U.S. government had clearly moved beyond the non-combat decorations associated with the heroics aboard USS *Stark* the previous May. Rinn was recognized with the Legion of Merit and a Navy Commendation Medal with Combat Distinguishing Device for his "superior performance and management of the wounded."[22] Following his naval service, he became a motivational speaker, and the lessons learned from saving the *Roberts* went on to influence Navy fleet-wide damage control training.

Roberts being transported back to the United States for repairs and eventual return to the fleet. The damage to the keel from the mine strike meant that the ship was no longer seaworthy. (National Archives)

The United States was then confronted with the question of what to do next. Deterrence had clearly "failed," as it appeared the Iranians were back to laying the same types of mines with the same ship. While a number of American sailors had been wounded—some seriously—none had been killed. Naval leadership in the region and at CENTCOM headquarters in Tampa came up with aggressive proposals that—in current parlance—might be termed "asymmetric." CENTCOM Commander Crist in Tampa proposed taking over the disputed Abu Musa Island, situated in the vicinity of the Strait of Hormuz and serving as both a surveillance location and a base for IRGCN small boat attacks. JTFME Commander Less in Bahrain advocated bombing the Iranian Navy headquarters in Bandar Abbas on the Iranian mainland, along with mining the entrance to Bandar Abbas Harbor and destroying three oil platforms in the Gulf. He also proposed striking the *Silkworm* launch sites along the Strait of Hormuz, which would have served the dual purposes of sending a signal as well as ridding JTFME of one of its principal planning concerns. All of these options were asymmetric only in the sense of what was to be targeted; none of these options envisioned going after the Iranian regime, thereby turning the conflict into an unlimited war.

As in the case of *Nimble Archer* and the response to the *Silkworm* strike on *Sea Isle City*, the focus in Washington turned to what was seen as a proportional, retaliatory attack. Chairman of the Joint Chiefs of Staff, Admiral William Crowe advocated destroying an Iranian warship as a sort of 1:1 exchange. His nominee was the *Sabalan* which—in addition to strafing the berthing compartments on merchant ships—had approached the *Roberts* as she appeared to be sinking on April 14. Rinn had run up an SM-1 missile—an anti-air missile that also had a surface-to-surface mode—on *Roberts*'s undamaged foredeck where the *Sabalan* could clearly see it; the Iranian ship left the area.[23] Secretary of Defense Carlucci, the former national security advisor who had relieved Weinberger as secretary of defense in December 1987—emphasizing that no Americans had been killed—advocated no loss of life on the Iranian side either and supported attacking more oil platforms with warnings provided ahead of time.[24] There was no Washington support for any attack on the Iranian mainland, except if the Iranians were in the process of firing their land-based *Silkworms* at U.S. ships. Nor was there any proposal to change the character of the war by targeting Tehran, which had already been on the receiving end of dozens of Iraqi SCUDs without noticeable strategic effect.

The bureaucratic conclusion was a classic Washington compromise: the retaliatory attack in response to the mining of the *Samuel B. Roberts* would be the sinking of one Iranian ship and the destruction of the Sirri and Sassan

A SERIES OF RETALIATORY EVENTS—OCTOBER 1987 TO APRIL 1988 • 87

"Before" shot of Iranian *Saam*-class frigate *Sabalan*, which acquired a reputation for strafing the bridge and crew quarters of targeted merchant ships following innocuous radio conversations. (National Archives)

oil platforms, and possibly the Rahkish oil platform. As official U.S. naval historian Michael Palmer tartly observed: "Despite the Reagan administration's rhetoric about never fighting another conflict the way the United States had fought in Indochina, the planned 'proportional response' against the Iranians was, in fact, a Vietnam-like controlled marginally escalatory use of military force."[25] That the end result was "the biggest battle the U.S. Navy has fought since World War II" was more attributable to the relatively large number of American and Iranian ships involved—and combat's inherent tendency to escalate—than to any specific U.S. intent.[26] By day's end, the U.S. Navy would engage in its first surface-to-surface missile exchange between ships and sink half of Iran's operational fleet, including its largest opposing warship since World War II.[27]

The retaliatory operation was codenamed *Praying Mantis*. The U.S. fleet subdivided into three Surface Action Groups (SAGs), each composed of three ships, designated to attack specific targets. SAG Bravo would destroy the Sassan oil platform, the westernmost target, as well as the Rahkish GOSP if no Iranian ships appeared as targets. SAG Charlie would destroy the Sirri oil platform. SAG Delta had a roving commission in the Strait of Hormuz to

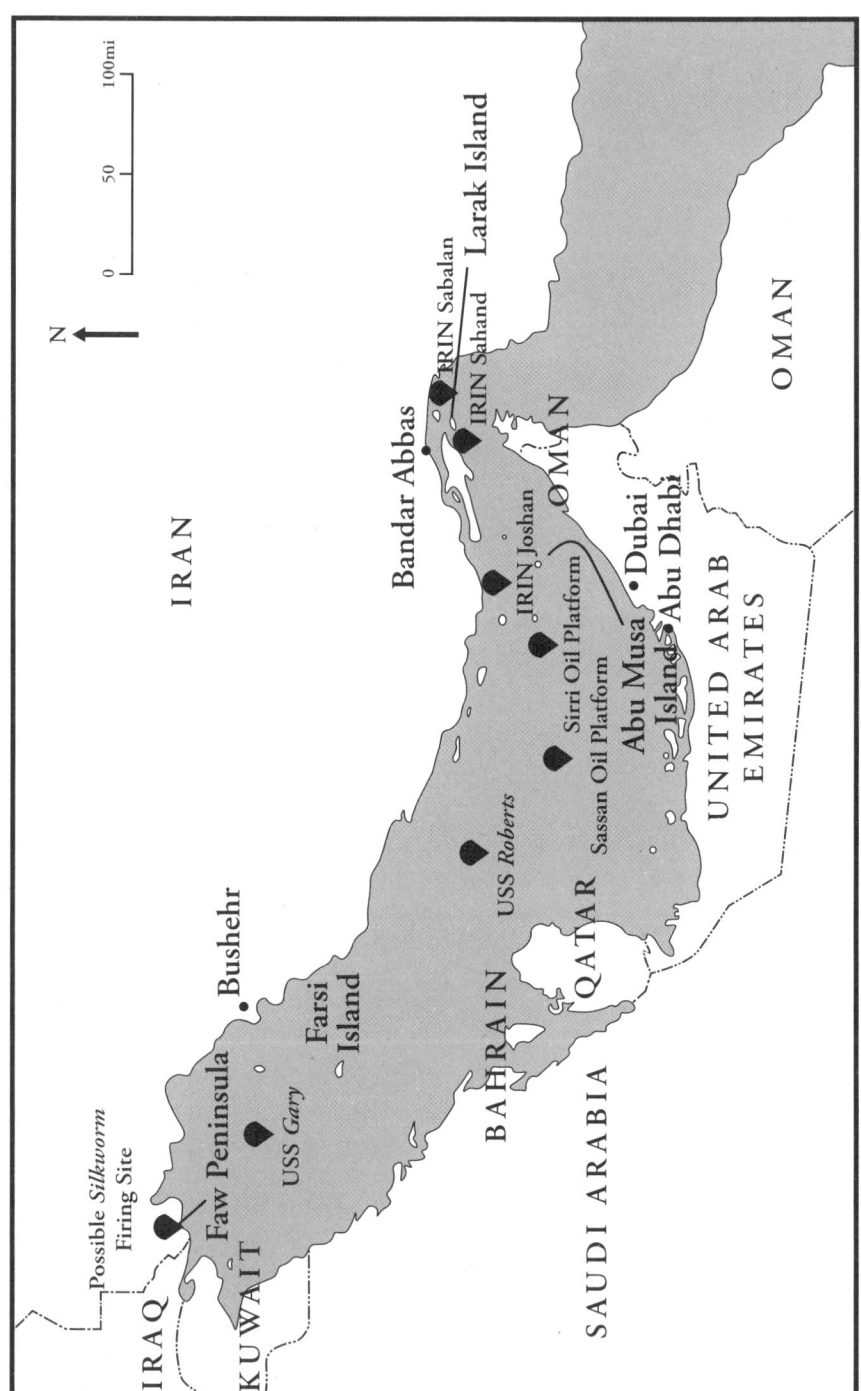

Operation *Praying Mantis* locations. USS *Samuel B. Roberts* struck a mine in the center of the Persian Gulf, but most of the retaliatory activity occurred to the east, in and around the Strait of Hormuz.

detect, engage, and destroy the Iranian naval ship *Sabalan*. The three SAGs would be backed up by additional Navy ships in the area, carrier aircraft from the USS *Enterprise* in the North Arabian Sea, as well as AWACs and refueling aircraft flying from Saudi Arabia.[28]

On the morning of April 18, SAGs Bravo and Charlie moved to attack their designated oil platforms. SAG Bravo, composed of USS *Trenton*, a large amphibious ship with Marines embarked, and the destroyers USS *Merrill* and USS *Lynde McCormick*, provided a 20-minute warning and then opened fire on the Sassan oil platform. Unlike *Nimble Archer*, this time the Iranians fired back—the first of what would be a day of reciprocal actions between the opposing sides. In this instance, American fire in response prompted a call for a cease-fire from the platform and several Iranians—described as "a large crowd of converted martyrs"—climbed aboard a waiting tug joining some colleagues who had moved after first hearing the 20-minute warning.[29] Those remaining on oil platform opened fire again; an AH-1 Marine Corps helicopter flying from the *Trenton* attacked and destroyed those defending the platform, allowing other Marines to board the oil island, gather intelligence

USS *Lynde McCormick* firing five-inch guns to starboard in 1988. *McCormick*'s guns and old-fashioned fired control system were instrumental in destroying Iranian oil platforms. (NHHC)

material, evacuate the wounded, and place charges that later destroyed the platform.

SAG Bravo was then directed to proceed to the neighboring Rakhish oil platform and destroy it as well. As SAG Bravo moved to the new target, two Iranian F-4E aircraft steered toward the Surface Action Group. *Lynde McCormick*—an older destroyer like its sister ship *Hoel*, but the only dedicated anti-air warfare platform in the SAG—directed its SPG-51C/D specialized missile fire-control radars at the Iranian aircraft. This is an unmistakable action that immediately proceeds an SM-1 missile launch; the Iranians broke off their run. As if any reminders as to the confusion inherent in war were needed, the SAG initially misidentified a nearby Soviet destroyer as an Iranian frigate—which would have made it a desirable target—and a UAE patrol boat as an Iranian *Boghammar* speedboat, but both initial targets were resolved before there were fired upon.[30] The Soviet captain, when queried on the bridge-to-bridge as to his intentions—which could easily have resulted in U.S. Navy ships engaging a Russian ship—said "he just wanted to take pictures for history."[31] In a move to limit any further escalation, the attack on Rahkish was called off, despite the fact that—at this point—no Iranian ships had been destroyed.[32]

SAG Charlie, made up of the cruiser *Wainwright* and frigate *Bagley*—both older ships with the same manned five-inch gun and gunfire-control director found on *Hoel* and *Lynde McCormick* that had proven useful in attacking the Rashadat oil platform in November—along with USS *Simpson*, another FFG-7, began their attack on the Sassan oil platform after providing additional time for Iranians to depart the platform. Several crewmembers remained upon the platform and the ships of the SAG opened fire. The SAG paused fire to allow the Iranian crewmembers to reconsider their options and an American helicopter dropped a raft nearby. When the SAG opened fire again, a round hit a compressed gas tank and incinerated the platform, making it both unnecessary and unfeasible to have the waiting SEAL platoon board the platform for intelligence exploitation.

The initial Iranian response to the attack on the Sassan GOSP might also be described as asymmetric—rather than confronting SAG Charlie, the Iranians instead deployed five IRGCN *Boghammar* speedboats into a separate area in the southern Persian Gulf. The *Boghammars* used their machine guns and rocket-propelled grenades to attack targets of opportunity: the U.S.-flagged oil rig supply ship *Willie Tide*; the Hong Kong-flagged, British-owned tanker *York Marine*; and the Panamanian-flagged *Scan Bay*, which had fifteen American crewmembers. Departing from the original *Praying Mantis* gameplan, JTFME commander Less authorized two A-6E aircraft based on USS *Enterprise* to attack the *Boghammars*. The lead speedboat was destroyed; the other boats ran themselves aground on Abu Musa Island.[33] Concurrent with the attacks on the two GOSPs, SAG Delta entered the Strait of Hormuz looking for the *Sabalan*. The Iranian ship, however, remained in port in Bandar Abbas, wedged between two civilian tankers that made for problematic targeting.

To the west, another Iranian ship made its appearance—the *Joshan*, a 275-ton fast-attack craft larger than the *Boghammars* but smaller than the 1350-ton *Sabalan*, the designated target ship for *Praying Mantis*. *Joshan* was armed with the same caliber gun—76 mm—as found aboard the American FFG-7s but, even more threateningly, carried Iran's last operational *Harpoon* missile. The *Harpoon* was a U.S.-made surface-to-surface missile, similar in explosive impact to the *Exocet*, but harder to decoy. Given that the orders associated with *Praying Mantis* only allowed for the targeting of *one* Iranian ship, there was some reluctance to have that ship be the *Joshan* rather than the larger and more notorious *Sabalan*. The *Joshan* continued on a course to intercept SAG Charlie, and the SAG commander aboard *Wainwright* was granted permission to engage the ship if necessary. *Wainwright*'s commanding officer later said that he would have engaged the *Harpoon*-carrying *Joshan* much earlier if he had not received guidance after the morning GOSP strikes to de-escalate.[34]

As the *Joshan* continued to close on SAG Charlie, the American ships broadcast warnings on bridge-to-bridge radio for the Iranian ship to turn away. *Joshan*'s fire-control radar then locked onto *Wainwright*, an action preparatory to launching the *Harpoon*. *Wainwright* announced on bridge-to-bridge, "Stop engines, abandon ship, I intend to sink you." *Joshan*, in response, launched a *Harpoon*. The missile rocketed past *Wainwright*'s starboard side; its guidance system either failed to activate—possibly because it was fired too close—or was lured away by the chaff systems that could have saved the *Stark* had they been deployed.

The Americans responded with overwhelming force. *Wainwright* and *Simpson* together fired five SM-1 missiles in surface-to-surface mode. What the SM-1s lacked in warhead size, they made up for in velocity and *Joshan* was quickly transformed into a mass of flaming, sinking metal.[35] A *Harpoon* fired for good measure by *Bagley* passed over the now close-to-the-water hulk. Fifteen of *Joshan*'s crew were killed outright; the commanding officer had his leg severed. The ships of SAG Charlie moved closer to what remained of *Joshan* and sank it with guns; there had been no American casualties in the exchange of fire.

Adams-class destroyer firing an SM-1 Missile; the ship's aft five-inch gun is to the right. Operation *Earnest Will* featured the first combat usage of the SM-1—normally regarded as an anti-air weapon—in surface-to-surface mode, where it proved devastating against Iranian ships. (Naval History and Heritage Command)

While the *Joshan* and the ships of SAG Charlie exchanged missiles, two Iranian F-4s were circling overhead. *Wainwright* carried guns aft and missiles forward; after warning the F-4s to depart, it fired two SM-2, extended range surface-to-air missiles. One missile hit an F-4, which still managed to make it back to land at Bandar Abbas, a tribute both to the skills of the Iranian pilot and to the resilience to battle damage of the American-made F-4s.

April 18 was only half over, but there was worse in store for the regular Iranian Navy. By noon, American intelligence ascertained that Iranian ships were preparing to sortie from Bandar Abbas. In the late afternoon, U.S. warplanes operating in conjunction with SAG Delta's *Joseph Strauss* picked up indications of a possible Iranian *Saam*-class ship—the class that included the specifically targeted *Sabalan*. The rules of engagement required American aviators to visually identify ships before attacking them—in pointed contrast to the Iraqis—and one of the aircraft flew toward the ship, which turned

Harpoon missile about to hit a target ship. The entire missile hits the ship, not just the warhead. Any unexpended fuel adds to the destruction. (Naval History and Heritage Command)

out to be the *Sahand*, a sister ship to the *Sabalan*. *Sahand* responded to the American fly-by with gunfire and hand-held surface-to-air missiles. The American aircraft maneuvered violently and avoided damage. Having been fired upon, the American ROE now permitted a forceful response. They, and other aircraft from the *Enterprise* air wing, then counterattacked with two air-launched *Harpoons* and bombs. *Joseph Strauss* added a surface-to-surface *Harpoon* to the mix. *Sahand*, like *Joshan*, was left a twisted, burning, hunk of metal—one of its magazines exploded and it sank, killing at least 45 of its crewmembers.

Sahand's fight finally drew *Sabalan* out of port. The attack on *Sahand* had used up much of the airborne ordnance carried by that wave of *Enterprise*'s aircraft, and there was a single A-6 on hand that still had unexpended weaponry. That aircraft flew close to *Sabalan* to perform the necessary visual identification; like the case with the earlier ship, *Sabalan* responded with hand-held surface-to-air missile fire. The A-6 dodged the fire, turned, and

Iranian Frigate *Sahand*, before and after Operation *Praying Mantis*, sinking after multiple *Harpoon* missile strikes and laser-guided bomb hits. (Official U.S. Navy Photograph, USNI)

dropped a single 500-pound bomb down *Sabalan*'s stack, destroying the engine room, leaving it on fire and dead in the water. By this point—in a scene reminiscent of its predecessor at the Battle of Midway—another wave of attack aircraft from *Enterprise* was inbound to finish off the *Sabalan* when Secretary of Defense Carlucci approved CJCS Crowe's recommendation to cease the attack with an un-Clausewitzian "Sir, I think we've shed enough blood today."[36] Iranian tugs brought the *Sabalan* back into Bandar Abbas, where it was repaired and eventually returned to service, carrying Chinese missiles. *Sabalan*'s commanding officer, Abdollah Manavi—callsign "Captain Nasty"—survived and later reached the rank of vice admiral.

***

The threat from *Silkworm* missiles had been an operational concern for the Americans from the beginning of the operation in 1987, especially those arrayed along the Strait of Hormuz. Other than the target-of-opportunity strike against *Sea Isle City* in Kuwait Harbor, the Iranians had not used these weapons against American targets; that was to change on April 18. In the realm of rumor, multiple witnesses aboard ships comprising SAG Delta operating in the Strait reported large objects flying past them emanating from Iran. A subsequent investigation did not find evidence of *Silkworm* launches in the Strait, although there was also speculation that there was little reason to make such a finding as it might have led to calls for a strike on the Iranian mainland. *Joseph Strauss* fired several SM-1s at an Iranian C-130 military cargo aircraft—another American-made platform in the Iranian inventory. The C-130 was thought to have been acting as a spotting aircraft for *Silkworm* launches; none of the SM-1 missiles hit, but the Iranian aircraft departed the area.

In the northern Persian Gulf, there was at least one verified *Silkworm* launch against an American ship. The FFG-7 USS *Gary*—on station to protect the barges supporting U.S. SOF operations—received indications of a *Silkworm* launch. The ship took evasive actions and fired at the missile, possibly shooting it down. The missile had been fired from the al-Faw peninsula; al-Faw's recapture by Iraqi forces later that very day obviated the need for any U.S. strike on the missile launch site.

The towing of the damaged *Sabalan* into Bandar Abbas concluded an eventful day. The Americans may have intended a proportional response, but the lop-sided results were a reminder of war's unpredictability and tendency to go to extremes. Newspaper headlines at the time spoke of Iran losing half of its Navy; the box-score is more complex. In 1988, the Iranian navies had hundreds of craft, ranging from several ex-World War II British and American destroyers to over 100 coast patrol craft. However, as *Janes Fighting Ships* for 1988/89 observed: Iranian "ships in commission suffer from two major problems—lack of maintenance and lack of spares. In the past, training of semi-literate conscripts was a major problem. Now, without foreign help, the dilemma must even be greater."[37]

Praying Mantis clearly took a severe toll on Iran's operational fleet. Of Iran's four newer, front-line *Saam* class frigates—delivered from the UK as Vosper Mk 5s in the early 1970s—*Sahand* was at the bottom of the Persian Gulf, *Sabalan* was a floating wreck in port at Bandar Abbas, and the other two may well have served mainly as sources of spare parts. Even after the sinking of *Joshan*, Iran retained another 10 *Combattante II* fast-attack craft, but their *Harpoon* missile launchers lacked any actual *Harpoon* missiles, and these ships presumably suffered from the same maintenance and spare part problems that afflicted the rest of the fleet.[38] After April 18, the IRGCN was credited with having 35 *Boghammars* and 35 *Boston Whalers*, but these were small platforms with endurance measured in hours rather than days. Iran retained minelayers such as the *Charak*, but the Americans had learned to close the surveillance gaps that allowed uninterrupted mining. It is hard to say whether the Iranians were deterred from further actions at sea; they may have not had any further effective platforms to put to sea at that point.

By 1988, the Iranians were a hardened military that had been involved in a major war for eight years. That said, the Iranians were used to fighting the Iraqis, and the warnings from the American-trained IRIN to the revolutionary IRGCN and Iranian political leadership, about American military capacity and lethality, had been dismissed. The lopsided results of *Praying Mantis*—American casualties were two aircrew lost in an accident when their AH-1 helicopter hit the water—were a consequence of the skill and resources of the Americans and the challenges Iran faced in adapting to their opponent.

By sheer coincidence, on the same day as *Praying Mantis*, the Iraqis opened a major offensive on the al-Faw peninsula at the northern end of the Gulf. The Iranians, who likely did not believe in coincidences, saw the Iraqi attack in the north and the American attack in the south as connected, suggesting that the Americans were now prepared to intervene in the Iran–Iraq War on the side of the Iraqis. The lack of American condemnation of Iraqi tactics—which included extensive use of chemical and nerve agents to take the peninsula—likely confirmed the Iranian mistaken belief in a changed U.S. policy.

As it happens, there had been a significant American policy shift in the midst of *Praying Mantis*—a consequential change that directly led to the *Vincennes* incident in July 1988. Right after the attacks on the GOSPs by SAGs Bravo and Charlie, Iranian *Boghammars* had attacked the *Scan Bay*, a non-U.S. flagged ship that nonetheless had American citizens aboard. A request was sent from the cockpit of an American aircraft all the way to the White House for permission to engage the Iranian small craft and protect U.S. citizens. Until that point, U.S. policy had been to protect only U.S.-flagged ships. President Reagan made a mid-battle decision to allow the A-6s to attack the *Boghammars*, which they did successfully.[39]

There had been a major question percolating for months about whether the U.S. Navy should protect non-U.S. flagged ships under attack by the Iranians in the Persian Gulf. U.S. ship commanders had advocated for the ability to open fire rather than simply having to stand by and watch the Iranians rake ships' crew quarters and bridges with small-arms fire. U.S. owners of non-flagged

U.S. ships pleaded for protection. The governments of Saudi Arabia and the United Arab Emirates urged the United States to take wider protective action. In January 1988, the French commander of naval forces in the Gulf announced the French warships would open fire on those attacking any merchant ships, not simply French-flagged ships, and urged other countries to do the same.[40] None of those other actors, however, had the numbers, capacity, or reach of the U.S. Navy. There were reports that Defense Secretary Carlucci, returning from during an early 1988 visit to the Gulf by way of Paris, had with the French, "raised what was described as his 'personal idea' of expanding the U.S. role in the gulf to include protection of neutral shipping," but Pentagon spokesmen at the time downplayed the report, saying, "that shouldn't be taken that changes are contemplated."[41]

The decision, therefore, announced by Secretary of Defense Carlucci on April 28, two weeks after *Praying Mantis*, was another turning point in the Tanker War:

> The president has decided to provide assistance under certain circumstances to ships in distress in the Persian Gulf and Strait of Hormuz in keeping with longstanding, time-honored Navy and maritime tradition. Such Aid will be provided to friendly, innocent, neutral vessels flying a non-belligerent flag outside declared war-exclusion zones that are not carrying contraband or resisting legitimate visit and search by a Persian Gulf belligerent. Following a request from the vessel under attack, assistance will be rendered by a U.S. warship or aircraft if this unit is in the vicinity and its mission permits rendering such assistance.[42]

Reading past the official, carefully hedged language of the announcement, this was a major expansion of the American rules of engagement. The new policy was not tested until July 2, when USS *Elmer Montgomery* came to the assistance of a Danish supertanker under attack by three of Iran's remaining speedboats, 13 miles from Abu Musa Island. That Iranian attack reportedly was in retaliation for an earlier Iraqi attack on two Iranian oil tankers. *Elmer Montgomery* arrived on the scene; two of the speedboats immediately departed, but one remained until after the U.S. ship fired warning shots.

With a new American policy in force, and with American shots already having fired in the vicinity of the Strait of Hormuz, the stage was set for the USS *Vincennes* incident and the end of the Iran–Iraq War.

CHAPTER 6

To End a War—April 1988 to August 1988

> The acceptance of the resolution was truly a bitter and tragic issue for everyone, particularly for me ... Happy are those who departed through martyrdom ... Happy are the disabled, the prisoners of war and the great families of the martyrs. And how unhappy I am because I have survived and have drunk the poisonous chalice of accepting the resolution ...
>
> —AYATOLLAH KHOMEINI ON UNSCR 598[1]

American policy toward the Iran–Iraq War in the late 1980s proceeded on two related, if not necessarily coordinated, tracks. The military track was *Earnest Will*, a U.S. Navy-led response to Iraqi and Iranian actions, which—while operationally successful—strategically was hostage to events and ultimately to a larger war over which the United States had very little influence.

The second track was diplomatic, centered in the United Nations Security Council in New York City. The United States is a permanent member of the UN Security Council, and both the Council and America had been working throughout the decade to create a diplomatic framework that could end the Iran–Iraq War. While the Council may have widely been regarded as largely moribund from its formation in 1945 until the Gulf War in 1991, it is arguable that it was the earlier Iran–Iraq War—and especially its end in 1988—that heralded a new period of relevancy for the UN Security Council.

Throughout the 1980s, the Council had passed a series of resolutions pertaining to the war between Iran and Iraq, overcoming a general Cold War stasis in order to do so. As early as September 28, 1980—six days after Iraq's initial invasion—the Council passed United Nations Security Council Resolution (UNSCR) 479, calling for both Iran and Iraq to "refrain immediately from any further use of force and to settle their dispute by peaceful means and in conformity with the principles of justice and international law." While it is easy to denigrate the resolution's high-flying language and immediate lack of results, it is worth highlighting that the Cold War UN Security Council was able to focus immediately on the Iran–Iraq War and, from the start, to frequently produce Security Council products on a way ahead.

Several years into the war, freedom of navigation in the Persian Gulf came to be another area of Council focus. In 1983, UNSCR 540 affirmed "the right of free navigation and commerce in international waters" and called for belligerents to cease attacks on maritime infrastructure. 1984's UNSCR 552 condemned "attacks on commercial ships en route to and from the ports of Kuwait and Saudi Arabia" and demanded "that such attacks should cease forthwith and that there should be no interference with ships en route to and from States that are not parties to the hostilities."

While the United States did not couch Operation *Earnest Will* in terms of enforcing UN Security Council resolutions—a practice that would become routine in the 1990s when it came to military operations against Saddam Hussein—it is clear that American actions were consistent with a general international attitude toward the war. On July 20, 1987—one day before the first *Earnest Will* convoy mission—the UN Security Council unanimously passed UNSCR 598. The Reagan administration had been subject to intense criticism after the *Stark* incident and was engaged in congressional hearings on the way ahead for the convoy operations, to say nothing of the concurrent Iran–Contra hearings that would be running all summer. Passage of an acceptable UNSCR in New York—even one not explicitly tied to U.S. military operations—would serve to show domestic American critics of the broad international support regarding the need to do something in the Persian Gulf.

UNSCR 598 (annotated text in Appendix 1) was a remarkable document, drafted by the five permanent members—the United States, the United Kingdom, France, China, and Russia, also known as the "the P5"—of the Security Council in close cooperation with the UN secretary-general.[2] Giandomenico Picco, a senior advisor to UN Secretary-General Javier Pérez de Cuéllar, wrote of the sense of opportunity: "In Pérez de Cuéllar's office, we thought that a single initiative by the secretary-general could amount to a political trifecta: we might rescue Washington from the humiliation of Iran-contra, test the new Soviet foreign policy, and unify the Security Council's Perm Five on a single political platform for the first time in UN history."[3] Picco was also serving as the UN's chief negotiator concerning the hostages in Lebanon; he was later able to unexpectedly draw from 598 in order to secure the cooperation of the Iranian government in helping to release some of the hostages that had helped to precipitate Iraq–Contra in the first place.[4]

Most UNSCRs start life at the initiative of a single Council member—for the P5 to cooperate in this fashion, especially in 1987, was unheard of and Secretary of State Shultz later commented on 598 in his memoirs: "A thaw in the Cold War was now clearly underway. Constructive action through the United Nations was now possible."[5] British Foreign Secretary Howe, present along with Secretary Shultz at the adoption of UNSCR 598 in the Security Council chamber in New York on July 20, 1987, was similarly complimentary, drawing attention to the unanimity of views of P5 members and observing that "clear consensus of this kind has been all too rare in the history of the Security Council."[6] To help place UNSCR 598 in context, it is worth recalling that in 1980, when the United States went to the Security Council to impose economic sanctions on Iran for holding American diplomats hostage, that move was blocked by the Soviet Union—seven years later, the mood in the Council had clearly shifted toward cooperation.[7]

Resolution 598—adopted citing articles 39 and 40 of Chapter 7 of the UN Charter, the Chapter that lays out the duties of the Security Council to take "Action with Respect to Threats to the Peace, Breaches of the Peace, and Acts of Aggression"—moved past the rhetorical exhortations of its predecessors. UNSCR 598 instead proposed a legally binding "demand" for the parties to "observe an immediate cease fire, discontinue all military actions" and "withdraw all forces to the internationally recognized boundaries without delay." UNSCR 598 differed from subsequent Iraq-oriented "use of force" resolutions such as UNSCR 678 that specifically authorized the use of military means against Saddam Hussein in 1991; that later resolution cited Chapter 7 in its entirety which—in addition to encompassing articles 39 and 40—triggered all twelve articles in Chapter 7, to include articles 41 and 42 that authorized economic sanctions and legal military action.[8] That said, UNSCR 598's language was about the most the market would bear in 1987 and—even more importantly—the demonstration of P5 unity made for a powerful diplomatic tool. The thinking was that enforcement of 598's demands would be achieved by a separate, stand-alone resolution to be adopted subsequently by the Council.

UNSCR 598 was put forward as a "presidential text"—a phrase that implied unanimity among Council members and obliged them to support the text as drafted in subsequent discussions. The actual formal Council session in which the resolution was adopted was overseen by several of the foreign ministers of Council members as well as U.S. Secretary of State George Shultz, a relatively rare event intended to demonstrate high national interest in the resolution being adopted—the overwhelming majority of Security Council resolutions

U.S. Secretary of State George Shultz at the adoption of UNSCR 598 in the UN Security Council on July 20, 1987. The U.S. delegation behind Shultz includes U.S. Permanent Representative Vernon Walters and Assistant Secretary of State for Near Eastern Affairs Richard Murphy; the Iraqi permanent representative is off to Shultz's right. (Secretary of State Photo Albums, 1987 July 20, Hoover Institution Library & Archives)

are passed simply with the presence of the New York-based ambassadors. Veteran American Security Council practitioner Cameron Hume, who wrote a negotiating history of UNSCR 598, summed up the scene:

> At the meeting, foreign ministers presented a tableau of council unity behind the new resolution. Two important precedents had been set: the permanent members had worked together as a group to lead the council, and the council had decided to use the powers of chapter VII to address an ongoing threat to international peace and security.[9]

The self-inflicted isolation that affected Iran's ability to get spare parts for its military equipment extended to its diplomacy as well; the Iranians had shunned the Security Council from the very start of the war and did not directly engage in the negotiations over UNSCR 598.[10] By contrast, the Iraqis, who had steadily engaged with Council members in the run up to the resolution's adoption and were present in the Council chamber at its adoption, quickly announced acceptance of its terms. On 598's adoption, Iran's permanent representative to the United Nations denounced it in New York as "a vicious

American diplomatic maneuver," and the official Iranian media response was instead to declare the resolution "null and void."[11] Strategically, in the words of a strategic assessment from the CIA at the time: "We judge that Iran's belief it can still achieve its maximum war goals—the ouster of Saddam Hussein and the ouster of the ruling Ba'ath party through military force represents the greatest obstacle to entering negotiations."[12]

The Iranian leadership in Tehran—significantly however—never actually officially rejected UNSCR 598 but rather offered commentary on its components and reordered how it should be implemented in practice. Tehran's eventual official response to 598's passage and contents, dated August 11, 1987, outlined their concerns, commenting that "as it reflects the Iraqi formulae for the resolution of the conflict, it cannot therefore be considered a balanced, impartial, comprehensive and practical resolution" and accusing the Security Council of turning "itself into a party to the conflict."[13] The Iranians, in particular, took issue with the Council's lack of identifying Iraq as the aggressor in the original attack, saying that 1980's UNSCR 479 effectively "called on Iran, a Member State of the United Nations, to practically submit to aggression."

Iran had many reasons to be dissatisfied with the language of UNSCR 598. The text called for immediate withdrawal from captured territory and the release of prisoners—both potential significant points of leverage for the Iranian regime in any negotiations, especially at the time of the resolution's adoption in mid-1987. The resolution's language contained very general language determining war guilt and predicated any such determination on cooperation with Iraq. The last paragraph of 598 spoke ominously of "further steps to ensure compliance with this resolution," a reference to the American-led efforts to pass an additional UNSCR that would have created an arms embargo against any country that did not accept UNSCR 598. If the Americans succeeded in passing the second resolution called for in 598, the quick Iraqi acceptance meant that the impact would have fallen solely on Iran, depriving it of the arms needed to fight Iraq.[14]

The capture by the U.S. Navy of the *Iran Ajr* in the act of laying mines two months after 598's passage did not help the Iranian case nor inspire countries to come to Iran's support. The P5 consensus that produced UNSCR 598, however, only went so far. United States' efforts to gain a commitment for the enforcement resolution, which had started prior to 598's passage, ran into consistent resistance from the Soviet Union.[15] Recollecting that all of this was still occurring during the Cold War, the Soviets instead advocated for the introduction of an international naval force into the Persian Gulf, interpreting

598's Operative Paragraph Five—calling upon states to "exercise restraint and to refrain from any act which may lead to further escalation and widening of the conflict"—to mean that U.S. naval forces acting unilaterally should withdraw from the Gulf. The Americans clearly did not agree; otherwise, they would not have supported UNSCR 598.[16]

That said, the political atmosphere leading to UNSCR 598 had fueled the idea of a multilateral UN escort force, an idea ironically initially proposed by an American congressman and then further developed by former U.S. senior national security officials—former Secretary of State Cyrus Vance and former Secretary of Defense Elliot Richardson—but then taken up by the Soviet Union.[17] Vance and Richardson advocated in a June 1987 *New York Times* op-ed that their "guiding principle" would be "diplomatic deterrence, which is likely to be more effective than military deterrence furnished by a nervous superpower."[18] The proposal illustrated the uneasiness about the potential escort mission and further underscored the faith that American policy makers had in deterrence; in retrospect—and perhaps only in retrospect—it would appear from subsequent mining operations that the Iranians were not to be influenced by any kind of deterrence.

The Vance/Richardson proposal did not rely on the use of naval vessels; rather, "a Council resolution should authorize seafaring United Nations peacekeepers to place a United Nations flag on vessels entering the gulf that asked a United Nations guarantee of safe passage and that submitted to United Nations inspection to insure [*sic*] that no war materiel was on board." This pre-Srebrenica proposal depended on the belief that United Nations "peacekeeping forces are widely respected and rarely attacked, even in zones of bitter conflict."[19] It also misunderstood the motivations of both the Kuwaitis—who felt that superpower involvement was *exactly* what was needed to end the larger war—as well as the Iranians, who knew full well that the tankers they were attacking did not contain war material; rather, they were attacking Kuwait's economic ability to fund the Iraqis. Vance and Richardson later met with Secretary of State Shultz to advance their proposal; Shultz replied that the area in which the United Nations could really be helpful would be in ending the Iran–Iraq War, and American efforts at the United Nations turned to promoting the follow-on, arms embargo UNSCR.[20]

The Soviets had their own smaller naval presence in the region. Warships of the Red Banner Fleet had escorted Soviet merchantmen since the Iranian boarding of a Russian ship in September 1986. Kuwait had reached out to both superpowers for protection later that year—while *Earnest Will* was a larger operation and had been predicated on the Kuwaitis abandoning their request to the Soviets, the Kuwaitis and the Soviets had in fact arranged for three tankers to operate under the Soviet flag. By June 1987, Soviet naval presence in the region included a *Kara*-class cruiser, a *Kashin*-class destroyer, three minesweepers, and associated support ships. That all said, the American naval presence dwarfed that of the Soviets, and the Americans had large assets—namely aircraft carriers—that were simply not to be found in the Soviet inventory.

The Soviets had a powerful strategic rationale to link American desires for an arms embargo UNSCR to P5 discussions regarding the creation of an at-sea UN peacekeeping force. The custom for UN Peacekeeping Operations (PKOs) up to that point was that such operations would not include military forces from the Permanent Five members of the UNSC; a UN at-sea peacekeeping force in the Persian Gulf would therefore serve Soviet (and incidentally Iranian) interests of displacing the U.S. Navy from the region.[21] Indeed, the Speaker of Iran's Parliament Ali Akbar Rafsanjani supported the idea of such a UN task force, so long as the superpowers were not part of the flotilla.[22] While a Soviet spokesman was briefing the Arab press that any task force would only include ships from "non-aligned states," Soviet General Secretary Mikhail Gorbachev announced that he was willing to envision the participation of both Soviet and American ships, likely counting on the Soviet UNSC veto to enable very close control over any actual UN task force deployment.[23]

The Soviet delegation in New York presented a non-paper in February 1988 (contained in Appendix 2) roughly laying out their proposal for a "United Nations Naval Force in the Gulf."[24] While the Soviet concept was relatively simple, the execution of a naval peacekeeping operation was so complicated that other members of the P5 were able to bring the proposal to a halt by insisting on answers to logistical, political, and financing questions that the Soviets had not effectively considered.[25] Additionally, the southern Gulf states viewed the replacement of Western naval forces with a UN task force or, indeed, the complete withdrawal of outside naval forces as a move favoring Iranian interests.[26] One of the effects of the Soviet ploy, however, was to consistently stall American efforts to pass the follow-on arms embargo resolution, mainly due to continuing Soviet objections.

As Security Council observer Cameron Hume summed it up:

> By the end of June 1988, what had resolution 598 accomplished? It had not ended the war, nor helped to protect shipping, nor led to imposition of UN sanctions … Resolution 598 nevertheless produced a framework … that acquired extraordinary legitimacy in defining the path to a settlement. As a guide for and expression of the foreign policies of other nations, resolution 598 subjected Iran and Iraq to pressure to end the war.[27]

UNSCR 598 remained on the books even as negotiating efforts in New York City ground to a halt. Instead, it would be military actions along the border between Iraq and Iran and in the Gulf itself that would be key to the resolution's implementation.

* * *

The extensive destruction of Iranian naval assets as a result of *Praying Mantis* in April coincided by sheer chance with a significant land operation by Iraq—*Blessed Ramadan*, a major offensive intended to recapture the Iranian-occupied al-Faw peninsula that the more secular Ba'athists launched against the Islamic Republic of Iran the evening of April 17—the night before the start of Ramadan. The two events were not linked—the Americans were retaliating in response to the April 14 mining of the *Roberts*, while the Iraqi multi-corps operation had been in planning for months. The Iranians were in a holiday standdown period and the massive Iraqi offensive—which featured the use of nerve agents—achieved tactical surprise, allowing the Iraqis to recapture the al-Faw peninsula, which had been under Iranian control as a result of a major Iranian military offensive in February 1986, and the overall operation arguably reversed Iran's most significant military accomplishment of the entire war. The Iraqi operation had been expected to take several weeks to reach its goals; in the event, they reconquered al-Faw in 35 hours, thereby emboldening the Iraqis to consider follow-on attacks.

The Iraqis continued their ground offensive the next month on May 25, attacking along a 15-mile corridor east of Basra, and counting upon heavy artillery barrages and extensive use of nerve gas. Iranian forces were driven back by the Iraqi combined-arms operations, and Iraq's use of chemical weapons drew little international condemnation, a measure of Iran's diplomatic isolation and a signal to the Iranians to expect more unfettered use of chemical weapons by the Iraqis. This Iraqi version of blitzkrieg repeated the rapid gains seen in April, with the Iraqis reaching their objectives in 10 hours. The momentum was clearly slipping from the Islamic Republic—Iranian gains achieved throughout 1987, at a cost of 50,000 dead, had been lost in a single day.[28] In the meantime, the Saudis severed diplomatic relations with Iran. From an Iranian perspective, the events of April and May 1988 seemed to suggest that an Iraqi–Saudi–American entente was emerging.[29] It is worth noting that Iraqi, Saudi, and American actions were occurring largely in isolation from each other, but that was not how there were necessarily being interpreted by the Iranians.

Domestically within Iran, support for the war was beginning to seriously deteriorate. In early June, Ayatolloh Khomeini appointed Parliamentary Speaker Hashemi Rafsanjani, a politician and religious figure with no military background, as acting commander of Iran's armed forces.[30] Former Prime Minister Mehdi Bazargan, who had served in 1979 as one of Khomeini's earliest appointees, published an open letter in early June:

> Since 1986, you have not stopped proclaiming victory, and now you are calling upon the population to resist until victory. Isn't that an admission of failure on your behalf? ... You have denounced the policy of the United States, and they are now installed solidly at our gates in the Persian Gulf. You have spoken of the failure of Iraq and the crumbling of its regime, but thanks to your misguided policies, Iraq has fortified itself, its economy has not collapsed, and it is we who are on the verge of bankrupcy [sic].[31]

On June 25, Iraq began its fourth major offensive of the year, attacking the Majnoon Islands and capturing them after about eight hours. The Iraqi superiority in weapons and training, along with the shift in momentum, was sufficiently guaranteed that Saddam Hussein himself was filmed leading a charge against Iranian forces.[32]

It was into this larger political context that the USS *Vincennes* entered the Persian Gulf in May 1988. While the captain and crew of the cruiser could not have been reasonably expected to be on top of Security Council negotiations—let alone Iraqi army moves on land or internal Iranian political machinations—the ship's efforts and actions turned out to be instrumental in achieving UNSCR 598's implementation. Their method of doing so, however, turned out to be an inversion of the language used in the citations for the awards eventually bestowed on the senior officers of *Vincennes*: their actions in fact reflected neither great credit upon themselves nor were they in keeping with the highest traditions of the U.S. Naval Service.

In the spring of 1988, Iran had begun to improve *Silkworm* launching facilities in and around the Strait of Hormuz, building new facilities on Abu Musa Island and resuming work on the Iranian mainland bordering the Strait. Upon completion, Iran would be able to fire *Silkworms* into the Strait with very little detection time. It was this threat that contributed to the deployment of the very capable USS *Vincennes* into the Persian Gulf.[33]

Vincennes represented a considerable technological upgrade from the U.S. Navy ships previously deployed to the Gulf. A *Ticonderoga*-class cruiser, *Vincennes* was designed around an AEGIS weapons system—the highly sophisticated integration of long-ranged, phased-array radars, missiles, and computer systems built to simultaneously handle the dozens of air and surface targets expected to be faced in any large-scale fight with the Soviet Union. AEGIS was particularly known for

> the extended range of its sensors, its fast reaction time, the capacity to track many targets at once, its ability to send this information automatically to other units, and its data displays which combine sensor information with other inputs and better convey it to the users. Because of its long range radar it gives operators additional time to react, to gather data, and to make considered judgments. Operating close-in to a land-based airfield, however, these advantages can be severely eroded. That problem is not the fault of the system but geography.[34]

If the FFG-7s represented low-mix ships, the *Ticonderogas*—with their billion-dollar-per-hull procurements costs—were striking examples of high-mix ships. Chief of Naval Operations Admiral Frank Kelso had objected when Deputy National Security Advisor Powell first proposed sending a "Tico" to the Gulf, asking, "Why would you want to put a diamond in a pigsty?"[35] The siting of *Silkworm* missiles so close to the Strait, and the rapid response time needed to combat such a threat, however, made for a compelling case to bring in such high-value assets. In his cover letter reporting the eventual outcome of the *Vincennes* incident to the secretary of defense, CJCS Admiral Crowe directly linked the deployment of AEGIS-equipped ships to the Gulf to the *Silkworm* threat: "Probably the most serious and destructive potential threat to both military and civilian shipping in the area is the *Silkworm* missile … Its flight time is a matter of seconds and it possesses an imposing destructive charge. It is an awesome weapon. The most capable platform in the U.S. inventory for handling this threat is the AEGIS cruiser."[36] Additionally, the Iranians had recently moved American-made F-14s from Bushehr south to Bandar Abbas; this increased air threat was something that AEGIS was specifically designed to handle.

The new AEGIS-equipped ships—they would go on to be the centerpiece of American ship production for the next 30 years—attracted ambitious officers and crews. After all, those schooled in AEGIS would be getting in on the ground-floor of a program clearly likely to define U.S. Navy surface warfare for the coming decades. Captain William Rogers, the commanding officer of *Vincennes*, was emblematic of this new wave of officers and saw in his Gulf deployment an early chance to prove the AEGIS system in combat—in fact, the *Vincennes* incident would represent one of the first tests of AEGIS in battle, especially when it came to the firing of its weapons.[37] *Vincennes*'s initial operating area placed the ship within the Gulf, but to the south, away from the day-to-day, face-to-face confrontations with Iranian naval assets, which were being handled by the older and less capable destroyers and

Artist's rendition of USS *Vincennes*, likely done before deployment, illustrating the two weapons systems essential to the Iran Air 655 shootdown—the helicopter, which precipitated *Vincennes*'s rapid move northward, and its missile system that shot down the airliner. (National Archives)

frigates already on station. The idea was to provide some stand-off distance and instead use AEGIS and its sophisticated command systems to coordinate the overall air and surface picture in the region. Rogers—who had received combat decorations for his service aboard ships in the Vietnam War—had other ideas and communicated frequently with JTFME Commander Less asking *Vincennes* to be redirected to "go into harm's way for which she was intended."[38]

In addition to demonstrating the apparent ubiquity of the John Paul Jones quote, Rogers embodied another cultural aspect of the U.S. Navy—a service in which enterprise and aggressive action counted for everything. *Vincennes*, its officers and crew, called to mind for some the "Arnheiter Affair" during the Vietnam War, in which USS *Vance* Commanding Officer Marcus Aurelius Arnheiter was relieved of command of his warship for, inter alia, having "apparently sailed into a prohibited position to shell the coast and sent false position reports to conceal these violations of orders and of the rules of engagement."[39] As Arnheiter was being led off the ship, his parting words to his crew were: "You'll never forget me. For I took you into harm's way."[40]

The recent change in the U.S. rules of engagement—which allowed for U.S. Navy forces to use force to now protect non-U.S. flagged ships under Iranian attack—intersected with the arrival of the *Vincennes*. In the Persian Gulf, Rogers and *Vincennes* earned the informal nickname "Robocruiser" from the other U.S. Navy ships operating in the area, a nod to the ship's tendency to push the ROE limits and the 1987 movie *RoboCop* in which a technologically advanced half-human/half-cyborg police officer aggressively approached crime control. *Vincennes*'s Robocruiser moniker was cemented on June 2 when, on its first patrol in the Gulf, Rogers aggressively maneuvered *Vincennes* and the frigate USS *Sides* while the remaining Iranian *Saam*-class frigate *Alborz* was conducting a (legal) visit and boarding of the bulk carrier *Vevey*; *Sides*'s commanding officer protested Rogers's actions in real time to JTFME in Bahrain, which directed both ships to stand down from their confrontation.[41] *Sides*'s skipper, David Carlson, would emerge as a critic of both *Vincennes* and of U.S. intelligence in the lead-up to the *Vincennes* incident; writing later in *Proceedings* magazine:

> The briefings that I received from two other commanding officers in the Gulf before taking command of the Sides in early June were invaluable. They essentially advised that I read the message traffic, absorb the contents, then go on deck and look around. Their message was clearly aimed at emphasizing the fact that—war or no war—life in the Gulf went on: fishermen fished; commerce continued; airliners flew ....
>
> All of us were done grave disservice by an intelligence system that covered its six by forecasting every possible worst-case scenario. Combined with heightened safety concerns (and not a few career concerns as well) in the wake of the *Stark*'s and *Samuel B. Roberts*'s, experiences, this aided in creating an undercurrent of tension and a sense of imminent danger.[42]

A month later, on July 2, the USS *Elmer Montgomery*—an older *Knox*-class frigate—came to the aid of the Danish ship *Karma Maersk*, under attack from Revolutionary Guard speedboats. The U.S. ship sped to the scene in accordance with the revised rules of engagement and fired warning shots that drove the Iranians off. The action placed the *Montgomery* in an area of high IRGCN activity and, on the following day, the frigate found itself in a similar position regarding a Pakistani-flagged ship. *Vincennes* was located to the south of the action, under the direction of JTFME in Bahrain, and dispatched its on-board helicopter to assist *Montgomery*, but then Rogers moved his ship nearly 50 miles north of his assigned station south of Abu Musa Island.[43] JTFME officials, while providing the orders regarding *Vincennes*'s helicopter, had directed the cruiser itself to remain well south of Abu Musa Island in order to deal with any possible IRGCN speedboats deploying from the island and also, presumably, to provide some stand-off range for *Vincennes*'s long-ranged sensors to be best positioned. Rogers disregarded those orders when moving farther north. *Vincennes*'s high rate of speed—the ship was moving at some 30 knots—was beginning to attract attention; the Omani Coast Guard at one point came up on bridge-to-bridge and warned *Vincennes* that "maneuvers at speeds up to 30 knots are not in accordance with innocent passage," and directed the ship to leave Omani waters.[44]

When JTFME in Bahrain discovered that Rogers was off station, the ship was ordered to return south to its assigned station. *Vincennes*'s helicopter moved toward the Iranian gunboats, where it was the subject of warning shots from IRCGN boats. Navy ROE mandated coming no closer than four miles to Iranian warships, but there were reports the pilots came as close as two miles.[45] In subsequent investigation, there were discrepancies in the statements made by the pilot of the helicopter regarding the aircraft's location and proximity to the IRGCN speedboats when fired upon, with some reports indicating the helicopter was provocatively closer to the Iranians than the rules of engagement permitted.[46]

Regardless of the distance between the helicopter and the Iranians, Rogers's reaction was to turn back toward the Iranians and increase the ship's speed back to 30 knots.[47] In taking this action, *Vincennes* itself entered Iranian territorial waters, which the Iranians were legally permitted to defend.[48] Significantly, this action—which was arguably in violation of standing guidance and changed the nature of the interaction with the Iranians, to include placing *Vincennes* under the flight path of Iran Air 655—was not mentioned in the official investigation nor in the immediate public statements. Indeed, CJCS Admiral Crowe's initial public statements and briefing devices clearly placed *Vincennes* in international waters in describing the subsequent events on July 3.

Vincennes's helicopter was directed to return to the ship, and Captain Rogers continued his course north. By this point, *Vincennes*'s helicopter had taken no hits and was no longer in range of the Iranian speedboats. Rogers's action, therefore, was not so much one of protecting an asset under fire as it was a retaliatory act for the Iranians having fired on his helicopter in the first place. While, overall, Operation *Earnest Will* unfolded in a series of retaliatory acts—such as *Nimble Archer* and *Praying Mantis*—those were the result of considered policy decisions made in Washington. Rogers's actions were more spur of the moment and, as *Vincennes* headed north, Rogers requested permission to engage the Iranian speedboats.

Overall, however, the pattern of retaliatory actions in *Earnest Will*—at both the policy and tactical levels—raises questions of efficacy. While the legal rationale for retaliation is instead generally phrased as "self-defense," it is presumably linked to deterrence (or "restoring deterrence"); however, it is far from clear that the Iranians were deterred from actions as much as they were deprived of assets with which to take future actions.[49] In other words, it is difficult to tell whether the Iranians made a decision not to take a given action because they were deterred or whether they simply no longer possessed the means to take those actions, even if they had the will to do so. In the case of the *Vincennes*, Rogers's retaliatory moves set up a chain of actions that had consequences far beyond the maintenance of deterrence. Reports are also inconsistent as to how much JTFME knew of the tactical situation when they granted Rogers permission to open fire on the IRGCN boats.

The result was a melee. In addition to sophisticated missiles systems, *Vincennes* mounted two five-inch, rapid-fire guns, fore and aft, and the forward five-inch gun began to fire at the Iranian small craft. The Iranians returned fire and, after firing several rounds, the cruiser's forward mount jammed. *Vincennes*'s second five-inch gun was mounted on the rear part of the ship, and the cruiser maneuvered violently to bring the after gun to bear.

In the midst of the surface battle, *Vincennes*'s sophisticated anti-air warfare system began picking up indications of possible Iranian warplane activity. While the small arms fire from the Iranian small craft may have represented a negligible threat to the 9,600-ton *Vincennes*, and the Iranian F-14 had no demonstrated capability to attack a surface vessel, there was always the possibility of a suicide attack. Further, as a consequence of the *Stark* attack, the rules of engagement provided to U.S. Navy ship captains were quite clear:

> If a potentially hostile contact persists in closing after you warn him away and if, in your judgement, the threat of attack is imminent, it is an inherent right and responsibility to act in self-defense. We do not want, nor intend, to absorb a first attack.[50]

The subsequent events of July 3 represented one of the first times the AEGIS anti-warfare system was to be used in combat—earlier actions by AEGIS-equipped ships off the coast of Lebanon had been more akin to air-traffic control. The results were a reminder that—no matter how sophisticated the weapons system—the ultimate decisions and responsibility were dependent on people, and most of the people participating aboard USS *Vincennes* that day were facing combat for the first time.

By all accounts—which include footage from a U.S. Navy combat media team filming on *Vincennes* bridge—the situation was chaotic. The ship's aggressive maneuvering and twisting course in order to keep the after five-inch gun on target caused books and papers to cascade throughout the ship; the noise and tumult meant the working conditions were more locker room than quiet, sterile operating theater. Sailors began to report what sounded like bullets hitting the hull.[51] While all of this was occurring, Iran Air 655—a regularly scheduled commercial Airbus A-300B—was preparing to take off for its short flight from Bandar Abbas to Dubai, with 290 civilian passengers and crew.

Aviation safety has a well-developed concept of "chain of events" that lead to airplane disasters and their interrelationship: "If any one of [the] ... cause factors had not been present, or if some of the factors had occurred in a different order, the accident would not have happened."[52] The chain of events on July 3 resulted in a tragedy for those aboard Iran Air 655, though Iranians have consistently questioned whether the destruction Iran Air 655 by USS *Vincennes* was actually an accident.[53] By contrast, the International Civil Aeronautics Organization (ICAO) investigation of the downing of Iran Air 655 drew from this sequential approach, going back to the start of U.S. military operations in the Gulf: "The incident on 17 May 1987 in which the USS Stark was severely damaged by two air-launched Exocet missiles was of particular relevance in the chain of events leading to the destruction of IR655."[54]

Iran Air 655 departed from Bandar Abbas, a "dual-use" airport hosting both military and civilian aircraft. A departure delay meant the aircraft took off just after *Vincennes* began opening fire on the Iranian speedboats; its route of travel took the airplane directly over the ship. It is unclear whether the Iranian air-traffic controllers knew of the at-sea fight and no "red alert" warning from Iranian authorities diverting civilian aircraft was in effect at the time of 655's flight.[55]

Vincennes picked up 655's take-off very quickly and began to query the aircraft via two radio channels—Military Air Distress (MAD), at 243 MHz, and International Air Distress, at 141.5 MHz. As the ICAO report noted, "As civil aircraft do not carry radio equipment capable of being tuned to 243 MHz, these [MAD] transmissions had no relevance as challenges to a civilian aircraft."[56] Similarly, illumination of 655 by the fire-control radars aboard *Sides* and *Vincennes*, which would have normally produced a defensive maneuver by a warplane, failed to produce any reaction from 655 "since civil aircraft did not carry [fire-control radar] detectors."[57]

The ICAO report went on to note: "There was no response to the four challenges made on frequency 121.5 [IAD], either by radio or by a change of course. This indicated that the flight crew of IR655 either was not monitoring frequency 121.5 MHz in the early stages of flight or did not identify their flight as being challenged."[58] This latter possibility was emphasized in other parts of the ICAO report, which commented that it was far from clear that the flight crew of IR655 would recognize that the U.S. Navy ships were addressing their flight based on the information contained in those Navy radio transmissions.[59] The "black box" for IR655, which would have included the doomed aircraft's cockpit voice recorder, was never recovered and there is no indication that the Airbus knew it was being addressed or targeted; the aircraft instead continued on course to Dubai airport.

As Norman Friedman—an expert in describing U.S. Navy technical systems—pointed out in later analyzing the incident:

> Although the [AEGIS] radar performs surveillance well (as demonstrated, for example, both off Lebanon and during the 1985 *Achille Lauro* incident), it is primarily a means of effective fire control, and the design is probably biased in that direction, naturally. In particular, the integration of the radar with its associated identification friend or foe (IFF) system was not very strong. For example, the IFF operator had to move a range gate manually to track an incoming target. He could, therefore, accidentally associate the IFF response of one aircraft with another.[60]

Aboard the ship, a backup "Identify Friend or Foe" (IFF) system—separate from AEGIS—picked up an IFF transponder signal correlating to an Iranian F-14 on the same line of bearing as the Airbus; the *Vincennes* operator in charge of the IFF system correlated the F-14's IFF signal with the Airbus. Radio transmissions from the Navy cruiser to the Iranian Airbus went unanswered. The threat geometry and lack of response led *Vincennes* to report to JTFME that the ship was being approached by an Iranian F-14 that was not answering radio challenges; the ship then announced its intention to fire on the aircraft. While other U.S. Navy warships monitoring the situation had their doubts about whether the plane was attacking or was, in fact, even a military aircraft, they deferred to the superior AEGIS technology aboard *Vincennes* and the ultimate responsibility of Captain Rogers to protect his own ship.

Vincennes launched two SM-2 missiles at the contact; both functioned as designed and destroyed the targeted aircraft. Aboard the *Vincennes*, "a lookout came in from the wing of the bridge. The target couldn't have been an F-14, he said. The wreckage falling from the sky, he murmured to the *Vincennes*'s executive officer, Cmdr. Richard Poster, is 'bigger than that.'"[61] The Commanding Officer of the nearby USS *Montgomery* watched from the bridge of his ship and saw an Airbus missing a wing and its tail spiral into

Video capture of SM-2 missile firing from USS *Vincennes* on July 3, 1988. Minutes later, it will bring down Iran Air 655 (U.S. Navy Photograph—USNI Photo Archives, 169065031)

the ocean; radar operators aboard the USS *Sides* announced, "He shot down COMAIR [commercial air]"—though, it has been noted, they made this determination only *after Vincennes* had shot the aircraft down.[62] Aboard the *Vincennes*, the ship ceased its surface engagement and Rogers turned the ship south, out of Iranian territorial waters. The news that *Vincennes* had shot down a civilian airliner was quickly communicated to JTFME headquarters in Bahrain and to Washington.

In his cover letter to the secretary of defense, forwarding the official U.S Navy report on the incident, JCS Chairman Crowe began by describing the threat environment after the strike on the USS *Stark* and subsequent clashes between U.S. and Iranian forces in the ensuing fifteen months, and defended Captain Rogers's decision-making, saying, "Given the time available, the Commanding Officer could hardly meet his obligation to protect his ship and crew and also clear up all of the possible ambiguities."[63] Crowe concluded: "I believe that the actions of Iran were the proximate cause of this accident and would argue that Iran must bear the principal responsibility for the tragedy,"

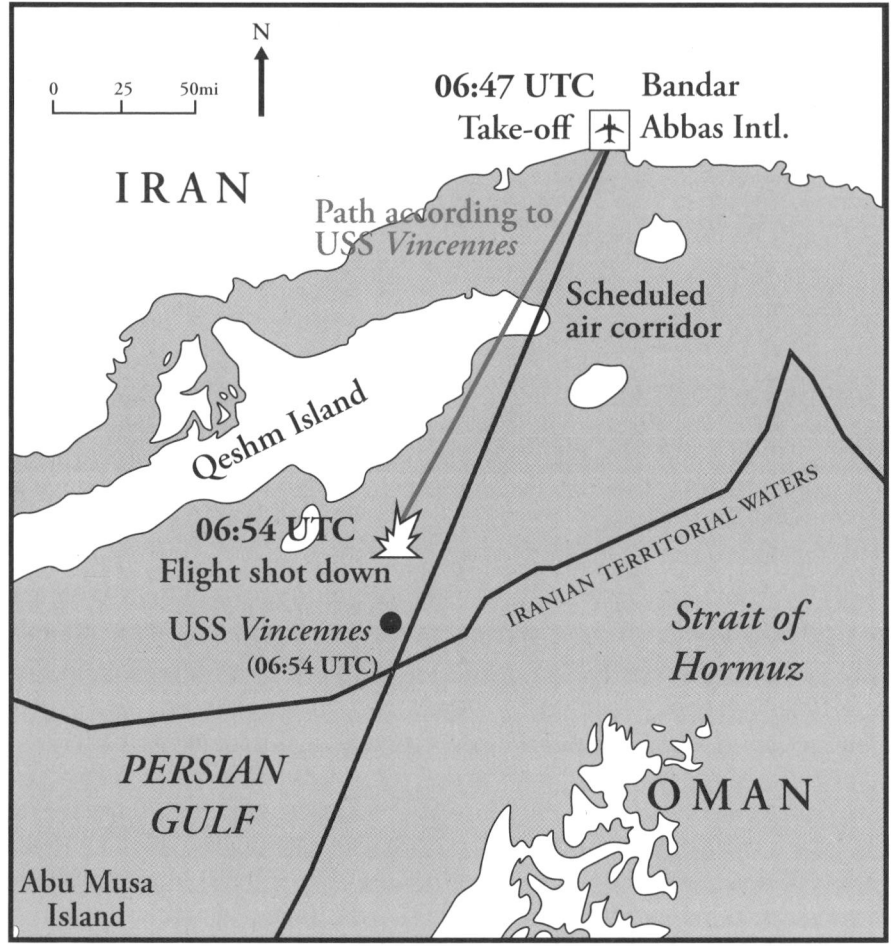

Threat geometry of the *Vincennes* incident.

saying that "it was especially reprehensible [for Iranian authorities] to allow an airliner to take off from a joint 'military/civilian' airfield and fly directly into the midst of a gunfight."[64]

The official investigation does not make note of the *Vincennes* crossing into Iranian territorial water—the tone is, instead, exculpatory in sympathy for a captain making quick decisions.[65] Indeed, the fact that *Vincennes* had crossed into Iranian waters—and thereby played a much bigger role in instigating the Iran Air incident than initially reported—remained quiet until *Newsweek* magazine broke the news some four years later.[66]

The official forbearance extended into decorations for Captain Rogers and his crew, with Rogers receiving a routine "end of tour" Legion of

Merit, and Commander Lustig, the air-warfare coordinator, receiving a Navy Commendation Medal for "heroic achievement," citing his "ability to maintain his poise and confidence under fire." The medal citations made no mention of the 655 shoot-down; rather, Rogers's medal covered his entire period of command—April 1987 to May 1989—while Lustig received two Commendation Medals—one end-of-tour covering 1984 to 1988 and a second for the specific action against the Iranian gunboats.[67]

To the working-level Navy's credit, the circumstances of the Iran Air 655 shoot-down and the resulting official statements and investigations have consistently been the topic of professional conversations, ranging from lessons learned regarding the AEGIS system to harsh critiques of Captain Rogers and senior Navy leadership.[68] To this day, there is a sense that the incident and the way it was handled mark a dark episode in the history of the U.S. Navy; it is also worth emphasizing that the Navy has not shot down any civilian aircraft since July 1988.

President Reagan, when it became clear that the target was civilian, expressed sympathy and condolences, but then went on to advocate for a cease-fire as soon as possible. International reaction varied by political propinquity to the Americans. UK Prime Minister Thatcher expressed profound regret. West German Foreign Minister Genscher expressed great shock; the Italian prime minister called it "an atrocious episode."[69] The Chinese government condemned the action and went on to express its opposition to "big-power military involvement in the gulf region."[70] The Russians used the opportunity to once again call for the removal of U.S. naval forces from the Persian Gulf and suggested darker motives behind the U.S. action: "The tragedy, responsibility for which is wholly with the American command, has been far from accidental. It has been, in effect, a direct corollary of United States actions over the past year to increase its military presence in the Gulf."[71]

On the Iranian side, regardless of the self-protective speculations of American intelligence regarding possible attacks over the July 4 weekend, authorities knew they had not modified an F-14 to attack American ships, let alone sent a civilian Airbus on a suicide mission. Rather, from Iran's perspective, there appears to be a conviction that the downing of the Airbus was a deliberate act and that the United States could be expected to stop at nothing to keep Iran from winning the Iran–Iraq War.[72] Iranian Foreign Minister Ali Akbar Velayati, entering the UN Security Council chamber on July 14 for the first time ever and speaking at length in front of representatives that included then-U.S. Vice President Bush, rebutted statements by President Reagan and Admiral Crowe that IR655 had been descending or flying outside a normal commercial corridor at the time the missiles were fired. Velayati observed that

Iranian Foreign Minister Ali Akbar Velayati, in his visit to the UN Security Council on July 14, 1988: "All available evidence suggests that the shooting-down of an Iranian civil airliner ... could not have been a mistake." (United Nations, UN7572450 / NICA ID 271404)

"F-14 fighters, as should be known most vividly to the Americans who made them, are designed for air-to-air attack and not air-to-surface operations."[73] He argued that the short duration of the flight argued against any expectation of the 655 pilots monitoring the International Air Distress frequency and questioned why none of the available transcripts of communications with the doomed airliner contained any record of the cited American warnings.[74] Velayati charged:

> All available evidence suggests that the shooting-down of an Iranian civil airliner flying on a scheduled flight known to the United States warships, using an internationally and published civilian airway and transmitting signals identifying itself as a civilian airliner could not have been a mistake.[75]

That Iranian belief that the United States had deliberately shot down the Airbus, combined with recent setbacks in the war and the parlous state of the Iranian economy, led to a consensus decision by the Iranian leadership to accept UNSCR 598 and its cease-fire. In particular, the capture of the al-Faw peninsula by the Iraqis, facilitated by widespread (and internationally un-condemned) use of chemical weapons by Iraqi forces brought the prospect of Iraq beginning to use chemical warheads on the SCUD missiles being launched at Iranian cities.[76] When Iranian political leaders went to the front and asked their military leaders for what would be needed to achieve victory, they were met with statements such as "no victories are in sight for the next five years" and unrealistic demands for large amounts of unobtainable sophisticated weaponry, as well as nuclear weapons.[77]

In his assessment of why Iran changed its position on accepting UNSCR 598, Hume credited:

> ... an accumulation of factors: the inability of the Iranian military to overcome losses suffered during the failed attack on Basra at the end of 1986; the Iraqi advantage in the tanker war, especially after the U.S. entry into the gulf; the demoralizing impact of Iraqi attacks on civilian targets during the war of the cities; the fear in the Iranian army that Iraq would again use chemical weapons; the destruction of the Iranian navy; the recent defeats of the Iranian army ... the shooting down of Iran Air 655, [and] concern for domestic politics and the future of the Islamic Revolution.[78]

Hume concluded: "With its military in retreat, its economy a shambles, and its civilian population demoralized, the future of the revolution required change."[79]

On July 18, four days after Velayati's appearance in front of the Security Council and nearly a year after UNSCR 598's passage, Iranian President Ali Khamenei sent a surprise letter to UN Secretary General Javier Pérez de Cuéllar, accepting the terms of UNSCR 598.[80] The text of the relatively short letter clearly linked the acceptance of the resolution to the downing of IR655.[81] In explanatory speeches in Tehran, Speaker of the Iranian Parliament Hashemi Rafsanjani said that the destruction of the Airbus prompted Iranian consideration of the cease-fire, that the downing had been a "turning point" in the war, and that the action taken by the *Vincennes* was seen as a "deliberate warning" that the United States would commit "immense crimes" if Iran were to go on with the war.[82] And, even if the *Vincennes* incident was being used by the Iranians as a face-saving way to end a very long war that had resulted in hundreds of thousands of deaths, the facts are that the government of Iran literally and repeatedly cited the incident as a reason to accept UNSCR 598—to use another *Caine Mutiny* reference, "as the massive door of a vault turns on a small jewel bearing."[83]

Khomeini went on to announce the acceptance of UNSCR 598 to an equally surprised Iranian populace on July 20.[84] A long speech that began with a commemoration of those killed during the 1987 Hajj riots and against

Iranian stamp commemorating the *Vincennes* incident. (Wikimedia Commons)

blasphemy and polytheism segued into a rationale for accepting UNSCR 598 and its attendant cease-fire:

> Due to some incidents and factors which, for the time being I will refrain from elaborating on and which—God willing—will be made clear in the future, and in view of the opinion of all the high-ranking political and military experts of the country, whose commitment, sympathy and sincerity I trust, I agreed with the acceptance of the resolution and the cease fire. At this juncture I regard it to be in the interest of the revolution and the system.[85]

It was later in this speech that Khomeini made his famous declaration of his requirement to "have drunk the poisonous chalice of accepting the resolution."

It is worth emphasizing the "collegiate nature" of the decision and announcement.[86] While Khomeini may have been the final approver, there was a clear sense among Iran's political elite that the war was no longer winnable. It would appear that—whether or not the Iranian leadership truly believed *Vincennes* had consciously shot down the Airbus—the incident provided a useful and widely acceptable rationale for the decision to end the war.

Khomeini's son Ahmad later wrote:

> When, on balance, he felt he should accept the ceasefire, when he drank the poisonous chalice, I was with him. The television was showing our soldiers and he kept hitting himself with fists saying "ah." No one dared to see him. After accepting the ceasefire he could no longer walk. He kept saying "My Lord, I submit to your will." He never again spoke in public. He never again went to speak at the Jamaran mosque and [eventually] he fell ill and was taken to the hospital.[87]

Khomeini died less than a year later. As Iran watcher Mark Axworthy summed it up: "As a display of cynicism, of irresponsibility, and of the failure of the international system to resolve conflict, the [Iran–Iraq] war set a depressing precedent. For many Iranians, the experience reinforced the belief that Iran could depend only upon her resources and that fine words in international institutions counted for little.[88]

The twist for the Iranians is that it was precisely the "fine words in international institutions" which made up the text of UNSCR 598 that constructed the parameters that ended the Iran–Iraq War. It was arguably Iran's lack of engagement with those institutions, and with the wider world, that ended the war on terms seen by the Iranians to be so unfavorable.

CHAPTER 7

The Other Navies in the Gulf

> A European force meant that participating nations "can't be singled out for raising tension and being provocative."
> —DUTCH DEFENSE MINISTER W. F. VAN EEKELEN

American military actions during the Tanker War did not occur in isolation—in addition to clashes with Iranian and Iraqi forces, the Soviets were an ever-present factor. Southern Gulf states, especially Saudi Arabia, had substantial military forces. But there were also important roles played by other outside forces, especially the navies of Europe.

From the start of Operation *Earnest Will*, there were questions of burden-sharing: while oil is a fungible commodity and a restriction of supply anywhere can affect global prices, it was also true that other countries depended more directly than the United States on oil products coming from the Persian Gulf—especially European countries and Japan. The most direct way to share the burden would have been the provision of naval assets, especially minesweepers, though financial contributions and diplomatic support in venues such as the United Nations would also have been welcome.

European navies had been operating in the region well before the start of *Earnest Will*. Great Britain's presence in and around the Gulf and Indian Ocean went back centuries. The announcement of the withdrawal of UK military forces from "east of Suez" in 1968 had significant political and military effects that were to affect *Earnest Will*. The British withdrew completely from their bases in Yemen and Bahrain; the latter's naval shore establishment—HMS *Juffair*—was taken over by a U.S. Navy presence that had to tread sensitively given Iran's longstanding desire for all foreign military forces to depart from the Gulf as well as claims on the island.[1] The Shah's overthrow solved the problem of the United States having to appease the Iranians regarding their longstanding claims to Bahrain, but the general unrest in the area—in addition to the taking of American hostages in November 1979, the Soviets invaded Afghanistan the following month—argued for returned Royal Navy presence, as did the outbreak of the Iran–Iraq War and the UK accordingly established the Armilla Patrol of two-to-four small combatants starting in 1980.[2] In addition to providing general naval presence, the Armilla Patrol protected UK-flagged and registered ships as they transited the Strait of Hormuz and the Royal Navy would allow other ships to tag along.[3]

The British took great pride in the Armilla Patrol and its deliberately low profile, which they believed had been "broadly successful in protecting British shipping."[4] An American 1988 congressional report on burden-sharing agreed: "The United Kingdom currently maintains what is arguably the most effective escort fleet in the Gulf. Although the number of naval vessels (9) is far fewer than the U.S. maintains (38), the U.K. is escorting 60 ships per month—three times the number escorted by the U.S. military."[5] The report went on to say, "The ships supplied to the region by the United Kingdom represent a greater percentage of the total fleet available to the U.K. than does the U.S. presence."

Such comparisons, however, only go so far—the Royal Navy and the U.S. Navy on the surface may have had the same missions, but the politics were very different. The Royal Navy was protecting UK-flagged and registered ships, often engaged in trade with Iran itself; the U.S. Navy was protecting formerly Kuwaiti tankers that had been the specific target of the Iranians. Further, it is likely that the British had significant overall policy differences regarding the U.S. approach to the Persian Gulf. As one article looking at recently declassified documents explained:

- The British were concerned that reflagging the Kuwaiti tankers in the first place had raised the likelihood of conflict with Iran;
- There were concerns that the Americans lacked staying power, especially after the example of the precipitate withdrawal from Beirut in 1983;
- Britain had an interest as being seen as neutral in the Gulf and as an independent actor, rather than acting as part of an American-led coalition;
- There was a concern that, in prosecuting *Earnest Will*, the Americans might engage in "Preemptive or Disproportionate U.S. Military Operations";
- It was initially unclear that minesweeping was either operationally viable or strictly necessary."[6]

So, while the British added an additional small combatant to the Armilla Patrol in the spring of 1987, there were limits as to how far they were prepared to go in response to American requests for cooperation.

Defense Secretary Weinberger, in a visit to NATO headquarters in May 1987 for a regularly scheduled meeting of defense ministers, made reference to the upcoming *Earnest Will* operation and asked for "any assistance they might be able to get after consultations with their governments."[7] In follow-on remarks with reporters, Weinberger would not specify countries or requests but named three general areas in which countries could provide assistance: additional naval assets, cooperation in air cover, or provision of existing infrastructure, which was assumed to mean bases.

Weinberger made the request at a NATO meeting, but it does not appear that he made the request to share the burden in the Gulf as an official NATO "ask." In other words, Weinberger's plea for assistance does not appear to have been a formal request for NATO "burden-sharing;" rather, it seems to have been to have treated the long-scheduled meeting of European defense ministers as a target of opportunity to raise the issue of maritime security in the Persian Gulf.[8] Weinberger does specifically discuss NATO and "out-of-area actions" in his memoirs, but in the context of the backfilling the Royal Navy for NATO duties during the earlier Falklands Conflict in 1982.[9] Weinberger's measured approach in 1987 may have set the stage for eventual, non-NATO cooperation.

The European countries were all NATO allies, but the Persian Gulf's location outside the region governed by the NATO Treaty area meant there were no formal obligations for NATO forces to join the United States in its Gulf operations. The May 1987 NATO meeting ended with no mention of the American request in the final communique nor any commitments on the part of the Alliance. NATO Secretary General Lord Carrington, speaking afterward to reporters, specifically cited the "out-of-area" nature of the request and said, "What happens in the gulf has a very considerable effect on members of the alliance. But when you get to doing anything about it in military terms, or in planning terms, then that has to be done either in a different forum or bilaterally."[10] Weinberger, for his part, was philosophical about the results; he mentioned the meeting in his memoirs only obliquely and, in parting remarks to reporters in Brussels, said simply, "We didn't come here with a satchel, expecting to fill it up and take it home."[11]

This lack of a formal joint response would appear to have several reasons. First, in 1987 and with the Cold War still going on, NATO's focus was on Europe. Second, across the board, there was a concern about signing on to what appeared to be a running bilateral fight between the United States and Iran; indeed, even among NATO states, there were different views about the best way to deal with Iran, with a number of countries maintaining diplomatic relations and embassies in Tehran. Some countries instead voiced support for an operation under UN auspices; given the political complications of setting up any such mission—especially in 1987—it is unclear whether such caveats were sincere or simply convenient. Third, echoing the concerns raised by Navy Secretary Webb, there were concerns about an open-ended military commitment—as one unnamed UK defense official put it: "We don't relish the idea of being sucked in and not being able to get out."[12] An opposition Labour spokesman was even blunter, warning against the British being dragged into "a naval, maritime Vietnam."[13]

NATO countries maintained their reluctance to deploy minesweepers even after the *Bridgeton* mining incident on July 24. The *Bridgeton* strike prompted Weinberger, working with Secretary of State Shultz, to have the Department of State make urgent, follow-on requests at the ambassadorial level—the seniormost possible level for the U.S. government in a foreign country—to the United Kingdom, France, the Netherlands, Italy, and West Germany for the specific dispatch of mine-clearing vessels to the Gulf.[14] The United States did not put the request in NATO-specific terms, but rather observed that such an effort would "portray a multinational commitment against the illegal mining of international waters."[15] The West Germans turned down the minesweeper request on July 29, 1987, though the German Navy eventually deployed naval forces to the Mediterranean to compensate for U.S. forces surged to the Gulf.[16] In a rare rebuff, the UK on July 30 turned down a public request made by the U.S. ambassador to British foreign secretary, with a Foreign Office spokesman saying, "It's better for us not to contribute to any escalation in tension."[17] On July 31, the Dutch rejected the request, saying that Dutch ships could only be sent as part of an (as yet non-existent and, in actuality, highly unlikely) UN peacekeeping force.[18]

The French had their own, ongoing dispute with the Iranians—having broken diplomatic relations in mid-July over a range of concerns—and increased their patrols in the region and unilaterally deployed the aircraft carrier *Clemenceau* with several escort warships. French efforts, however, remained focused on escorting French-flagged ships and did not include minesweepers. Additionally, while it verges on cliché to state that "you can't surge trust," there is a potential reciprocal dynamic that bears keeping in mind—past efforts that have not gone well can lead to *distrust* that affects future operations. Such a dynamic appears to have been in place in the Franco–American relationship, with memories of the abortive effort in Lebanon in 1983 not only affecting the American need to demonstrate resolve in the Persian Gulf but also contributing to a reluctance on the part of the French to engage in future French–American cooperative efforts.[19] Their response to the Weinberger/Shultz request was instead an offer to sell the two French minesweepers, manned by non-uniformed French crews until U.S. sailors could take their places.[20] The U.S. Navy had little interest in taking French ships into the U.S. force structure; the lack of the French tricolor vitiated the hoped-for multinational cooperative signal, and an effort by JCS Chairman Crowe to instead have the Kuwaitis take up the offer went nowhere.[21]

American paucity in ship-based minesweeping assets appears to have more to do with unilateral force structure decisions than as a result of a failure in any formal burden-sharing arrangement with NATO. While there may have been informal expectations of NATO provision of complementary assets—even if out of area—the U.S. Navy has a long history of neglecting mine countermeasures until faced with an actual mining crisis.[22] U.S. helicopter assets were on-station and available, but—as one authoritative study put it—from "the mid-1960s the Navy had fallen far behind its NATO allies in MCM development, particularly in fiberglass shipbuilding technology and small drone boat minesweeping systems. European nations, notably France, had successfully developed increasingly sophisticated versions of tethered dual mine hunting and mine-neutralizing Remote Operated Vehicles."[23]

The United States had long sought to remedy this gap with the *Avenger*-class, ocean-going mine countermeasure ship—first proposed in the late 1970s and ordered in the early 1980s—but the lead ship in the 14-ship class was commissioned two years behind schedule and not until *Earnest Will* was well in progress. USS *Avenger*, in fact, did not deploy until Operation *Desert Shield* in 1990.[24] The Navy had run into similar development and cost overruns with a smaller, coastal mine countermeasure ship, the 12-ship *Osprey* MHC program—which, while started in the early 1980s, did not commission its lead ship until 1993.[25]

The intended future force structure of the U.S. Navy would suggest that the United States was not counting on foreign countries to solely handle minesweeping—as there were, in fact, plans for a 31-ship strong force dating from the start of the build-up of the "600 Ship Navy" of the early 1980s. Instead, the complexity of building mine-warfare ships combined with inefficiencies within the American ship-building enterprise meant that the ships whose need had been identified and funded simply hadn't been produced on schedule and were therefore not available.[26] In the meantime, European refusals in July meant there was a substantial gap in surface minesweeping assets in the Gulf and the Navy was forced to sortie its 1950s-vintage MSOs to the region.

***

As happened regularly during the Tanker War, events drove policy more than policy drove events.

On August 10, the U.S.-owned tanker *Texaco Caribbean*—which had just taken aboard a cargo of Iranian crude oil—struck a mine about eight miles off the Emirati port of Khor Fakkan, in the Gulf of Oman and therefore outside the Persian Gulf. While nothing in the geopolitical landscape had changed—the region remained "out-of-area" for NATO and concerns continued over involvement in a U.S.–Iran war—the mine strike physically outside of the Persian Gulf significantly widened the mine danger area for everyone. A presumably inadvertent Iranian mine strike on a ship carrying Iranian cargo raised the specter of catastrophic damage to every ship in the area. The European countries accordingly changed their positions in August 1987—deciding to share the burden of minesweeping, even if that burden-sharing was not done in a NATO context or as part of any formal cooperative agreement. The next day—on August 11—the governments of both France and Great Britain in uncoordinated announcements said they would send minesweeping assets to the Middle East.[27]

Three interviewers from the German magazine *Der Spiegel* later asked British Prime Minister Thatcher about the UK's change in position, saying in reference to the Gulf, "You said the important thing is to keep calm and to deescalate things. Some days later, you sent your minesweepers over there. Is there any contradiction between those two positions?" Thatcher replied:

> None at all … Your questions amaze me! Look at the facts! You know what happened, more mining down the Straits of Hormuz and actually outside. … My supposition that the first [mine] laying may have been a one-off was wrong, so the answer was different, and look who else has followed: in the morning France, in the afternoon Italy now [*sic*], and I think that some others may be thinking about it.[28]

Thatcher had benefited from a UK general election in June 1987 that returned a 102-seat Conservative majority in the House of Commons. Speaking in September to a UK general interest magazine, she contrasted the British style of government with those on the Continent, remarking, "It was we who went first to send the minesweepers to the Gulf. Others followed but we had a clear majority and therefore we were able to make decisions knowing that we would have the majority in Parliament behind us."[29]

Thatcher, focused on the larger situation in the Middle East and the importance of U.S.–UK relations, appears to have had second thoughts about the July British refusal, telling her cabinet that the deteriorating security situation in the region had led to a qualitative change in the Persian Gulf.[30] Additionally, she was concerned that the well-publicized refusal had sent an international signal of disunity and raised questions of Britain's dedication to freedom of navigation; the August 10 mining incident therefore provided the chance for a new start. The British Defence Secretary, in making his announcement about the revised decision to send four *Hunt*-class, state-of-the-art minesweepers, clearly linked the change to the August 10 mining and declared: "Sweeping mines is the least aggressive and least escalatory of all operations of war."[31] The British force of minesweepers and support vessels joined the Royal Navy destroyer and frigate already on station as part of the Armilla Patrol.

French officials delinked their decision from the July American request and emphasized that their minesweepers would not enter the Persian Gulf. American Defense Secretary Weinberger nonetheless welcomed the news, saying, "Anything that adds to the minesweeping capabilities of free nations is a most welcome important and welcome addition."[32] A Pentagon official went on to comment that "the military would prefer such efforts not include the Soviet Union" and added, "Since a United Nations effort to clear mines would have to include Soviet assistance, the United Nations should not run the operation."[33]

***

Continued mining incidents in the raised the stakes. Emirati coastguardsmen found and defused two mines; the Emirati government, eager to return to business as usual near this important port, quickly declared the area mine-free. On August 15, however, *Anita*—an offshore supply ship captained by a UK citizen—hit another mine off Fujairah, killing the skipper and four other crewmembers. A British official in an August 17 BBC program accused Western Europeans of "free riding" when it came to benefiting from Middle Eastern oil while not helping to address the mine threats.[34]

During an August 20 meeting of the Western European Union hosted in The Hague—likely influenced by the earlier unilateral deployment decisions made by France and the United Kingdom—the Dutch announced their support in principle for sending minehunters in conjunction with other Western European countries. The Belgians made a similar announcement on August 31. Dutch Defense Minister W. F. van Eekelen commented that a combined European force was preferable, as it meant a single nation "can't be singled out for raising tension and being provocative."[35] A cooperative effort would also allow participants, van Eekelen said, "to share logistical support and air cover."

The Dutch and Belgian effort—announced on September 7, 1987, and codenamed Operation *Octopus*—focused on minesweeping in the Gulf of Oman and the southern Persian Gulf and featured some unusual command relationships. The Dutch sent two minesweepers, as did Belgium. A Belgian naval captain was in charge of the ships in the area, while the commander of the Royal Netherlands Navy—from the Naval Headquarters in Den Helder, the Netherlands—oversaw the operation as a whole.[36] Britain's Royal Navy provided air cover, but only as a third priority after protecting British warships and merchant vessels, which prompted some questioning regarding how highly Britain would prioritize non-British ships; the Dutch accordingly reinforced their ships with *Stinger* anti-air missile teams.[37] Logistics support depended upon the French base in Djibouti, via a Belgian supply ship. In May 1988, the task force transitioned to an overall British command and was redesignated Operation *Calendar II*.

The combined Dutch–Belgian flotilla took some time to reach the Gulf; minesweepers are not known for their high rate of speed and some of the ships were quite old. As Dutch naval writer Anselm van der Peet emphasized in his work looking at the Royal Netherlands Navy and NATO out-of-area operations:

> In times of crisis in the Middle East, what always made the fleet attractive to the Dutch authorities as a political instrument was the fact that the ships were not only relatively rapidly deployable, but that as tools of first response they also left ample room for political fine-tuning of the mission during the weeks in which they were on their way to the deployment area. While the Netherlands gave a political signal by taking part in these operations, at the same time the country did not run any significant military risks and the ships remained under the country's full control at all times on account of their ability to operate independently as well as progress in communication technology.[38]

Running parallel to—and therefore separate from—the American, French, and Dutch/Belgian efforts were those of the Italian Navy which, after an IRGCN gunboat attack on the Italian container ship *Jolly Rubino* on September 3, sent three minesweepers and three frigates.[39] The Italians, like other Western

European governments, had been approached by senior USG officials in late July for minesweeping assistance requests; like those other governments, the Italians turned down that request.[40] However, the September attack on the Italian ship, along with the news of the moves by other Western European governments in August, set the stage for a change in the Italian position. As one commentator put it, in an observation that is unlikely to apply solely to Italian politics: "As is often the case in Italy, the ostensible reason for taking one position or another on a substantive issue such as this masks the subtle political machinations of the parties in their external struggle for temporary advantage in a complex political system."[41]

The Italian flotilla, designated the *Eighteenth Naval Group*, entered the Persian Gulf on October 3, and began a system of informal cooperation with the other Western naval task forces in the region. As one analysis of Italian decision-making put it: "It appears that each European country in the Gulf attempted to maintain essential independence of action, but also maintained technical cooperation and assistance with other friendly navies operating in the area."[42] The Italian naval presence over time was reduced to two frigates, two minesweepers and a supporting vessel, and then withdrawn entirely in the fall of 1988 after the end of the Iran–Iraq War.[43]

By 1988, the navies of the NATO member states were working effectively together. In fact, in the wake of the mine strike against the *Samuel B. Roberts* in April—thereby both demonstrating that the Iranians had resumed their mining operations, which had been in abeyance since the *Iran Ajr* episode, as well as the resulting mine threat to anything that floated—a flotilla of 13 minesweepers from Belgium, France, the UK, Italy, the Netherlands, and the six old MSOs of the U.S. Navy and Navy EOD personnel were able to effectively inspect and clear the mine danger area.[44] The combined force ended up detecting and destroying 10 Iranian mines.[45]

These separate but related efforts underscored a number of points. First, while the initial discussion may have been held at NATO headquarters and the navies followed NATO procedures and standards while operating, this was in no-way a NATO operation—unlike subsequent NATO out-of-area operations in the following 30 years such as those in Afghanistan, Iraq, or off the coast of Somalia. Second, the ad hoc cooperative nature of the navies operating in the same space illustrates some unique aspects of maritime operations—especially the ability of tactically relevant units to operate effectively in the same battle space without an explicit political mandate like a Security Council resolution or an overarching command-and-control structure. Third, and most importantly, the navies were fighting different fights.

For the United States, the exchanges of fire between Iranian and American forces clearly demarcated the action as a war. The Americans may have gone in believing in the efficacy of deterrence and signaling, but in practice American forces used a lot of violence and caused a lot of Iranian casualties—it was a combination of luck and skill that avoided reciprocally large numbers of casualties on the American side. The British, by contrast, prided themselves on being "the only country which has conducted an extremely successful low-profile operation for years."[46] The United Kingdom had a different political relationship with Iran than did the Americans; the Royal Navy also likely benefited from the fact that violent U.S. actions served both to reduce the Iranian military capability in the Gulf as well as a political point of contrast. France, Italy, the Netherlands, and Belgium similarly represented different aspects of political relations with Iran despite their navies performing, on the face of it, roughly similar missions. Apart from warning shots, it would not appear that any of the other navies "fired shots in anger" or caused any Iranian casualties.

The question naturally arises as to whether, that being the case, the U.S. Navy could not have performed its similar mission without causing loss of Iranian lives. In a sense, the answer is unknowable—not only is the question a counterfactual one, but it is possible that the other navies were able to operate with lower levels of force precisely *because* the Americans were engaged in combat. Ultimately, the Europeans were not tested the same way the Americans were. Setting aside the *Vincennes* incident, it is worth noting that American actions were in reaction to Iranian acts. Regardless of whether retaliation falls under the legal cover of self-defense, it is a fact that none of the European naval ships were actually damaged by Iranian missiles or mines. As a matter of history, no one knows how the Europeans would have reacted to the damage or loss of one of their naval ships because it never happened. It is worth emphasizing, however, that the deployments of all of these ships—as well as of Soviet ships—were in reaction to Iranian attacks on merchant ships, and usually merchant ships flying the flags of the deploying navies.

The United States Congress, always interested in the costs of military operations and looking for ways to spread the burden, tasked the U.S. General Accounting Office (GAO) with examining Operation *Earnest Will*; that report came back largely laudatory, crediting the European navies with providing the majority of the "relative value of contributions":

1990 GAO Report on "Relative Value of the Contributions of the Six Countries with Ships Operating in the Persian Gulf" (between October 1987 and August 1988)[47]

Country and Ships	Estimated months deployed	Relative Contribution Value
Belgium/Netherlands		9%
1 Minesweeper (10/87-3/88)	6	
1 Minesweeper (10/87-7-88)	10	
2 Minesweepers (10/87-8/88)	11	
France		34%
1 Aircraft carrier (10/87-8/88)	11	
7 Combatants (10/87-8/88)	11	
3 Minesweepers	11	
Italy		7%
1 Combatant (10/87-1/87)	3	
2 Combatants (10/87-8/88)	11	
3 Minesweepers (10/87-8/88)	11	
United Kingdom		10%
3 Combatants (10/87-8/88)	11	
3 Minesweepers (10/87-8/88)	11	
1 Command ship (10/87-8/88)	11	
United States		40%
1 Aircraft carrier (10/87-8/88)	11	
8 Combatants (10/87-8/88)	11	
1 Combatant (5/88-8/88)	4	
6 Minesweepers (10/87-8/88)	11	
1 Command ship (10/87-8/88)	11	

Notes: time period covers period of international naval deployments rather than Operation *Earnest Will* and does not factor in support or amphibious ships. Relative value figures derive from U.S. operating cost estimates for differentiated classes of ships.

The report contains several caveats for the data, noting that "establishing a common measure of the cost of naval operations was difficult," observing that some countries already maintained a regional presence, that dissimilar ships made comparisons difficult, and highlighted the high costs associated with U.S. and French aircraft carrier deployments. The report goes on to say the table "identifies the naval assets, time frames, and values assigned. Under this methodology, the allied contribution is about 60 percent and the U.S. contribution is about 40 percent. The United Kingdom, which had a large number of ships in the region, suffers under this methodology because it did not assign an aircraft carrier to the Gulf."[48] While any measure is imperfect, the report does reflect how U.S. government entities viewed some of the financial costs associated with Operation *Earnest Will* and emphasized the preponderant material contributions of NATO allies, even if they were not operating under a NATO mandate.

***

The Soviets played an important role, with concerns about their growing influence in the Persian Gulf motivating both the Carter Doctrine and the U.S. decision to approve the 1986 Kuwaiti reflagging request in an attempt to forestall a Russian presence. Soviet naval ships began deploying to the region in 1968, shortly after Britain announced the withdrawal of its military forces from "east of Suez." Three Soviet combatants and a support ship began a continuing naval presence in the Indian Ocean region.[49] Measured by presence, by 1973 the Soviets would end up spending 8,543 ship-days in the region, four times that spent by U.S. ships, according to a U.S. congressional report.[50] Soviet naval presence in the region was assessed by the U.S. Department of Defense as spiking to about 30 forward-deployed ships rotating about the same time as the Russian invasion of Afghanistan, dropping after 1982 to about 20 ships on continuous deployment.[51]

At the same time, it is helpful to recall that the Soviet and the American navies operated differently. While the most visible differentiating characteristic of the U.S. Navy may be its large aircraft carriers, the USN is also backed up by a less prominent but critical logistics support network and especially the practice of underway replenishment, perfected during World War II. This logistics system, in which ships steam tethered together to transfer fuel, food, parts, mail, and personnel, is capable of literally keeping a warship at sea for years without anchoring or entering a port. The Russians, by contrast, mainly supplied their ships in port. Therefore, while the Soviets had access to ports such as Aden in the then-People's Democratic Republic of Yemen or the Dahlak Archipelago off the coast Ethiopia (lost as a result of Eritrea's independence in 1993), they still faced significant transit times; the nearest major ship repair facility for the Soviets was in Vietnam's Cam Ranh Bay, over a week's sailing time away. Faced with the need to keep ships on station further north, in the vicinity of the Strait of Hormuz, and without access to port facilities in Iran or from the Arab Persian Gulf states, the Soviets instead had to station an *Oskol*-class repair ship to act as an afloat mobile logistics base and floating workshop in the Gulf of Oman.[52] Soviet sailors characterized their attempts at underway refueling—literally routine for American warships—as "a dangerous procedure" which led to "many collisions."[53]

Threats to Soviet merchant ships in connection with the Iran–Iraq War resulted in a regular Russian naval Persian Gulf presence starting in 1986, prompted by the boarding and searching of a Soviet cargo ship carrying arms to Iraq.[54] The request by the Kuwaitis for Soviet naval protection for oil cargos in the fall of 1986 presented an opportunity for Soviet foreign policy—an invitation from a southern Gulf state rather than the result of a Soviet initiative or pressure. The Russians first agreed to make Soviet tankers available for charter and, when the Kuwaitis further proposed reflagging Kuwaiti hulls, the Soviets readily accepted.[55] The American eventual agreement to the Kuwaiti request in March 1987 was predicated on none of those Kuwaiti ships sailing under the sickle and hammer, an arrangement the Kuwaitis honored. The Kuwaitis and Russians did, however, agree to the separate chartering of three Russian tankers—a development that, when CJCS Admiral Crowe (a former MIDEASTFOR commander) learned about, reportedly prompted him to consider canceling the American *Earnest Will* escort mission.[56] The Russians were also able to complicate the politics for the Americans by continuing to press at UN headquarters in New York for a UN-flagged naval escort mission.

The Soviet deployment, like those of the European sending states, featured minesweepers, frigates, and destroyers, along with salvage tugs. The total number of Russian ships averaged around a dozen, with most anchored in the Gulf of Oman outside the Persian Gulf. The typical force level featured three surface combatants, several mine countermeasures ships, an amphibious warfare ship, a command-and-control ship, and various support ships, sourced from the Baltic, Black Sea, and Pacific Fleets.[57]

The Russian Persian Gulf deployment did not feature larger combatants or groups configured to take on a U.S. carrier battle group, with some speculating that the USSR was hoping to avoid provocation with either the Americans or the Iranians.[58] Subsequent events supported Russia's dispatch of warships—in early May, a Russian cargo ship was raked by machine-gun fire from IRCGN gunboats and on May 17—the same day as the *Stark* incident—the newly chartered tanker *Marshal Chuykov* struck an Iranian-laid mine off the Kuwaiti port of al-Ahmadi.[59] Russia borders Iran—in addition to increasing the Soviet naval presence in the Gulf, the Russians reportedly sortied 50 military aircraft into Iranian airspace in response to the machine-gunning incident, along with diplomatic warnings. Some commentators attributed the lack of a more forceful response by the Soviets to "the increasingly toothlessness of the

Soviet Navy" in the last years of the USSR.⁶⁰ While Russian merchant ships were not subject to further machine-gunning or mine attacks, there would continue to be incidents of close calls and aggressive maneuvering between Russian and Iranian ships; overall, the Soviet Navy was credited with 178 convoys escorting 374 merchant ships.⁶¹

While there were indications that the Russians were ready to expand protection to non-Russian ships—along the lines of policy changes seen in other navies—it does not appear that such an ROE expansion actually occurred.⁶² There was also one near-miss between the Soviets and the United States during Operation *Praying Mantis*, in which a fast-moving contact originally designated as an Iranian frigate—which would have made a highly desirable target—turned out to be instead a Russian *Sovremenny*-class destroyer that said it was seeking to document the action.⁶³

Much like their American P5 opposite numbers, the Russians were also running a parallel diplomatic line of effort at the UN in New York. While cooperation resulted in products such as UNSCR 598, the more typical competition manifested itself in gamesmanship. The Russians initially were encouraged by the initial disunity among the Western powers, particularly the frictions caused within NATO by differences over out-of-area operations. The subsequent, if informal, cooperation among Western navies being sent by NATO member states in the late summer of 1987 was an apparently surprising show of solidarity.⁶⁴ It is worth noting that the Soviet proposal for a UN naval task force was first officially proposed at the UN in September 1987, shortly after the parameters of Western European naval deployments became clear.

***

The Japanese and German navies both present interesting cases—while both countries now routinely deploy their ships to the Middle East, that was not the situation in the 1980s.⁶⁵ So, in that sense, neither of those navies were running the same risks as the European or U.S. navies—their lack of physical presence meant that there was no chance whatsoever they would be the subject of an Iranian mine or missile attack, targeted or not.

For the Japanese, some 64 percent of their oil supply derived from the Persian Gulf, but post-WWII restrictions on the use of their military made deployment of Japanese naval vessels a non-starter. Japan, instead, sought to provide support in other arenas, announcing in October 1987 a "Persian Gulf Package" of $500 million in aid to Oman and Jordan, an increased

$100 million in support of U.S. forces stationed in Japan, and $7–9 million in electronics to enhance the navigational systems in the Gulf.[66]

The then-West German Navy similarly faced national and constitutional constraints in using its military forces outside the territory of NATO. In what was widely seen as a "substantial change for Germany," the West German Navy deployed warships to the Mediterranean to offset NATO ships deployed to the Persian Gulf.[67] The Germans had only recently expanded their area of deployed naval operations from the Baltic into the North Sea, and the move farther south prefigured future naval deployments after the end of the Cold War.

The same GAO burden-sharing report that examined the deployment of NATO navies commended the contributions of extra-regional countries that did not deploy military forces:

> Japan, Luxembourg, and West Germany provided indirect support. In reporting its contribution, Japan included credit for a $300 million loan made to Oman and a $200 million loan to Jordan, which is not a Gulf state. These concessional loans provide favorable terms and low interest rates.
>
> Japan also agreed to provide a precision navigation system in the Gulf. Beacons are almost completely installed along the friendly states' coast-lines and, by cross-fixing signals, will enable accurate ship location. This system will not only aid in navigation but also enhance mine-clearing capabilities should other conflicts arise in the future.
>
> Luxembourg, which has no navy, provided $400,00 for the upkeep of forces.
>
> West Germany interpreted its constitution as prohibiting a naval presence. It fulfilled a US-NATO commitment to provide naval forces in the Mediterranean, thereby freeing other naval forces for relocation to the Gulf.[68]

The countries of the southern Gulf states also made significant contributions—as might have been expected, given that the actions were occurring off their coastline and affecting their commerce. Their constraints tended to be capacity as well as political concerns—while all the countries were members of the Gulf Cooperation Council (the GCC, made up of Bahrain, Kuwait, Oman, Qatar, Saudi Arabia, and the United Arab Emirates), an organization formed in response to the threats posed by the Iranian Revolution, each individual country could also be expected to have its own national policy concerning Iran, just as the European countries had their own national policies. In another analogy with Europe and the hosting of NATO, one also needs to account for the provision of other tangible support, such as port facilities, fuel, and enabling services such as those provided by Saudi AWACS aircraft and the various Coast Guards of GCC member states. The southern Gulf countries additionally provided financial support to Iraq—an issue that was later to be associated with Saddam's 1990 invasion of Kuwait over repayment concerns—as well as intangible political support for Iraq and those countries providing intervening naval forces, which triggered Iranian political and military reactions.

Of the six countries making up the GCC, Saudi Arabia always stood out in terms of geographic size, population, and military capacity. Questions about possible minesweeping contributions from Saudi Arabia arose almost from the start—one of freshly sworn-in Navy Secretary Webb's initial lines of questioning involved making use of relatively new Saudi minesweepers instead of old, mal-positioned American assets.[69] It is important to recall that the regional attitude toward hosting outside military forces and participating in multilateral military operations was very different in 1987 than it would be three years later in connection with Operation *Desert Storm*. Indeed, one of the measures of success for *Desert Storm* was the ability to assemble a 42-nation coalition and to overcome regional concerns about hosting Western military forces. Those fears about the presence of foreign military forces were not necessarily misplaced—one of the strategic narratives used by Osama bin Ladin during the 1990s in popularizing al-Qaeda was to sharply criticize the Saudi government for "allowing the enemy Crusader American forces to occupy the land" in the aftermath of Operation *Desert Storm* and the prosecution of Operation *Southern Watch*.[70]

Given Saudi Arabia's geographical location, the country's potential contribution to military operations was not limited to their Navy. However, initial requests to the Saudis to use their F-15s to help provide air cover for convoys were rebuffed; a similar response greeted the request to station American F-15s at Saudi bases.[71] Both requests presumably triggered concerns over the political liability that would be incurred by offering overt or offensive military support. The Saudis, however, did agree to cooperate in the use of their AWACS surveillance aircraft and to provide initial minesweeping services off Kuwait.[72]

A key aspect in depending upon Saudi minesweeping services, however, was the training and skills needed to detect and neutralize mines. It is one matter to *own* the equipment; it is another matter to be able to *operate* the equipment.[73] Royal Saudi Navy priorities regarding the threat of mine warfare were in practice not that much different from the benignly neglectful attitude of the U.S. Navy. As a late 1984 CIA assessment summed it up:

> U.S. Navy reporting from both 1983 and 1984 rated the mine warfare skills of the Saudi squadron of four minesweeping ships as generally low. The ships have fairly modern equipment, but personnel deficiencies remain the primary barrier to an effective Saudi minesweeping capability. The limited education of most Saudi recruits, normal attrition,

and widespread personnel shortages ... often result in the transfer of trained personnel to positions where they are more urgently needed ...[74]

While Saudi minesweeping contributions were eventually folded into the multinational minesweeping operations that evolved through 1988, it is important to remember that the Saudis were making contributions, running risks, and taking casualties. In August 1987, a Saudi EOD diver was killed and another injured in a demining effort off the port of Ras Tannurah, and the Saudis would continue to live and work in the area long after the end of the operation, having to deal with any post-war unexploded ordnance.[75]

***

The improvisational, ad hoc nature of the international naval response to the Tanker War mirrored that of the United States. There was never a clear, single policy, or organization behind the growing international naval presence, which instead developed in response to a series of events. The Gulf states themselves also faced an array of difficult choices. While no country welcomed a predominant Iranian presence, none sought a predominant Iraqi presence either—it was, after all, the fear that Saddam would continue charging south in 1990 that caused the Saudis to finally welcome land-based American forces into the Kingdom as part of *Desert Shield*. Decades later, regime change in Baghdad and Kabul removed Iran's natural predators, allowing the Iranians to instead devote their energies to supporting regional proxies, some of which then turned on individual GCC countries such as Saudi Arabia. In addition to those regional concerns, the Gulf states also had to keep in mind the Cold War and competing American and Soviet desires to bring countries into their respective orbits.

In dealing with this complicated situation, naval forces provided a number of attractive aspects. Naval deployments created the opportunity for countries to demonstrate their interest, relevance, and concern while simultaneously limiting the political liability that may have come with land-based forces. As the Dutch experience illustrates, the long timelines associated with deployments "leave ample room for political fine-tuning," which provide a range of attractive possibilities for political leaders looking to keep their options open until the last possible moment. The naval forces could effectively cooperate without requiring an overarching political structure—for example, these were not peacekeeping forces with regular reporting requirements to the UN Security Council.

By focusing international efforts on sea-oriented threats, the outside countries could respond with sea-based forces. While those sea-based forces may not have been able to end the Iran–Iraq War, they did allow for a range of possibilities when the war did finally conclude, positioning those countries to benefit from the post-war situation—even if that peaceful period was over more quickly than anyone expected.

CHAPTER 8

The Outcomes of Operation *Earnest Will*

> Finally, on 15 August 1988 the Iranians gave up. Khomeini said it was like swallowing bitter poison but agreed to comply with UN Resolution 598 ... It was then we could answer the Navy Secretary's question—when would we know we had won? Clearly we have won, at least for now.
> —DEFENSE SECRETARY CASPER WEINBERGER, "THE PERSIAN GULF SUCCESS STORY"[1]

> In war the result is never final ... even the ultimate outcome of a war is not always to be regarded as final. The defeated state often considers the outcome merely as a transitory evil, for which a remedy may still be found in political conditions at some later date.
> —CLAUSEWITZ[2]

The Duke of Wellington, prompted by a writer for his recollections about the 1815 Battle of Waterloo, replied: "The history of a battle is not unlike the history of a ball. Some individuals may recollect all the little events of which the great result is the battle won or lost, but no individual can recollect the order in which, or the exact moment at which, they occurred, which makes all the difference as to their value or importance."[3]

The battles in *Earnest Will* are, in a sense, different. First, they were obviously fought at a much smaller scale than Waterloo. But they were also fought at sea, almost entirely by ships, and those types of battles have always been easier to reconstruct in terms of movements, ships, and which cannon started firing when. The ships' logs at the naval battle of Trafalgar—10 years before Waterloo—still allow a sequential study of the battle, even if they are limited in providing a detailed guide as to what happened on each individual ship. The progress in technology by the late 20th century means that—in looking at the participation of U.S. Navy ships in *Nimble Archer*, *Praying Mantis*, and the *Vincennes* incident—there is actually quite a lot of data about the order and moments in which actions occurred—in the case of *Vincennes*, there are detailed computer logs and actual video camera recordings. On the other hand, time brings with it new information and new discoveries, such as the recent work regarding the attack on the USS *Stark* being perpetrated by a modified civilian jet rather than an Iraqi *Mirage*.[4]

What these battles share with Waterloo is recognizing that there are still some essentially unknowable aspects to the war. What was the so-called "theory of victory" when the Iranians first targeted Kuwaiti tankers? Why and when did the Iranians decide their mining campaigns? Why did the Iranians actually accept UNSCR 598 and end the Iraq–Iran War in 1988? It is worth recalling from the start that any military history will necessarily be based on incomplete information, not unlike trying to reconstruct a ball at which the Duke of Wellington once danced.

The timeline on page xv makes the Tanker War appear as a logical series of events. That linear approach, however, disregards the ever-present role of chance. What if the Iraqi pilots had *not* fired on *Stark*? What if the *Silkworm* strike that precipitated *Nimble Archer* had *not* hit an American-flagged ship? What if a *European* ship had steamed into the minefield that damaged the *Roberts* or what if the *Roberts*, like the models predicted, had snapped in half and taken most of the crew with it? What if *Vincennes* had held its missile fire? What if the Iranians did *not* accept UNSCR 598? The "what-ifs" are plentiful—and yet they are countered with numerous examples of what actually did happen. The Tanker War and Operation *Earnest Will* were actual events, and we know enough about them to benefit from a descriptive approach, one in which an examination of what actually occurred provides insights usable today.

The role of politics in *Earnest Will* illustrates why it is a nonsense statement for a military officer to describe themselves as "apolitical." Politics pervades *Earnest Will*, from the American decision to act in the first place, to the constraints of the American War Powers Act, to the concurrent holding of the Iran–Contra investigations by the United States Congress. The decisions of the Europeans to send assets to the Gulf was as much a factor of intra-European power jockeying—and individual domestic politics—as it was a military one. One sees the power of an individual political leader, as was the case with British Prime Minister Thatcher when she overruled her ministers and decided to send Royal Navy minesweepers to the Gulf in August 1987. And less clear, but no less important, are the little understood back and forth of Iranian political calculations, from the start of the war to the acceptance of UNSCR 598. Military officers should be non-partisan—they should not align with any political party—but it beggars the imagination to figure out how they could do their jobs without an appreciation for politics.

***

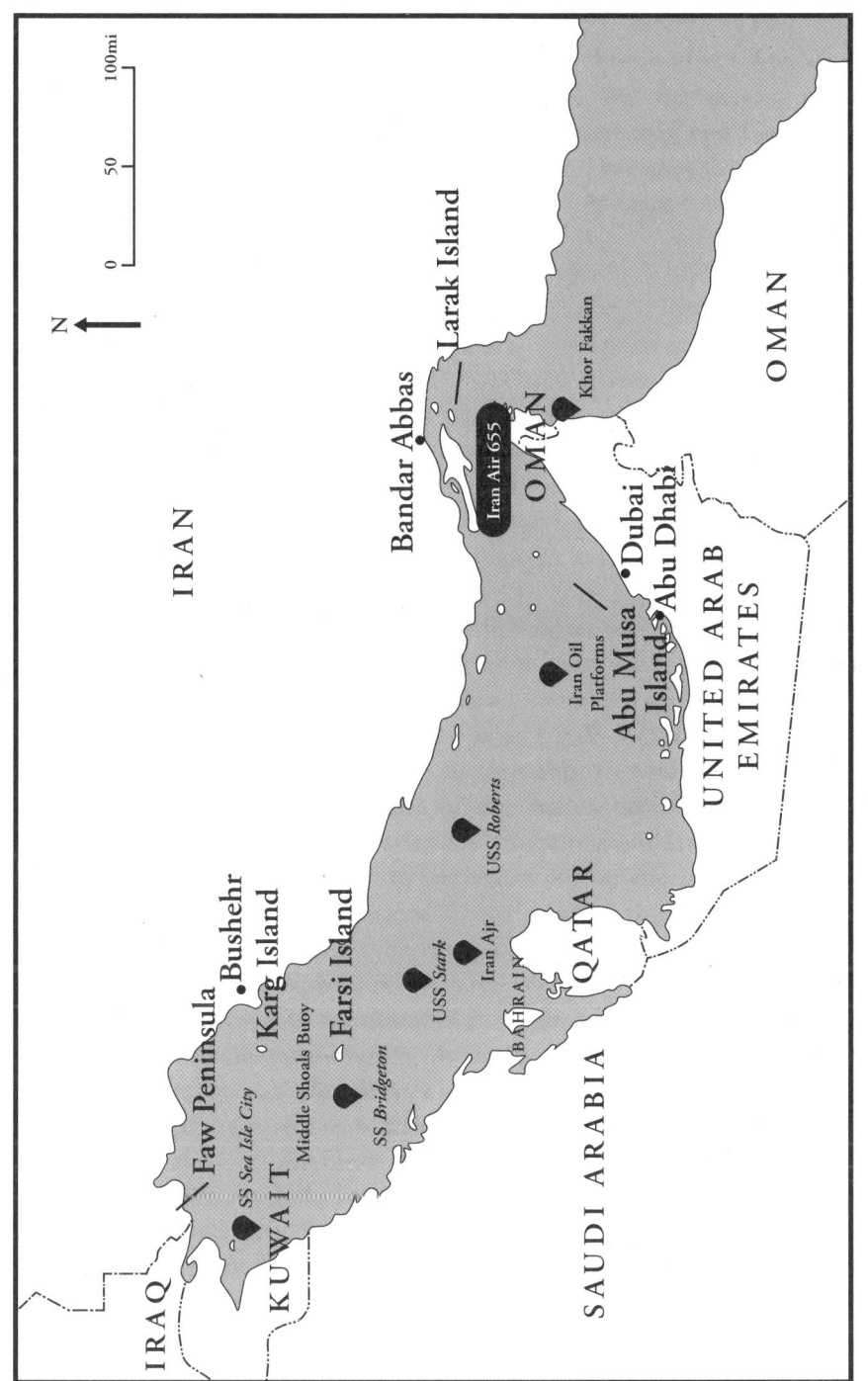

Major incidents in connection with Operation *Earnest Will*.

Earnest Will represents a maritime strategy in practice—it was a war completely fought at or above the sea and a vivid demonstration of the utility of seapower. The operation is a clear example of "strategy as the use of war for the purposes of policy," one of the distinctions that Scottish military historian Hew Strachan lays out as a difference between "Strategy in Theory; Strategy in Practice."[5] This focus on strategy and its connection to violence may seem obvious but it is not. The opening words of 2023's *The New Makers of Modern Strategy*—"the next generation of the definitive work on strategy, essentially the latest version of the textbook for strategists"—which includes a chapter dedicated to American maritime strategist Alfred Thayer Mahan, but not one on Corbett—declares, "Strategy is what allows us to act with purpose in a disordered world; it is vital to out-thinking and out-playing our foes."[6] This is strategy as a euphemism for planning, which is a common-enough way to use the word, but one which loses the link between violence and strategy.[7] *New Makers* does go on to say, speaking of international competition, "In this sense, strategy is intimately connected to the use of force, because the specter of violence hangs over any contested relationship," but those caveats are revealing: strategy, in this formulation has many senses *other* than violence, and the mere threat of force is seen as virtually the coequal of the use of force. While all these observations make sense in theory, it is not all clear they work in practice.

Earnest Will is the story of the actual conduct of a war, not the avoidance of war.[8] Much of American strategic discourse may well focus on deterrence—as was clearly the case going into the Tanker War—but it is an open question as to whether the Iranians were deterred from actions as much as they were deprived of assets via the efforts of the United States military. There is no sense that the Americans had the day-to-day fidelity in understanding the Iranian decision-making process that would make a strategy of deterrence actually work in practice. A researcher later asked Admiral Bernsen, U.S. Middle East force commander, whether he had "any internal intelligence on what was going in on Iran?" Bernsen replied: "Damn little. Oh, sure, there was some reporting, but it was very difficult to ferret out specific details concerning leadership decision making … So what you really did was you sort of made your assumptions based on what you knew about them, their track record."[9] Bernsen's unvarnished remarks would likely be echoed by most operational commanders in almost any conflict and are a reminder of the difference in perspective between those making policies in capital and those carrying out those policies on the scene.

The operation also represents *a* maritime strategy as compared to *the* Maritime Strategy, the highly visible series of briefings, speeches, equipment acquisition, and deployments associated with the Reagan administration throughout the 1980s that one may have expected to guide U.S. naval operations occurring in the same decade. The Maritime Strategy worked very effectively as a strategic narrative, explaining how an aggressive, forward-deployed Navy could materially affect a notional land-war in Europe. The Maritime Strategy certainly worked as a budget narrative— "perhaps the most successful employment and force structure plan in the Navy's history"—and provided the strategic context for the funding of the "600-ship Navy."[10] Admiral James Watkins, American Chief of Naval Operations during critical years for the Maritime Strategy, is said to have viewed the document as the "bedrock of planning, programming, and operations throughout today's Navy."[11] Watkins himself, in his 1986 unclassified articulation of the Maritime Strategy, stressed, however, that the document did "not purport to be a detailed war plan with firm timelines, tactical doctrine, or specific target sets. Instead, it offers a global perspective to operational commanders and provides a foundation for advice to the National Command Authorities. The strategy has become a key element in shaping Navy programmatic decisions."[12]

Even by the late 1980s, the very general nature of the Maritime Strategy was identified as a possible weak point, particularly as the Cold War was seen to be winding down. Prominent naval affairs commentator Ron O'Rourke warned as early as 1988 of "a situation in which "the Maritime Strategy" refers to all of the Navy's possible peacetime and wartime operations, and thus to none of them in particular. By stretching the concept in this manner, "the Maritime Strategy" could come to mean everything, and thus nothing."[13]

Above all, the Maritime Strategy cannot be described as a war-*winning* strategy, because of the obvious point that it was never actually used in a war—as an actual war-fighting approach, it remains an untested hypothesis. One might argue that the entire point of the Maritime Strategy was deterrence and that its success was measured by ensuring that a war was never actually fought, but that success also means that the strategy was never demonstrated in war. In reality, it may be fortuitous that the Maritime Strategy was never actually executed. Contemporary critics who argued that the strategy's actual implementation against the Soviet Union would be "highly destabilizing" and—when "coupled with the threat of nuclear escalation ... potentially dangerous" —may have been correct if recent Russian reports about the linkage between naval losses and nuclear weapons release authorization are to be believed.[14] In terms of actual war-fighting then, the Maritime Strategy remains a strategy in theory. It is also worth noting that the Maritime Strategy, given its focus on an affecting short-term decision-making by the Soviet leadership, did not represent a classic, economically focused maritime strategy either.

That all said, *Earnest Will* is clearly a "maritime strategy in practice" mainly in retrospect. American decision-makers did not quote Clausewitz or Corbett in their announcements or their deliberations in 1987 and 1988—nor, for that matter, did they draw from the Maritime Strategy in using, say, the Strategy's highly stylized progression of phases ("Phase I: Deterrence or the Transition to War/Phase II: Seizing the Initiative/Phase III: Carrying the Fight to the Enemy").[15] If anything, the initiative rested with the Iraqis in attacking Iranian ships, followed by Iranian retaliation. American actions were by contrast, almost entirely *reactive*. *Earnest Will* was fought at sea, but not for lack of thinking about how to fight ashore—senior U.S. military leaders repeatedly pressed for strikes on land; several advocated for the invasion and takeover of Iranian-held islands. Like most military history, it only makes sense in looking backwards. Going back to Wellington, it was only in retrospect that it becomes clear that the Battle of Waterloo ended the threat of Napolean. So too, it is only in looking back that one sees how the events of *Earnest Will* contributed to the end of the Iran–Iraq War.

***

This sense of fortuitousness in results was present from the war's end. A 1989 analysis—titled "The Wrong Strategy in the Right Place"—expressed a sense of happenstance at the establishment of the cease-fire called for in UNSCR 598, charging that the American approach was "poorly conceived, ineffective, and dangerous."[16] A later analysis of the war was titled "Better Lucky Than Good: Operation Earnest Will as Gunboat Diplomacy."[17] Another contemporary account emphasized "the role of luck in this case."[18]

In terms of minimizing impacts to world oil prices, a 1990 U.S. General Accounting Office report scored the operation as a success: "One of the objectives of operation Earnest Will was to maintain the free flow of oil from the Persian Gulf area …. the operation was successful. Oil disruptions did not occur, and Persian Gulf oil production actually increased slightly."[19] That same report also addressed the counterfactual:

> If a disruption had occurred, the near-term impact on oil-consuming economies would have been serious. Dramatic increases in oil prices have historically affected the economies that rely on oil or its products. For example, following the 1973–74 embargo, crude oil prices nearly

tripled. This increase contributed to a 1.1-percent decrease in the real gross national product of the United States in 1975. Further, in the year following the 1979 Iranian shutdown, oil prices nearly doubled, contributing to a 13.5-percent inflation rate and a 7.1-percent unemployment rate in 1980 in the United States.[20]

American decision-makers in the mid-1980s thus had very clear recent examples of the economic and political consequences of oil flows from the Middle East.

Secretary of Defense Caspar Weinberger, commenting in his 1990 memoirs on Iran's acceptance of UNSCR 598 and the end of the Iran–Iraq War, directly addressed Navy Secretary James Webb's questions from the beginning of *Earnest Will* in a chapter he—significantly—titled "The Persian Gulf Success Story":

> Finally, on 15 August 1988 the Iranians gave up. Khomeini said it was like swallowing bitter poison but agreed to comply to UN Resolution 598 and to accept a ceasefire with the Iraqis. The lengthy negotiations toward the final settlement of the Iran–Iraq war then began. It was then that we could answer the Navy Secretary's question—when we would know we had won? Clearly we have won, at least for now, in the sense of achieving our objectives that non-belligerent, vitally important commerce can and will flow freely in the open international waters of the Gulf without being subjected to mines or indiscriminate attacks by Iran.[21]

Weinberger went on to place *Earnest Will* in a larger context:

> This whole Gulf action and our role in it seems to me to be another proud chapter in the history of our military. We worked with many of our allies in a well-conducted activity in an area of high strategic importance. We kept the Soviets out, despite their historic ambition for a larger role and a port in the Gulf region. In so doing we reconfirmed our forty-year role in the Gulf. We helped our Gulf Arab friends to survive, and to see the possibility of a brighter future with Khomeini dead and the war over. Most important of all, we demonstrated to our Arab friends that they could indeed rely on a strong, resolute, and effective America.[22]

Weinberger was careful to caveat this American success story—he went on in his memoirs to stress "I am not entirely convinced that this is the end of the issue," going on to discuss actions by the Iranians such as the fatwa on writer Salman Rushdie and the specific nature of the Iranian revolutionary regime.[23] Indeed, Weinberger went so far as to compare Ayatollah Khomeini with "Captain Nasty"—"his ship's captain who 'cleared' innocent merchant ships and then fired on them."[24] Weinberger emphasized that the only way to preserve the gains of *Earnest Will* was to continue to work closely with the southern Gulf states.

Navy Secretary Webb's persistent questions about the wisdom of intervening in the Tanker War had been anchored in the context of the "Weinberger Doctrine" for the use of military power, laid out in a notable speech delivered by the Defense Secretary at the National Press Club in Washington, D.C. in

November 1984, some two years before the beginning of *Earnest Will*.[25] The Weinberger Doctrine was articulated after the 1984 landslide election returning President Reagan to power, but also in the aftermath of the withdrawal of U.S. Marines from Beirut—an intervention Weinberger had opposed because of its ill-defined parameters. In his speech, the defense secretary adversely compared missions such as that which brought the Marines to Beirut—a classic, interpositional peacekeeping force not intended for combat but rather to keep two warring factions apart while peace negotiations took place—with actions such as Operation *Urgent Fury* in Grenada, an action that took place two days after the barracks bombing, and one for which forces were equipped and oriented toward combat.[26]

Weinberger argued the post-World War II period had provided several lessons and that he had therefore "developed six major tests to be applied when we are weighing the use of combat forces abroad":

1. The United States should not commit forces to combat unless the vital national interests of the United States or its allies are involved. Referring back to the possibility that South Korea had been invaded in 1950 because of an ill-phrased public announcement, he emphasized the United States should not characterize a given area as outside its strategic perimeter.
2. Combat troops should only be committed when there is "a clear intention of winning," though the modalities of winning are not defined in the speech—the implicit comparison is instead to static situations such as peacekeeping. Referencing Hitler's 1936 remilitarization of the Rhineland, Weinberger allowed that a limited force—which he went to further define as a "small combat force"—could "perhaps prevented the holocaust of WWII."[27]
3. Forces committed to combat require clearly defined political and military objectives and "we should know precisely how our forces can accomplish those clearly defined objectives." Here, Weinberger literally quoted Clausewitz: "No one starts a war—or rather, no one in his senses ought to do so—without first being clear in his mind what he intends to achieve by that war and how he intends to conduct it."[28] He went on to warn that we "not assign a combat mission to a force configured for peacekeeping."
4. "The relationship between our objectives and the forces we have committed—their size, composition, and disposition—must be continually reassessed and adjusted if necessary." Weinberger proposed two "basic questions: is this conflict in our national interest? Does our national interest

require us to fight, to use force of arms? If the answers are 'yes,' then we must win. If the answers are 'no,' then we should not be in combat." It is worth noting that there is a tension set up between the two parts of this test—a continual reassessment could well mean that an answer that was initially a "yes" could, on reassessment, turn into a "no."
5. "Before the United States commits combat forces abroad, there must be some reasonable assurance that we will have the support of the American people and their elected representatives in Congress."
6. "The commitment of U.S. forces to combat should be a last resort."

Colin Powell—future national security advisor, chairman of the Joint Chiefs of Staff, and secretary of state, serving at the time of the speech as the two-star military assistant to the secretary of defense—was asked by Weinberger to circulate the initial draft of Weinberger's points, which he directly connected to the secretary's reaction to the 1983 Beirut Marine Corps barracks bombing.[29] Powell was present at the National Press Club when the remarks were delivered and later wrote: "When it became my responsibility to advise Presidents on committing our forces to combat, Weinberger's rules turned out to be a practical guide."[30]

The problem is that—while the tests made sense in the abstract—their practical application unraveled in the face of how wars actually unfolded, particularly if the wars were protracted. Military historian Hew Strachan observed:

> [In] both the Weinberger doctrine of 1984 (in whose formulation Powell is presumed to have played a leading role) and the Powell doctrine of 1992 [in line with presentations Powell made that year as Chairman of the Joint Chiefs of Staff] ... all that is required for success is the establishment of clear aims and the provision of overwhelming force to achieve those aims. As a theoretical requirement of policy, that is fair enough; as a statement about war's true nature it is demonstrably false.[31]

The Weinberger and Powell doctrines set up inherent civil–military tensions—in essence, reserving the Army only for "popular, winnable wars," to be fought symmetrically against foes structured like the U.S. armed forces.[32] As Strachan notes, "Because America's generals would only countenance the employment of military forces in the sorts of operations for which the army was optimized, they effectively rendered them unusable."[33] The question arises as to what the military would do if ordered—as their civilian masters have the legal right to do—to participate in unpopular wars without a clearly identifiable end.

In response to the question of Weinberger's Test #2 regarding the need for winning—the counterfactual question arises of what if, in 1936, President Roosevelt *had* decided to send forces to the Rhineland to combat Hitler?[34] The requirement for the permanent demilitarization of the Rhineland was laid out in the Versailles Treaty and the Locarno Treaties—agreements to which the United States was not a party, notoriously in the case of Versailles. Weinberger did not specifically call for the use of American military forces, which is just as well—Army Chief of Staff General Douglas MacArthur, speaking in 1935 of the 119,000 soldiers that comprised the entire regular U.S. Army, observed that his whole service "could be crowded into Yankee Stadium."[35] As a domestic political matter, would such a deployment have had "the support of the American people and their representatives in Congress?" It's worth recalling that in August 1941, with Hitler's invasion of Russia well underway, the U.S. House of Representatives passed a military draft bill by only one vote.[36] One also encounters the "then what?" question—would American forces have stayed in the Rhineland indefinitely? What was "winning" in 1936?

While the Weinberger's tests may have made sense in a short, sharp conflict such as the eight-day-long American invasion of Grenada, they lose their meaning in more protracted conflicts against more effective foes. Weinberger addressed this type of criticism head on, in his concluding sentence to the "Persian Gulf Success Story:"

> In view of the long weeks and months of superb service given by our forces, I was, somewhat sardonically I fear, amused by another of the post-Grenada criticisms: "Well, anything we can do quickly, such as Libya or Grenada, we do reasonably well, but we have no staying power." We had enough staying power in the Gulf to win and to ensure that "Freedom of the Seas" is more than a slogan.[37]

The challenge is in how one measures staying power. Navies operate in peacetime much as they do in wartime—if staying power is measured as a function of time spent in lengthy deployments, then Weinberger was absolutely correct. However, if staying power is instead measured as a function of ability to absorb large numbers of casualties then—fortuitously—this was never put to the test, despite Iranian actions that had the potential to inflict high losses. Once the violence starts, war itself can act as an independent factor that changes the aims and expectations of the participants—in other words, the actual fighting of war can double back to affect the policies that sought to instrumentalize war in the first place. The mutation of objectives derided as "mission creep" is in fact inherent in any protracted conflict. As Strachan

Defense Secretary Caspar Weinberger (center) at the swearing-in of future Navy Secretary James Webb. Webb asked all the right questions about the wisdom of American involvement in the Tanker War, but Weinberger's gamble ultimately paid off. (NHHC)

argues elsewhere, "The dynamic and reciprocal nature of war shapes strategy more than strategy shapes war."[38]

Newly sworn-in Navy Secretary James Webb had gotten at these gaps between Weinberger's tests and what faced the United States in the Persian Gulf in a series of classified memos to Weinberger. Webb, in a *New York Times* profile later assessing his first year as Navy Secretary, was described as "uncomfortable with what he considered to be the loosely defined, haphazardly executed expansion of the Navy's role in the Gulf" and was quoted as saying "I really learned in a couple of months how Vietnam got so screwed up by watching the way that decisions were made on the Persian Gulf."[39] In reaching out to the defense secretary, Webb acknowledged that he "had no operational authority as secretary of the Navy, but I at least could give him some policy advice."[40] Webb started with questions as early as May 1987 in meeting with Weinberger: "How will we know when we've won? What is victory? Why are we getting involved in the middle of a war in the Persian Gulf?"[41] In a July memorandum, Webb was said to have continued his sharp line of questioning, with a reporter saying that the navy secretary continued to push as to "whether the policy had been adequately justified and the mission fully defined, and whether the public would support it."[42]

In more measured public remarks on the communication in September, after news of Webb's concerns reached the public, the Navy Secretary said:

> The concern that I and many people had was that we would be pulled into an obligation that did not have specific goals attached to it so that we couldn't measure when the goals had been met and we could then downsize our forces ... Without being able to clearly articulate what our goals, what our objectives, are politically, it's difficult to measure the military commitment.[43]

Webb himself made subsequent supportive public announcements, saying by September that "the assistance of other nations in escorting ships safely through the Persian Gulf had largely resolved his early reservations about the American presence there."[44] While these public remarks served to mollify concerns that there was a split between the secretary of the navy and the secretary of defense, in private Webb was still said to have harbored doubts.[45] As it happens, none of the promised additional European ships had actually reached the Gulf at the time of the September statement, and Webb himself stepped down as navy secretary over proposed cuts to overall U.S. Navy ship numbers in February 1988, two months before *Praying Mantis*.

As an exercise in logic, Webb was right—Operation *Earnest Will* arguably did not come close to meeting all of Weinberger's six tests.[46] Those tests, which had to do with only using force in areas of vital interest to the United States, were clearly met in word and deed, with multiple, high-level announcements from leaders of both political parties as well as in staying the course, despite taking casualties in situations such as that of the USS *Stark*. The other tests, however, were arguably not met, hence the power of Webb's questions.

As the navy secretary pointed out, there was no ultimate criteria for winning, other than via an open-ended metric of attacks on merchant ships—a dynamic that was completely beyond American control. Test 3's requirement for clear military and political objectives—beyond the operationally focused metric of merchant ship attacks—was never met. Test 5's requirement for congressional and public support was never definitively put to the test—a comparison would be the later congressional votes regarding Iraq in 1991 and 2003, which never happened in 1987. Finally, it was never clear that the commitment of American forces was the last resort to be tried after all other options had failed—there was never, for example, a high-profile effort to compel the Iraqis to cease the attacks on Iranian merchant ships that led to the retaliatory Iranian attacks responsible for bringing in Western navies.

***

And yet, despite Webb asking all the right questions for all the right reasons and despite *Earnest Will* arguably failing at least four of Weinberger's six tests, the operation was a success—seen so at the time and even more evident in retrospect. Iranian attacks on ships did drop off and the Soviet Union was never able to secure a foothold in the Persian Gulf. Weinberger, operating from necessarily incomplete information when it came to discerning Iranian motives and future actions, guessed correctly and gambled successfully that the operation would pay off.[47]

Weinberger, Powell, and Webb were reacting both to recent events such as Beirut and Grenada but also to America's strategic defeat in the Vietnam War and came out of it determined to ensure such a defeat never happened again. The challenge is that these leaders were talking about war, a human institution which is simultaneously rational, irrational, and non-rational.[48] Highly structured approaches such as political doctrines are understandable and likely vital when it comes to budget battles and securing domestic political support. Yet, in their actual application to war itself, it becomes clear how crude these models and structures actually are—they cannot come close to comprehending all the variables and chance in war. The same observation could be made of nuclear deterrence—the "strategic logic" of nuclear-deterrent thinking may make sense in the abstract, but one does not actually know how or whether it works in practice.

In the case of the Iran–Iraq War, the two sides ended the conflict in 1988. The *Vincennes* incident may have only served as a pretext serving to preserve Iranian Revolution, but in fact, it did serve as a politically acceptable reason for the Iranians to accept UNSCR 598.[49] Attacks on merchant ships perpetrated by either side dropped to zero, and American force levels dropped down to pre-*Earnest Will* levels.

While senior American military officers in the field—for very good operational reasons—had urged attacks on the Iranian mainland, the American political leadership always ultimately chose not to do so. Part of this was circumstances—had there been a successful land-based *Silkworm* strike that sank an American ship and killed hundreds of sailors in the process, the Reagan administration would have been hard-pressed not to attack *Silkworm* sites on the Iranian mainland. But secondly—and perhaps more importantly—the

Reagan administration never tried to make *Earnest Will* anything more than a limited war; there was no loose talk over overthrowing the Islamic Republic of Iran. Again—as a counterfactual—a large American death toll may have changed that calculation but—in the actual event—it didn't, and that was a key factor in America winning this conflict.

While it is true that war quickly returned to the region—a number of the American ships that withdrew in 1988 returned in 1990 in connection with Operation *Desert Storm*, including an enhanced minesweeping component—the political circumstances of that return are important. *Desert Storm*, after all, was a war against Iraq, not Iran. While the subsequent American policy in the region in the 1990s may have been "dual containment" against Iraq and Iran, it is also worth noting that—much as was the case with the earlier Twin Pillars policy—the dualities were not symmetrical. In other words, much as Iran and Saudi Arabia were treated very differently under Twin Pillars, so too were Iraq and Iran treated very differently under dual containment.

In the case of Iraq, the ultimately unsatisfactory outcome of *Desert Storm* meant that American and—at least initially—coalition forces were engaged in ongoing uses of force against Iraq for the following decade, leading to Operation *Iraqi Freedom* in 2003 and a subsequent forceful U.S. military presence in Iraq for decades to follow.[50] The contrast with Iran is pretty stark—despite rhetorical clashes and occasional military encounters, the use of force against Iran has dropped to virtually zero in decades since 1988; it remains to be seen whether the June 2025 air strike against Iranian nuclear facilities by U.S. military forces is a one-off affair. One could argue that the Iranians have engaged in a forward strategy of their own, pushing their armed conflict with the United States into other countries using proxies such as Iranian-associated militias in Iraq, the Houthis in Yemen, and Hezbollah in Lebanon, but it is worth recalling that those proxies are also fighting for their own political reasons in their own countries. When it comes to force-on-force conflicts between the American and Iranian militaries themselves—fights which featured very prominently in and around the roughly two years of Operation *Earnest Will*—there has arguably been a status quo that has lasted for nearly 40 years.

That status quo between the United States and the Islamic Republic of Iran is what victory looks like in limited wars. The Iranian revolutionary regime has not been toppled but, at the same time, commerce continues to flow through the Persian Gulf and the area—especially at sea—is neither under the control of the Iranians nor any other country or coalition of countries hostile to the United States and all of that has been accomplished at an acceptable and sustainable cost. Especially when contrasted with the results seen in Iraq and Afghanistan, it is hard not to see Operation *Earnest Will* as a win.

CHAPTER 9

Why the Tanker War Matters Today

> I know that when I put on a blue uniform, I'm expected to stand in harm's way.[1]
> —REAR ADMIRAL ALLEN BERGNER, MEMBER OF USS *PUEBLO* COURT OF INQUIRY
>
> In strategy there is no such thing as victory.
> —CLAUSEWITZ[2]

The Tanker War was completely fought at sea.

In one sense, that's a statement of the obvious—the conflict, after all, is named after a class of ocean-going ship. At another level, however, it is a remarkable statement. Despite the first taste of U.S.–Iranian clashes fought via proxies on land in and around Beirut in the early 1980s, this first conflict between the actual uniformed, national forces of the United States and the Islamic Republic of Iran was confined exclusively to the maritime.

That's not to say that there were no plans to extend the fight onshore—Admiral Ace Lyons was fired, in part, because of that and even CENTCOM General Crist, CJCS Admiral Crowe, and JTFME Admiral Less advocated plans to strike targets ashore in Iran that were never approved. In the series of actual historical events in 1987 and 1988, though—in looking at what actually happened, not what *might* have happened—all the action occurred at, below, or above the sea. If the Maritime Strategy of the 1980s—in which the United States would deploy its fleets against the Soviet Union in order to either deter World War III or materially affect the NATO–Warsaw Pact land battle—represented maritime strategy in theory, then *Earnest Will* represented maritime strategy in practice. Virtually every part of the operation involved the sea—the major actors were ships, and the fight was for the sea lanes and maritime trade.

Geoffrey Till writes of the efficiency of seapower—that there is "something uniquely cost-effective about seapower, as compared to landpower."[3] He was speaking mainly of the economic aspects "that those nations best able to exploit its attributes profited hugely over those who did not," but there is another measure of efficiency at play. In the eight years of the Tanker War, 432 sailors lost their lives.[4] On land, during the Iran–Iraq War, those numbers would have summed up one bad morning.

The Tanker War was recognizably a sideshow of a larger war, but this is a case where the sideshow brought down the curtain. It was the end of the larger, Iran–Iraq War that brought a conclusion to the Tanker War but—in the end—the American military involvement occurred on and over the sea, and there are some lessons to be learned from this unusual fight. Michael Howard, founder of the discipline of War Studies and writing about why to study military history, emphasized that—while each war is unique, "After all allowances have been made for historical differences, war still resemble each other more than they resemble any other human activity."[5]

The way that *Earnest Will* unfolded—lurching from event to event—is a case study in operating under incomplete information. Navy Secretary James Webb was right in pressing Defense Secretary Weinberger about the endgame questions at the beginning of the operation; one of management guru Stephen Covey's dicta is after all to "begin with the end in mind."[6] Clausewitz put this more formally in the words quoted by Defense Secretary Caspar Weinberger in his six criteria speech: "No one starts a war—or rather, no one in his senses ought to do so—without first being clear in his mind what he intends to achieve by that war and how he intends to conduct it."[7] Yet this is one of those examples in which corporate strategy diverges from military strategy. Both deal with situations of acting under incomplete information, but war adds not only violence but the creational aspect that derives from that violence—once people start getting hurt and killed, the stakes and methods change. In a world where one must continually operate in dimly understood circumstances, it makes sense to limit liability where possible.

Earnest Will represents a compelling example of such a "limited liability" approach to warfare, one highlighted by British writer Basil Henry Liddell Hart as England's preferred "British Way of Warfare": the UK should focus on what it could do by sea, leaving the grinding land operations to continental partners. While Liddell Hart did not credit Julian Corbett for that insight, it was in fact Corbett who originated that line of thinking and who commiserated with Admiral Jackie Fisher over what both men saw as a misguided British strategy in creating a large British Army and deploying it on land in the Western Front during World War I.[8] Geoffrey Till, writing on Corbett's focus on maritime strategy—as opposed to a narrower, naval strategy—recognized that "sea powers could not defeat land powers on their own but, in conjunction with allies on land, they could determine the outcomes of wars and the nature of the peace."[9] In the case of ending the Iran–Iraq War, Iraq proved to be an ally in practice of the United States in the campaign against Iran, even if there was no actual Iraqi–American alliance or, indeed, any sustained operational coordination of military activities between the two countries. While it is possible Iraq, with its operational surge in 1988, could have ended the Iran–Iraq War on its own, it seems certain that the United States could not have concluded the Tanker War without the impact that Iraqi land offensives were having on Iran.

Elizabethan statesman Sir Francis Bacon observed: "He that commands the sea is at great liberty, and may take as much and as little of the war as he will."[10] This political flexibility clearly applied to the United States in the Persian Gulf which, through both expanded rules of engagement and increased force levels, chose to keep taking more and more of the war. Had American actions not been successful—as was the case in Beirut—the ship-focused presence would have allowed for a much less politically visible withdrawal than had been the case in 1983. There are, of course, limitations to this sea-based approach—as one critic of the concept of the British Way in Warfare put it: "Taking as much or as little of the war as one will" is never to be despised, but it never enabled us to *win*."[11] Except that—in this case—a sea-based approach *did* enable the United States to win.

In retrospect, Operation *Earnest Will* was a success, but no one could have accurately forecast that result at the outset—hence the force of Secretary Webb's questions. The risks to ships and crew from Iranian mines and missiles were clear, but it is also worth the effort to consider the risks of doing nothing. In a Cold War context, the Soviets were clearly ready to seize an opening. By 1985, of all the southern Gulf states, only Kuwait had diplomatic relations with the USSR, and no one was expecting the Berlin Wall to fall in 1989.[12] A Soviet flotilla was already operating in the region, and Kuwaitis in fact did utilize several additional tankers flying the Sickle and Hammer. If the end of the Cold War was due in part to crisis in confidence on the part of the Soviets— including, as John Lehman (Webb's predecessor as navy secretary) argued, a critical role played by aggressive American forward naval operations—then who knows what the effect would have been of the Russians supplanting the Americans in the Gulf, just as the Americans had supplanted the British.[13]

From an Iranian perspective, a maritime version of the 1983 USMC barracks bombing—in which mass casualties helped to precipitate a full military withdrawal—could have both satisfied longstanding Iranian desires to help expel foreign forces from the Persian Gulf, as well as provided a significant morale boost to the still-nascent Iranian Revolution. The potential impact on the southern Gulf can only be imagined, but it is hard to believe that the Iranian Revolution would have simply frozen in place as American ships steamed back over the horizon. Longstanding Iranian designs on majority-Shia Bahrain seem like an obvious place to start, not to mention the Eastern Province of Saudi Arabia—home to both Saudi oil production as well as the majority of Saudi Shia—which had already been the target of thwarted Iranian military operations in October 1987.

The truth is that it is simply unknown what would have happened if the Reagan administration had not taken the steps that it did in 1987 and 1988—speculation deals with counterfactuals, in pointed contrast to what actually occurred. The facts of *Earnest Will* are that there were fights between the Iranians and the Americans and that the Americans achieved their policy goals while working in a high-stakes situation of having to make decisions with only some parts of the story understood. Not for nothing does Clausewitz say in describing the uncertainty of war, "From the very start there is an interplay of possibilities, probabilities, good luck and bad that weaves its way throughout the length and breadth of the tapestry. In the whole range of human activities, war most closely resembles a game of cards."[14] Or, as a more contemporary writer put it, "Poker players like me, and the accomplished risk-takers from astronauts to venture capitalists I've talked to for my research, understand the importance of working with incomplete information. And they understand that sometimes doing nothing is the riskiest plan of all."[15]

***

The Tanker War was unmistakably an actual war—Operation *Earnest Will* participants, after all, met that most exacting of bureaucratic standards, eligibility for U.S. "veteran's preference" reserved for those with wartime service.[16] The word "war" is not being used here as some euphemism for concentrated and sustained effort, such as a "war on poverty" or a "war on inflation"—this operation was "an act of force to compel the enemy to do our will."[17] While the deployment of U.S. forces was not intended to provoke a war with the Iranians, it was not intended to avoid war either. Instead, *Earnest Will* represented the deployment of combat forces, in line with Defense Secretary Weinberger's use of the phrase in the speech announcing his doctrine: these forces were not intended to play an interpositional role between the Iraqis and the Iranians, but rather to use force—if necessary—to keep the sea lanes open as well as serving to keep the Soviets out.

Operation *Earnest Will* illustrates—along the lines of former American Defense Secretary Donald Rumsfeld's "you go to war with the Army you have" observation—how much wars are actually fought with older equipment.[18] In the case of the Tanker War, one can see significant roles played by mines first designed 80 years previously, as well as the effective employment of older American ships without the benefits of the latest technology. It is worth recalling that the United States straight up lost wars to the Taliban and the Viet Cong, both of which depended on light infantry armed with vintage-design weapons. Had the Iranians succeeded with their mining efforts, their 1908-model mines would have expelled modern, billion-dollar warships.

***

Thinking about limited and unlimited wars the way that Corbett described them—as an approach focused on political *ends* rather than military *means*—has applicability far beyond Operation *Earnest Will*. It was command of the sea that helped to shield the United States during its wars in Korea, Vietnam, and the Middle East. Recalling Corbett's explanation:

> Limited war is only permanently possible to island Powers or between Powers which are separated by sea, and then only when the Power desiring limited war is able to command the sea to such a degree as to be able not only to isolate the distant object, but also to render impossible the invasion of his home territory.[19]

It is clear that—no matter how the battles overseas were going—there was never any question of the North Koreans, the Viet Cong, or any Middle Eastern military invading the United States. This intrinsic characteristic of command of the sea is worth keeping in mind as America ponders a potential conflict with the People's Republic of China. It seems clear that American military leaders are planning for this possibility: in the words of former U.S. Navy Chief of Naval Operations Lisa Franchetti: "The Chairman of the People's Republic of China (PRC) has told his forces to be ready for war by 2027—we will be more ready."[20]

Any conflict with China would not be solely a Navy fight—the American joint approach to war codified in the 1986 Goldwater–Nichols Act and subsequently structured into American military commands would see to that, and Admiral Franchetti identified a multiplicity of possible Chinese threats: "The PLA Navy, Rocket Force, Aerospace Force, Air Force, and Cyberspace Force are coalescing into an integrated warfighting ecosystem specifically designed to defeat ours, backed by a massive industrial base."[21]

And yet, it is hard to dispute that any American–Chinese conflict would be primarily maritime—while there may be a lot of loose talk about replacing the Chinese Communist Party, no one is advocating that the United States Army march to Beijing in order to do so. In Clausewitzian and Corbettian terms, therefore, the option exists of a limited war focused on territory rather than an unlimited war focused on the overthrow of the Chinese government. The recent unsatisfactory history of American military interventions in the Middle East should provide plenty of incentives to keep wars limited and this is where Operation *Earnest Will* remains relevant today.

Earnest Will was overshadowed by the much larger Operation *Desert Storm* occurring several years later, which is unfortunate—while *Desert Storm* in retrospect ended up being the opening campaign of a much longer and, ultimately, unsuccessful war, *Earnest Will* led to results that favored the United States for decades to come. Part of this overshadowing was the larger scale of *Desert Storm*, but one should not overlook the marketing aspects of that 1991 operation and its immediate results. The new "Big 5" combat systems of the U.S. Army were demonstrated and validated.[22] Air power seemed to again have its day.[23] Most critically, the new "joint" system appeared to have been tested and also validated.[24] The combination was a triumph for continentalist, land-based thinkers, given the joint system's deep roots in U.S. Army doctrine.[25]

As navalist Steve Wills observed regarding *Desert Storm* that "few if any elements of the Navy's Maritime Strategy were utilized. There was no vast clash of naval arms as envisioned by the U.S. Navy's Cold War strategy adopted in the 1980s."[26] Part of this was the nature of the conflict—what little Navy the Iraqis did possess had largely been wiped out by the Iranians in the early stages of the Iran–Iraq War, but part was also the nature of the Maritime Strategy itself.[27] The Maritime Strategy worked extremely well as a "pleading document" for budget and programing decisions but wasn't really adaptable to a war-fighting, operational strategy against a target that did not depend upon access to the sea and which was simultaneously vulnerable to an overwhelming land attack.[28] The U.S. Navy was also distracted by a number of internal scandals that had repercussions for top-Navy leadership.[29] The combination of the appearance of not having been seen to play a major role in what appeared to be a once-in-a-generation war, the dissolution of the Soviet Union (along with its galvanizing strategic challenge), and Navy leadership focused on legal challenges and responding to calls for a "peace dividend" by redirecting Navy strategic intellectual focus toward industrial management techniques, enabled a post-Cold War American strategic environment dominated by continentalist, land-based thinking—one that arguably tops out at the operational level of war.

Wills details the impact of the 1986 Goldwater–Nichols Act in diminishing the impact of maritime strategy on American national security thinking: "In strengthening regional commanders' authority, joint leaders altered long-held concepts of maritime strategy and redrew the Navy's theater map of the world." and encouraged subsequent naval "strategy" documents that "focus on the operational level rather than the strategic level of war."[30] In the immediate post–Cold War world, maritime strategy lost out in the "defense marketplace of ideas."[31] U.S. Naval War College professor Sam Tangredi asks some hard questions regarding the outcomes of the post–Goldwater–Nichols world: "Has Joint ideology improved U.S. decision-making and ensured victory? Look at Afghanistan, Iraq, interventions in Kosovo, Libya, and elsewhere—did the U.S. achieve its strategic goals?"[32] The sense of frustration underlying Tangredi's questions undergird a line of thinking that suggests American strategic thinking and planning could use a rethink.

***

Given how poorly recent American wars have turned out, it may be time to reconsider the overall approach and to recognize the advantages inherent in maritime strategy. First, a reconsideration of how one defines limited and unlimited wars is in order, moving the discussion away from a focus on means and scale and instead focusing on ends. Clausewitz's differentiation of two types of wars does not specify maritime strategy, but Corbett's further elaboration certainly does. The point here is not simply that Corbett, a maritime strategist, defined the terms limited and unlimited war—it is that Corbett pointed out that *only* maritime powers can truly engage in limited war. His observation has significant consequences for the United States, which is unusually both a continental *and* a maritime power.

Corbett differentiated the Maritime and Continental schools of strategy, associating the first with a clear seapower—Britain—and the second with a clear landpower—Germany.[33] The United States is arguably both, even if the immediate post-*Desert Storm* period was biased toward landpower. A recognition that America is also a seapower, with much to gain from using maritime strategy, widens the range of options in the coming years. Take, for example, an application of Corbett's limited war approach to possible U.S. disputes with the People's Republic of China regarding Taiwan. From an American perspective, a fight over Taiwan clearly approaches Corbett's conditions for a limited war: the United States may be able to use maritime power to "isolate the distant object"—Taiwan—from an invasion by the PRC, but it can also use that same maritime power to "render impossible the invasion of [American] territory." In this sense, American war aims would be consciously limited, both in terms of political outcome—specifically defeating a sea-borne invasion of Taiwan rather than overthrowing the Chinese Communist Party—and in terms of the types of forces dedicated to achieving that plannable outcome.

Corbett warns of at least two challenges to thinking about limited war. First, while Taiwan might be a "limited object" for the United States, that thinking does not apply to the Chinese, for whom Taiwan would appear to meet Corbett's example of "objects that are not truly limited … of so much importance to him that he will be willing to use unlimited effort to retain it."[34] A second challenge to Corbett's way of thinking about limited war is doctrinal—as he put it, limited war was a "direct negation of the current doctrine" at a time in which it was believed that "in war there can only be one legitimate object, the overthrow of the enemy's means of resistance and that primary objective must always be his armed forces."[35] This preference for unlimited war—expressed emblematically in General Douglas MacArthur's farewell address, "In war there is no substitute for victory"—is arguably a Continentalist way of viewing war, and one that may be more ingrained in American thinking than is recognized.[36]

The other doctrinal consideration is the current American joint approach to warfare which—formed in no small part because of the outcome of Operation *Desert Storm* and Army General Colin Powell's position as JCS Chairman at the time of the conflict—is dominated by Army thinking. While an Army-derived joint system has produced a series of successes at the tactical and operational levels of war—and none of those successes should be taken for granted—the system has a conspicuous lack of success at connecting those battlefield successes to sustainable political outcomes favorable to the United States. Goldwater–Nichols and the joint system it engendered date from 1986—it is likely time for a relook.

Corbett was writing at sunset of the nearly century-long Pax Britannica, but he is also associated with the sea-based British Way of Warfare that contrasted with the Continentalist method the British ultimately ended up employing on the Western Front in World War I. That move to a large (for Britain) land-based force, away from an approach that centered on naval mastery, economic power, and adroit political movements is connected by some to the end of Pax Britannica.[37]

That idea of a British Way of Warfare is connected to the concept of "limited liability"; for the United States, the liability to be limited is both political and financial. The political consequences of limited war—which, in the case of

Taiwan, would be restricted to the defense of the island—play to American strengths. The United States has demonstrated the ability to win limited wars, of which Operation *Earnest Will* is a recent example. *Earnest Will* not only validates America's ability to succeed in fighting limited wars, it showcases that such wars can be fought with older, existing equipment.

Limiting financial liability may also become a key strategic concept for the United States in coming years. An American aversion to taxation combined with the political untouchability of "non-discretionary" social welfare programs such as Social Security and Medicare will likely drive the seeking of savings elsewhere in the federal budget. The largest discretionary part of the U.S. budget—by far—is the U.S. defense budget. High levels of spending and investment in the U.S. military since the 1980s are at odds with traditional American suspicion regarding military spending and large standing armies. At some point, those budgetary and political lines may very well unite. A 2016 Congressional Research Service report regarding the 30th anniversary of the Goldwater–Nichols Act pointedly asked, "Why, after the expenditure of nearly $1.6 trillion and over 15 years at war in Iraq and Afghanistan, has the United States had such difficulty translating tactical and operational victories into sustainable political outcomes?"[38] Those types of questions are likely only to become sharper in coming years.

A transition to a less ideological foreign policy, twinned with declining defense budgets, offers a chance to reconsider a range of options. Americans tend to associate ideological motivations with their foes—the Marxists are a prominent example—but the United States itself has its roots in a revolutionary 18th-century political movement that re-emerges from time to time. A recent notable occurrence was seen early in the Biden administration, where senior Biden foreign policy officials faced off with their Chinese counterparts in Anchorage, Alaska, in March 2021, presumably seeking to establish the boundaries that would guide future interactions.[39] Secretary of State Blinken opened the televised part of the meeting with a defense of the American-originated "rules-based international order" and National Security Advisor Sullivan commended the "can-do spirit of the world's democracies," along with lightly veiled accusations about Chinese economic and military coercion as well as their assaults on "basic values."

Their Chinese counterparts were clearly taken aback by the language and the tone of the American introduction—at one point, Director of the Office of the Central Commission for Foreign Affairs Yang Jiechi chided the Americans: "Well, isn't this the intention of the United States—judging from what, or the way that you have made your opening remarks—that it wants to speak to China in a condescending way from a position of strength?" But—in the main—the Chinese did not respond ideologically by citing the universal applicability or inherent superiority of "Socialism with Chinese characteristics"; rather, they responded with straight-up geopolitical rejoinders. Yang, in addition to putting the bilateral relationship in "position of strength" terms, said, "What China and the international community follow or uphold is the United Nations-centered international system," and "The United States has United States-style democracy and China has Chinese-style democracy." Of note, when Yang was still China's foreign minister, he famously observed to his Singaporean counterpart in 2010 that "China is a big country and other countries are little countries, and that's just a fact."[40]

The American secretary of state and national security advisor were in turn irritated by the extended Chinese remarks. Blinken and Sullivan directed the cameras to stay in the room and delivered what was obviously a heartfelt response, with Blinken quoting from the United States Constitution to describe America's "constant quest to, as we say, form a more perfect union" and Sullivan speaking of "the secret sauce of America."[41] In other words, the Americans continued to respond publicly to Chinese geopolitical observations in generally abstract and ideological terms.[42] It is a consistent and evidently bipartisan view: in the words of Blinken's predecessor, former Secretary of State Mike Pompeo's Policy Planning Staff: "In the face of the China challenge, the United States must secure freedom."[43]

The challenge for these sentiments in warfighting terms is measurement—how does one determine that sufficient "freedom" has been achieved? A war driven by political ideology is not dissimilar from a religious war—how does one determine that they have "won?" Viewed in this light, it is not hard to see how America tends toward unlimited wars as laid out by Clausewitz and Corbett. That ideological predisposition of the United States—which does, after all, have intellectual roots in the Enlightenment—is essentially within the DNA of the country. In strategy terms, it is helpful to recognize that dynamic, as it tends to drive the nation's wars into unlimited directions.

The stakes for the United States keeping any war with China limited—both in scope and in politics—are enormous. The "classical strategists" could talk the way they did because nuclear weapons did not yet exist. War in their time could widen in technology and geographic scope and become very bloody, but they did not have potentially planet-ending consequences. Given war's tendency to expand to its technological limits, this is a major factor to keep in mind—and an incentive to keep any war as limited as possible and likely as maritime as possible.

An additional challenge in any maritime war with China will be the burden of history—while *Earnest Will* could have gone the other way had the Iranians been successful with their mine strikes, the point is that the U.S. Navy once again prevailed. One has to go back to the opening days of World War II to find an instance in which the U.S. Navy indisputably lost a naval battle. Yet, it defies both history and logic to assume that they will always be successful in all future battles, and here-in lies the root of a powerful potential political problem—what will be the American domestic political reaction to being on the losing side any fight at sea?

British novelist Patrick O'Brian captured a sense of the despair resulting from the preeminent naval power losing battles to an upstart challenging country in his Jack Aubrey/Stephen Maturin series. In the opening chapters of the War of 1812, large American frigates prevailed in a succession of individual ship-on-ship battles: the USS *Constitution* defeated HMS *Guerriere*, the USS *United States* prevailed over HMS *Macedonian*, and the USS *Constitution* went on to maul HMS *Java* so badly that the British ship was destroyed in place as unsalvageable. The British Admiralty ended up issuing orders forbidding British ship captains from one-on-one battles with American frigates.[44]

O'Brian has Doctor Maturin writing of Captain Aubrey's despondent condition:

> This series of defeats, without a single victory, in the first months of a war is striking enough, particularly since the frigate is the very type of the fighting ship; but it is of no real consequence … The British army may be defeated again and again; that can be accepted; but the Navy must always win. It has always won these last twenty years or so; nor is there any record of serious naval defeat since the Dutch wars. The Navy has always won, and it must always continue to win, to win handsomely whatever the odds.[45]

The Dutch Wars of which Maturin speaks occurred principally between 1652 and 1674—over 138 years prior to the War of 1812. The last straight up defeat of the U.S. Navy at sea—at the hands of the Imperial Japanese Navy at the Battle of Savo island in 1942—is now over 80 years in the past. One wonders at the potential American reaction to the unanswered loss of a U.S. Navy ship at the hands of the People's Liberation Army Navy, especially if it is something major such as an aircraft carrier. It is worth noting that Aubrey is later aboard HMS *Shannon* when the British turn the tide of the naval aspect of the War of 1812 by defeating USS *Chesapeake* and that, overall, the British are assessed as coming out ahead in the War of 1812. When it comes to the U.S. Navy, a similar unbroken record of success is bound to be challenged at some point. It is impossible to predict whether the American national response to a large naval defeat will be more similar to the reaction after USS *Stark*—to stay the course—or instead to be more akin to the reaction after the 1983 USMC barracks bombing, where United States forces literally sailed away.

***

Operation *Earnest Will* is a solid example of the United States getting the use of force right. By no means did the U.S. Navy decide the war by itself; Iraq played the major military role, and the United Nations provided a structure that appears to have surprised everyone with its utility. Corbett reminds us, "We speak glibly of sea-power and forget that its true value lies on the operations of armies."[46] Elsewhere, he writes that the first function of the fleet was "to support or obstruct diplomatic effort."[47] Above all, Corbett—writing in the years before World War I—stresses the need for what might now be termed a "whole of government" approach to warfighting: "In time of war or of preparation for war ... arrangements must always be based to an exceptional degree on the mutual relation of naval, military, and political considerations ... of which no one service is master."[48] Logically, a situation "of which no once service is master" supports a new approach where an army-dominated "joint" approach to warfare is no longer intellectually unassailable.

It is important to recognize—and preserve—the improvements achieved at the operational level of war since the implementation of Goldwater–Nichols in 1986. Several reviews of U.S. military operations in the decades prior to the legislation repeatedly identified shortcomings when disparate U.S. military services were thrown together to accomplish a mission—examples would include the rescue of the SS *Mayaguez* in 1975, the abortive rescue of American hostages in Iran (Desert One) in 1979, and Grenada in 1983.[49] It is clear that, since the adoption of Goldwater–Nichols, the ability of the U.S. military services to cooperate in battle has significantly improved. The weakness, rather, is one of conceptualization at the higher, strategic level of war—as the Report of the 9/11 Commission phrased it: "It is therefore crucial to find a way of routinizing, even bureaucratizing, the exercise of imagination."[50] This critique of Goldwater–Nichols is one of an inability to conceptualize maritime approaches to national security decision-making because the army-dominant joint process structurally biases toward land operations, producing sub-optimal political results.

It is time for a rethink of how seapower and maritime strategy can serve a country's interests as well as recognizing that—while making the best operational use of what each service can offer—the current approach to Joint strategy only goes so far and, when looking at its employment in wars such as Iraq and Afghanistan, tops out at the operational level of war. The fact that the word strategy is now so widely used militates against its return to its use only in classical and force-oriented terms, but it is worth keeping "strategy with a capital S" in mind. There is an argument that our modern, very broad concept of national security strategy, encompassing not only the use of military force but also economics and domestic political and social considerations, in fact has its roots in the way maritime power works and has even been characterized in a twist on the title of Alfred Thayer Mahan's most famous work as "the influence of seapower on strategic thought."[51] Looking afresh at maritime operations such as *Earnest Will* demonstrates how seapower can succeed in practice and provides lessons directly applicable to ongoing and future national security discussions.

Glossary

AEGIS—An American naval weapons system that uses advanced computers and radars to track and destroy targets. AEGIS features the SPY-1 phased array radar, Naval Tactical Data System links, and associated advance fire-control and weapons-control systems and a Command and Decision Suite to enable effective use of naval guns, missiles, and self-protective systems simultaneously against large numbers of targets.

Boghammar—a high-speed patrol boat used by the Iranians, originally manufactured by the Swedish company Boghammar Marin AB. *Boghammars* feature a crew of six and are generally armed with light weapons such as rocket launchers, machine guns, and recoilless rifles.

CENTCOM—United States Central Command, a military headquarters overseen by a four-star officer located in Tampa, Florida. CENTCOM, established in 1983, has command authority over all American military forces in the Middle East—the "central" area between the other U.S. military commands responsible for Europe, Africa, and the Pacific areas. The passage of the Goldwater–Nichols act in 1986 significantly strengthened CENTCOM's power and influence. *Earnest Will* was one of its first tests.

CIC—Combat Information Center, the "nerve-center" of a warship that draws from radar, sonar, electronic warfare systems, radios, datalinks and other sensors to provide a comprehensive picture of the overall tactical situation, enabling the officers and crew to use its weapons systems most effectively and to coordinate actions with other units.

Carl von Clausewitz—Prussian military theorist best known for his posthumous work *On War*, first published in 1832. The book, known for its unflinching recognition of the roles of violence, chance, and politics in war, languished in obscurity until victorious Prussian generals linked it to their victory in the Franco–Prussian War of 1870 and was first translated into English in 1873. A 1908 revision in English formed the basis for key concepts in Corbett's *Some Principles of Maritime Strategy*; a 1976 updated translation by Michael Howard, Peter Paret, and Bernard Brodie was extensively used by the U.S. military seeking to make sense of its defeat in Vietnam.

CNO—Chief of Naval Operations for the U.S. Navy, the four-star, senior staff officer of the organization. Despite the word "operations" in the title, by the time of *Earnest Will* the CNO had relinquished any operational or command authority over American military units and instead concentrated on funding, manning, training, and equipping the U.S. Navy.

Sir Julian Corbett—English lawyer and novelist now best known for his 1911 work *Some Principles of Maritime Strategy*; the book vastly expanded Clausewitz's conception of limited and unlimited wars and argues that only seapowers can truly fight limited wars. Corbett's influence on England's Royal Navy was enabled by the patronage of First Sea Lord Admiral Jackie Fischer; both men were bitterly disappointed by England's land focus in the World War I, which they believed needlessly dissipated the advantages to be gained by the maritime-centric "English Way of War."

Desert Shield/Desert Storm—The codename for U.S. military operations from August 2, 1990, to February 28, 1991, intended to expel Iraqi forces from their occupation of Kuwait.

Earnest Will—The codename for a U.S. military operation responsible for the protection of reflagged Kuwaiti tankers and overall freedom of navigation in the Persian Gulf in the late 1980s. The official dates of *Earnest Will* run from the date of the first convoy operation—July 22, 1987, until August 1, 1990, the day before the subsequent Iraqi invasion of Kuwait and the beginning of Operation *Desert Shield*. As a practical matter, however, most observers date the end of the Tanker War with the end of the Iran–Iraq war itself, with Iran's acceptance of UNSCR 598 in July 1988. The U.S. Navy played a key, if inadvertent, role in the end of this major conflict.

Exocet **missile**—a French-made anti-ship missile used by the Iraqis. It is capable of being fired from ships or aircraft and carries a 364-pound warhead. When fired from a ship, it has a range of 25 miles; when launched from an aircraft, its range increases to 45 miles. The *Exocet* is an "active" missile in its terminal phase, homing in on its target without external assistance and uses solid propellant.

FFG-7—An FFG is a frigate armed with guided missiles. FFG-7s were also known as the *Oliver Hazard Perry* class after the lead ship in the series, hull number 7. FFG-7s were "low-mix" ships, intended to be produced relatively cheaply in large numbers and used for convoy defense and anti-submarine warfare. In addition to SM-1 and *Harpoon* missiles, FFG-7s were armed with a 76 mm (three-inch) gun and helicopters.

Goldwater–Nichols—The Goldwater–Nichols Act of 1986 was a major piece of legislation that reorganized the U.S. Department of Defense away from single military services and toward joint military organizations and operations. Goldwater–Nichols enabled a direct chain of command from the president through the secretary of defense to the "warfighting" joint combatant commanders, bypassing the military service chiefs. *Earnest Will* was the first major U.S. military operation to occur after the passage of Goldwater–Nichols. It was, however, the much better-known Operation *Desert Storm* that cemented the army-centric "joint" approach to military operations that characterized the post-Cold War world.

Harpoon **missile**—An American-made anti-ship missile of the same general type as the *Exocet* used by the United States and Iranian navies. It is capable of being fired from ships or from aircraft and carries a 488-pound warhead. When fired from a ship, it has a range of 75 nautical miles; when fired from an aircraft, its range increases to 120 miles. The *Harpoon* is known as an "active" missile—it has a radar built into the front that enables the missile to home in on its target without an external illumination source; it is also known as a "fire and forget" kind of missile.

JTFME—Joint Task Force Middle East, established on September 20, 1987, in line with defense reorganization after Goldwater–Nichols and joint operations in support of the *Earnest Will* tanker escort missions. Coexisting initially with MIDEASTFOR (responsible for operations in the Persian Gulf while the JTFME oversaw operations outside the Persian Gulf, a consequence of the DOD seam line of the dividing line between CENTCOM and Pacific Command), a single dual-hatted naval commander, Commander, Middle Eastern Force (COMMIDEASTFOR), was appointed by February 1988.

M-08 mine—a moored, contact mine first designed by Imperial Russia in 1908 and later used by Iran in and around the Persian Gulf. The mines are spherical in shape and have detonators studded on the upper half of the mine that have to be in contact with ship's hull in order to detonate.

MIDEASTFOR—Middle East Force, U.S. Navy command established August 16, 1949, headquartered and responsible for military operations in the Persian Gulf.

Naval guns—the U.S. Navy classifies naval artillery principally by the diameter of the gun; a "five-inch gun" therefore refers a gun that fires projectiles five inches in width; a "76 mm gun" fires projectiles 76 mm in width. The guns can be used against air and surface targets and are integrated with radar-based fire-control systems to counter the ship's roll and direct the projectiles to their most effective course and range. A five-inch projectile weighs about 70 pounds and can reach nearly 13 miles when fired at a 45-degree elevation; a 76 mm projective weighs about 27 pounds and can reach about 10 miles. Both weapons have shorter effective ranges.

Nimble Archer—Codename for U.S. military operations conducted on October 19, 1987, in retaliation for a *Silkworm* missile strike on the reflagged Kuwaiti tanker *Sea Isle City*. U.S. naval forces shelled two Iranian oil platforms in central Persian Gulf, variously known as Rostam and Rashadat.

Praying Mantis—Codename for U.S. military operations conducted on April 18, 1988, in retaliation for the mining of the USS *Samuel B. Roberts*. While American intentions were to keep the operation proportional and limited to destruction of one oil platform and/or one ship, by the end of the day the tally was two destroyed Iranian oil platforms, two sunken Iranian warships, several destroyed Iranian *Boghammar* speed boats, and two damaged Iranian fighter jets. *Praying Mantis* remains the largest surface fight since World War II.

Prime Chance—Codename for U.S. special forces operations in the Persian Gulf from August 1987 to June 1989. *Prime Chance* was a secret operation at the time, complementary to *Earnest Will*, with U.S. Army Special Operations Forces helicopters, SEALs, Special Boat Units, and U.S. military Explosive Ordnance Disposal specialists playing key roles surveilling and attacking Iranian forces.

Silkworm Missile—Chinese version of 1950s-era Soviet anti-ship missile, deployed on both mobile and fixed sites. *Silkworms* are based on old technology but can be very destructive if they hit their targets, as they carry an 1,100-pound warhead. *Silkworms* have a maximum range of 95 km (56 mi) but are most effective under 40 km (25 mi). Different versions have different guidance systems; some require an outside radar to illuminate the targets; others have onboard homing systems that require no external assistance. The liquid propellant used by *Silkworms*—in contrast to the solid propellant used by the other missiles in the Tanker War—requires a lengthy, dangerous, and observable fueling period measured in hours before the missile is ready to fire.

SM-1 Missile—Also known as the *Standard Missile*, the SM-1 is an American-made medium-range surface-to-air missile intended to shoot down aircraft and used by the U.S. Navy. At the time of *Earnest Will*, the SM-1 had a range of approximately 30 miles, could reach an altitude of 80,000 feet, and featured a roughly 120-pound warhead. The SM-1 also has a surface-to-surface mode, in which it can be used against ships. The SM-1 is known as a "semi-active" missile—targeting requires a ship-based fire-control radar to illuminate the target, allowing the seeker head on the missile to home in on the target. The solid propellant powering the missile provides stable storage and immediate usability.

SM-2 Missile—An improved version of the SM-1 Missile, able to engage over twice as far and designed for AEGIS equipped ships such as the USS *Vincennes*.

TAO—Tactical Action Officer, the senior officer normally on watch in CIC responsible for fighting a warship. The ship's captain bears ultimate responsibility for the warship's performance, even if they are not in CIC when the TAO makes decisions.

UNSCR—UN Security Council Resolution. The resolution is adopted with the affirmative votes of at least nine UN Security Council members, provided that none of the five permanent members vote against (more commonly known as a veto). UNSCRs are legally binding on all member states of the United Nations. UNSCRs adopted under Chapter 7 of the UN Charter can authorize sanctions and the legal use of force.

UNSCR 598—UN Security Council Resolution passed unanimously on July 20, 1987. It was intended to provide a framework to end the Iran–Iraq War.

Appendix 1: Text of UNSCR 598

The Security Council,

Reaffirming its resolution 582 (1986)

Deeply concerned that, despite its calls for a cease-fire, the conflict **between Iran and Iraq** continues unabated, with further heavy loss of human life and material destruction,

Deploring the initiation and continuation of the conflict,

Deploring also the bombing of purely civilian population centers, attacks on neutral shipping or civilian aircraft, the violation of international humanitarian law and other laws of armed conflict, and, in particular, the use of chemical weapons contrary to obligations under the 1925 Geneva Protocol,[1]

Deeply concerned that further escalation and widening of the conflict may take place,

Determined to bring to an end all military actions between Iran and Iraq,

Convinced that a comprehensive, just, honourable and durable settlement should be achieved between Iran and Iraq,

Recalling the provisions of the Charter of the United Nations and in particular the obligation of all member states to settle their international disputes by peaceful means in such a manner that international peace and security and justice are not endangered,

Determining that there exists a breach of the peace as regards the conflict between Iran and Iraq,

Acting under Articles 39 and 40 of the Charter of the United Nations,

1. *Demands* that, as a first step towards a negotiated settlement, Iran and Iraq observe an immediate cease-fire, discontinue all military actions on land, at sea and in the air, and withdraw all forces to the internationally recognized boundaries without delay;
2. ***Requests* the Secretary-General to dispatch a team of United Nations Observers to verify, confirm and supervise the cease-fire and withdrawal and further requests the Secretary-General to make the necessary arrangements in consultation with the Parties and to submit a report thereon to the Security Council;**
3. *Urges* that prisoners of war be released and repatriated without delay after the cessation of active hostilities **in accordance with the Third Geneva Convention of 12 August 1949;**
4. *Calls upon* Iran and Iraq to cooperate with the Secretary- General **in implementing this resolution** and in mediation efforts to achieve a comprehensive, just and honourable settlement, acceptable to both sides, of all outstanding issues in accordance with the principles contained in the Charter of the United Nations;
5. *Calls upon* all other States to exercise the utmost restraint and to refrain from any act which may lead to further escalation and widening of the conflict and thus to facilitate the implementation of the present resolution;
6. *Requests* the Secretary-General to explore, in consultation with Iran and Iraq, the question of entrusting an impartial body with inquiring into responsibility for the conflict and to report to the **Security** Council as soon as possible;
7. *Recognizes* the magnitude of the damage inflicted during the conflict and the need for reconstruction efforts, with appropriate international assistance, once the conflict is ended **and, in this regard, requests the Secretary-General to assign a team of experts to study the question of reconstruction and to report to the Security Council;**
8. *Further requests* the Secretary-General to examine in consultation with Iran and Iraq and with other states of the region measures to enhance the security and stability of the region;
9. *Requests* the Secretary-General to keep the **Security** Council informed on the implementation of this resolution;

10. *Decides* to meet again as necessary to consider further steps to ensure compliance with this resolution.

Adopted unanimously by the Security Council at its 2750th meeting on 20 July 1987

1. League of Nations, *Treaty Series*, vol. XCIV (1929). No. 2138
2. United Nations, *Treaty Series*, vol. 75. No 972.

Portions in **bold** reflect proposals made by non-permanent members of the Security Council.[2]

Appendix 2: Text of Russian February 1988 Non-Paper on Proposal for a Naval Presence[1]

The United Nations Naval Force in the Gulf: revised elements

1. Task: ensuring the safety of commercial navigation in international waters and passage to ports of Gulf states.
2. Composition: naval vessels comprising the UNNF are to be provided by international States.
3. Number: the number of vessels should be reasonably sufficient to carry out the task outlined in para 1.
4. Types: vessels suitable for escorting ships, and other operations which may be necessary to carry out the task, including minesweeping.
5. Financing: costs are covered by the States providing the vessels and also through deductions from users of sea routes (States, shipping, and insurance companies).
6. The UNNF is granted the right to self-defense.
7. The Security Council will decide the questions of establishing the Force, its composition, tasks, functioning, and command, as well as financial aspects.

Endnotes

Prologue

1. The U.S. military frequently refers to itself as "apolitical"; what it means is that it is "non-partisan"—it is not supposed to identify with partisan, political parties. Given the relationship between war and politics, it could not be apolitical and still do its jobs, especially at the senior ranks.
2. David Crist, *The Twilight War: The Secret History of America's Thirty-Year Conflict with Iran* (Penguin Press, 2012), 251. Webb's questions and concerns may have been broader than the Secretary of the Navy; asked for his views on the initial reflagging plan, U.S. Marine Corps Commandant General Kelly was quoted as complaining that "life is full of lousy options." Bernard E. Trainor, "U.S. Officers Troubled by Plan to Aid Gulf Shipping," *New York Times*, June 29, 1987. An unnamed admiral was quoted in the same article saying, "It would be stretching it to say that the [Joint] Chiefs [of Staff] were in on the decision, or even asked their opinion on it."
3. Michael Howard, "The Use and Abuse of Military History," in *The Causes of Wars and Other Essays*, 2nd edition (Harvard University Press, 1984), 188–197.

Acknowledgements

1. Cecil Woodham-Smith, *The Reason Why: The Story of the Fatal Charge of the Light Brigade* (Constable, 1953). Professional historians may differ with her conclusion that the Allies lost the Crimean War, but "history is a debate without end" as Andrew Lambert notes in his foreword to John Brooks's *Dreadnought Gunnery and the Battle of Jutland: The Question of Fire Control* (Routledge, 2005). There is hope for all of us considering the impact of the body of work of an influential writer such as Woodham-Smith, whose highest earned academic credential was a bachelor's degree in English.
2. Brian Bond, *Military Historian: My Part in the Birth and Development of War Studies, 1966–2016* (Helion, 2018), 18. Bond goes on to conclude: "[I] encountered individuals on the MA course who initially thought Clausewitz's *On War* was a load of (Prussian) rubbish and I was delighted if I could convert them in time for the exam," 138. Bond also describes the extraordinary expansion of the King's College London War Studies program. When the author attended in 1988/89, there were 40 MA students and 12 PhD research students, overseen by six faculty members. (September 1988, King's internal handout). By 2018, the War Studies department hosted 756 BA students, 580 MA students, and 200 PhD candidates overseen by 70 faculty members. Bond, 133.
3. The relationship is exactly reversed when it comes to understanding the individual human condition, hence the old saying, "It's better to be court-martialed by colonels than by lieutenants."

4   Sir Julian Corbett, *History of the Great War*, quoted in Kevin D. McCranie, "Theory meets the reality of war," in *Planning for War at Sea: 400 Years of Great Power Competition*, ed. Evan Wilson and Paul Kennedy (Naval Institute Press, 2025), 77.

Chapter 1

1   Sam Jones, "Klaus Schwab's Step Back Prompts Fresh Questions Over Davos," *Financial Times*, May 30, 2024.
2   "The outcome/resolution of [the] Iran–Iraq war is the key ... the sheer scale of the land war makes it apparent that the Persian Gulf [tanker] war is, ultimately, a *sideshow* to the war that counts between the two protagonists." OP-60 [Navy political-military staff in the Pentagon] unclassified brief, March 1988, emphasis in original; quoted in Michael A. Palmer, *Guardians of the Gulf: A History of America's Expanding Role in the Persian Gulf* (Freepress, 1992), 292.
3   Steven T. Wills, *Strategy Shelved: The Collapse of Cold War Naval Strategic Planning* (U.S. Naval Institute, 2021), 103. Wills goes on to say, "As Chief of Naval Operations, Adm Frank B. Kelso (1990–1994) took the opportunity offered by the end of the Cold War to fundamentally reorganize OPNAV [the staff of the Chief of Naval Operations in the Pentagon] along lines more favorable to the maintenance of the existing fleet strength rather than a continued focus on strategy," 6.
4   See discussion in D. C. Hefkin, "The Navy's Quality Journey: Operational Implementation of TQL," The Industrial College of the Armed Forces, National Defense University, Fort McNair, Washington, 1993. As it happens, American business writers specifically disassociated TQM from strategy, singling it out instead as a tool to increase operational effectiveness, and then going on to emphasize that "operational effectiveness is not strategy." Michael E. Porter, "What Is Strategy? *Harvard Business Review* 74, no. 6 (1996), 62.
5   Wills, *Strategy Shelved*, 211.
6   Michael Howard *The Strategic Approach to International Relations*, British Journal of International Studies 2, no.1 (April 1976), 67.
7   Lawrence Freedman, *Strategy: A History* (Oxford University Press, 2013). The term "magisterial" comes from the review of the book in *The Economist* and is at the top of the front cover.
8   Beatrice Heuser, *The Evolution of Strategy* (Cambridge University Press, 2012), 3. Emphasis added.
9   Hew Strachan, "The Lost Meaning of Strategy," *Survival* 47, no. 3 (2005), 49.
10 Michael E. Porter, "What Is Strategy?" *Harvard Business Review* 74, no. 6, 61–78.
11 W. Chan Kim and Renee Mauborgne, *Blue Ocean Strategy: How to Create Uncontested Market Space and Make Competition Irrelevant* (Harvard Business Review Press, 2005).
12 Michael Howard, "The Classical Strategists," in *Studies in War and Peace* (Viking Press, 1971), 154. Upon Michael Howard's death in 2019, the International Institute for Strategic Studies (IISS) selected "The Classical Strategists" as one of his 29 lifetime works to emphasize—*A Historical Sensibility: Sir Michael Howard and the International Institute for Strategic Studies* (Routledge, 2020)—"The Classical Strategists" is Chapter 11.
13 Michael Howard, *Captain Professor: A Life in War and Peace* (Continuum, 2006), 160.
14 Howard, *Captain Professor*, 154–155.
15 Then-Secretary of State John Kerry's comments on the initial Russian invasion of Ukraine in 2014 are illustrative: "You just don't in the 21st century behave in 19th century fashion by invading another country on completely trumped up pre-text," Kerry said. "It is serious in terms of sort of the modern manner with which nations are going to resolve problems. There are all kinds of other options still available to Russia. There still are. President Obama wants to emphasize to the Russians that there are a right set of choices that can still be made to address any concerns

they have about Crimea, about their citizens, but you don't choose to invade a country in order to do that." Secretary Kerry interview with Bob Schieffer, CBS *Face the Nation*, March 2, 2014. Bob Schieffer interviews Secretary of State John Kerry—CBS News.
16 Howard, "The Classical Strategists," 154.
17 "Clausewitz," in *Makers of Modern Strategy: Military Thought from Machiavelli to Hitler*, edited by Edward Mead Earle (Princeton University Press, 1943), 93.
18 "The aggressor is always peace-loving (as Bonaparte always claimed to be); he would prefer to take over our country unopposed." Carl von Clausewitz, *On War*, edited and translated. Michael Howard and Peter Paret (Princeton University Press, 1976), 370. Michael Howard emphasized Lenin's "sardonic approval" of this particular passage in *Clausewitz: A Very Short Introduction* (Oxford University Press, 2002), 57. Howard went on to write: "The frequent and flattering references to Clausewitz that are to be found in Lenin's writings were to make his ideas acceptable to Marxist–Leninists in spite of his bourgeois militarist background, much as Aquina's homage to Aristotle made that pagan philosopher acceptable to the medieval Church. The new army reconstituted by the Soviet Union after the Revolution and the Civil War thus took the Clausewitzian doctrine about the relationship of war to policy as the foundation for its own military thinking." 69–70. Lenin's fondness for Clausewitz should be of interest to those who believe the Chinese Communist Party is devoted to Marxism–Leninism and to Lenin in particular. "… Clausewitz functioned as a link in the development of Marx-Leninist and Mao Zedong's military thought, a status that no other foreign military theorist enjoyed or could compete for. Mao Zedong's military thought is still the guideline of China's military strategy and military doctrine today. It may be reasonable to draw a conclusion that so long as Marx-Leninism and Mao Zedong thought remain the orthodoxy ideology in China, Clausewitz and his *On War* will keep on enjoying a privileged and unparalleled position compared with other Western military thinkers in the future." Yu Tiejun, "The Western Master and Bible of War: Clausewitz and his On War in China," In Reiner Pommern, ed., *Clausewitz Goes Global* (Carola Hartmann Miles-Verlag, 2014), 47.
19 Clausewitz, *On War*, 144.
20 Bernard Brodie, "The Continuing Relevance of *On War*," *On War*, 50.
21 Clausewitz, *On War*, 50. Emphasis in original.
22 Brodie, "Relevance," *On War*, 53–54.
23 U.S. Special Operations Commander General Joseph Votel, quoted by Admiral Eric Olson in "America's Not Ready for Today's Gray Wars," *Defense One*, December 10, 2015.
24 Adam Elkeus, "Abandon All Hope, Ye Who Enter Here: You Cannot Save the Gray Zone Concept," *War on the Rocks*, December 30, 2015; also quoted in Donald Stoker and Craig Whiteside, "Blurred Lines: Gray-Zone Conflict and Hybrid War—Two Failures of American Strategic Thinking," *Naval War College Review* 73, no. 1, 2020.
25 Hew Strachan, "The Lost Meaning of Strategy," *Survival* 47, no. 3 (2005), 48.
26 Strachan, "Lost Meaning of Strategy," 47–48.
27 Donald Stoker, "Everything You Think You Know About Limited War is Wrong," *War on the Rocks*, December 22, 2016; Donald Stoker, *Why America Loses Wars* (Cambridge University Press, 2022), 5.
28 Clausewitz, *On War*, 69. Emphasis in original.
29 "[Michael Howard] confessed that, apart from the prefatory note of 10 July 1827 not much in *On War* addressed the notion of limited war." Hew Strachan, Sir Michael Howard Centre Annual Lecture 2020, "Michael Howard and Clausewitz." While notions of limited and unlimited war are mentioned in other parts of *On War*, the full consideration of what Corbett later defines as limited war appears to have been a casualty of Clausewitz's early death—in Corbett's words, "[Clausewitz's] death condemned his theory of limited war to remain in the

inchoate condition in which he left it." Sir Julian Corbett, *Some Principles of Maritime Strategy* (Naval Institute Press, 1988), 52.
30 Kevin D. McCranie, *Mahan, Corbett, and the Foundations of Naval Strategic Thought* (Naval Institute Press, 2021), 231.
31 Michael Handel, "Corbett, Clausewitz, and Sun Tzu," *Naval War College Review* 53, no. 4 (Autumn 2000), 10. D. M. Schurman details Corbett's role as intellectual innovator: in writing about Drake and the war against the Spanish, "Corbett revealed a growing maritime self-awareness that had begun to give rise to strategic concepts. That Corbett over-played his hand is arguable; the fact that he invented the game is not … In this field, Corbett was the complete pioneer." D. M. Schurman, *The Education of a Navy: The Development of British Naval Strategic Thought, 1867–1914* (Cassell, 1965), 152. Don Stoker points out that both Clausewitz and Corbett stressed that "limited" war applies to the political aim, not to the means with which the war is fought and that—especially when considering nuclear war—Americans often think of limited war as applying to means rather than the political end. Donald Stoker, "Everything you think you know about limited war is wrong," *War on the Rocks*, December 22, 2016.
32 Corbett, *Some Principles*, 57. Handel also argued that Corbett's limited war thinking applies to air power: "As an afterthought, it is interesting to note that in the age of modern airpower, Corbett's theory of limited war can acquire a degree of relevance perhaps exceeding that which its author envisioned. Today, the sustained projection of airpower, combined with the use of precision guided munitions, presents conditions that fit Corbett's requirements: namely, a remote overseas battlefield that can be isolated by naval superiority and that allows the projection, insertion, and removal of land forces at will. The sustained command of the air—together with day and night fighting capabilities and long-range, precision firepower— can create the isolation necessary for a limited war in any region of the world." Handel, "Corbett, Clausewitz, and Sun Tzu," 21.
33 Corbett, *Some Principles*, 55.
34 Ibid., 54–55. See also the argument in Handel, "Corbett, Clausewitz, and Sun Tzu," 13.
35 Corbett, *Some Principles*, 55.
36 Ibid., 57.
37 Ibid.
38 Ibid.
39 Steve Coll, *The Achilles Trap: Saddam Hussein, the CIA, and the Origins of America's Invasion of Iraq* (Penguin Press, 2024), 198.
40 Coll, *Achilles Trap*, 200.
41 Ibid.
42 *FRONTLINE*, "The Gulf War," Public Broadcasting Service, 1996, Pt. 2.
43 Quoted in Samuel Helfont, "The Gulf War's Afterlife: Dilemmas, Missed Opportunities, and the Post-Cold War Order Undone," *Texas National Security Review* 4, no. 2 (Spring 2021), 25–47.
44 Kevin Woods, IDA Paper P-4217 *Iraqi Perspectives Project Phase II Um Al-Ma'arik (The Mother of All Battles): Operational and Strategic Insights from an Iraqi Perspective Volume 1* (Revised May 2008), 346.
45 Woods, *Mother of All Battles*, 397.
46 Secretary of State Madeleine K. Albright, *Remarks at Georgetown University*, Washington, D.C., March 26, 1997.
47 United States Congress, Iraq Liberation Act of 1998, H.R.4655.
48 Colonel Joel D. Rayburn and Colonel Frank K. Sobchak, *The US Army in the Iraq War, Volume 2: Surge and Withdrawal 2007–2011* (Strategic Studies Institute and U.S. Army War College Press, 2019), 639.

49　Michael Howard, "Mistake to Declare This a War," *Royal United Services Institute Journal*, December 2001.
50　Secretary of Defense Caspar Weinberger was explicit on this point in his memoirs. Writing of his response to Navy Secretary James Webb who, among other points, said he was violating his own "Weinberger Doctrine," the Defense Secretary wrote: "Thus the answer to Jim was simple. I said we would consider we had achieved our objective, or 'won,' every time a commercial ship with non-belligerent commerce went back and forth in the international waters of the Gulf without being subjected to indiscriminate attacks from Iran." Caspar Weinberger, *Fighting for Peace: Seven Critical Years in the Pentagon* (Penguin, 1990), 282.
51　While there may have been some discussion of the general desirability of regime change in Iran during the Reagan administration, there was not the same type of policy emphasis such as that seen regarding the Sandinista regime in Nicaragua and the arming of the Contras. Some examples of those internal policy discussions can be seen in Peter Kornbluh and Malcolm Byrne, *The Iran–Contra Scandal: The Declassified History* (New Press, 1993), 370, 394.
52　Andrew R. Marvin, "Operation Earnest Will—The U.S. Foreign Policy behind U.S. Naval Operations in the Persian Gulf 1987–89; A Curious Case" *Naval War College Review* 73, no. 2 (Spring 2020).
53　Michael Dunn, "Hiding Our Gulf Success?" *Washington Times*, September 23, 1988.
54　The phrase is from the opening words of Geoffrey Till's magisterial *Seapower: A Guide for the Twenty-First Century*, 4th edition (Routledge, 2018), 1.
55　It's also worth considering whether military history is fundamentally different from the study of other historical topics. Howard, in "Use and Abuse of Military History," goes on to write: "Unlike politics, or administration, or economic activity, which are continuing and constantly developing processes, war is intermittent, clearly defined, with distinct criteria of success or failure. We cannot state dogmatically that Britain is better governed now, or that her economy is more flourishing, than it was in 1761. We can disagree as to whether certain historical events—the Reformation, or the Glorious Revolution, or the Great Reform Act—were triumphs or disasters. The historian of peace can only chronicle and analyse *change*. But the military historian knows what is victory and what defeat, what is success and what failure. When activities do thus constantly recur, and their success can be assessed by a straightforward standard, it does not seem over-optimistic to assume we can make judgements about them and draw conclusions which will have an abiding value." Michael Howard, "The Use and Abuse of Military History," 193. Emphasis in original.

Chapter 2

1　"Our own role in the Gulf is vital; it is to protect our interests and to help our friends in the region protect theirs. Our immediate task in the Gulf is clear and should not be exaggerated. It is to escort U.S. flag vessels, a traditional role for the Navy and one which it has carried out in the Gulf as well as in other areas. Most recently there's been some controversy about 11 new U.S. flag vessels that've been added to our merchant fleet. Let there be no misunderstanding: we will accept our responsibility for these vessels in the face of threats by Iran or anyone else. If we fail to do so simply because these ships previously flew the flag of another country, Kuwait, we would abdicate our role as a naval power, and we would open opportunities for the Soviets to move into this chokepoint of the free world's oil flow. In a word: if we don't do the job, the Soviets will. And that will jeopardize our own national security as well as our allies." Ronald Reagan, "Address to the Nation on the Venice Economic Summit, Arms Control, and the Deficit, June 15, 1987," Archives, Ronald Reagan Presidential Library & Museum.

2   "Telegram From the Commander-in-Chief, Strike Command (Throckmorton) to the Joint Chiefs of Staff, November 18, 1970, 2350Z, Subj: Soviet and Friendly Naval Involvement in the Indian Ocean Area," *Foreign Relations of the United States, 1969–1976, Volume XXIV, Middle East Region and Arabian Peninsula, 1969–1972; Jordan, September 1970*, Office of the Historian (U.S. Department of State).
3   "Address by President Carter on the State of the Union Before a Joint Session of Congress Washington, January 23, 1980," *Foreign Relations of the United States, 1977–1980, Volume I, Foundations of Foreign Policy*, Office of the Historian (U.S. Department of State).
4   James Morris, *Farewell the Trumpets: An Imperial Retreat* (Harvest/HBJ, 1978), 511.
5   Margaret Thatcher was scathing in her memoirs on this decision: "We developed what might be called the 'Suez Syndrome': having previously exaggerated our power, we now exaggerated our impotence … Defeats, which in reality were the results of avoidable misjudgment, such as the retreat from the Gulf in 1970, were held to be the inevitable consequences of British decline." Margaret Thatcher, *The Downing Street Years* (HarperCollins, 1993), 8. Commenting on her visit to the Gulf in 1980, shortly after becoming prime minister in 1979, "I always regretted, even at the time, the decision of Ted Heath's Government not to reverse the Wilson Government's withdrawal of our forces and the severing of many of our responsibilities east of Suez. Repeatedly, events have demonstrated that the West cannot pursue a policy of total disengagement in this strategically vital area." Ibid., 162. Thatcher would later make key decisions in 1987 broadening international naval participation in the Gulf.
6   Roham Alvandi, "Nixon, Kissinger, and the Shah: The Origins of Iranian Primacy in the Persian Gulf," *Diplomatic History* 36, no. 2 (April 2012), 339.
7   See discussion of Iranian actions and international acquiescence in Cameron Hume, *The United Nations, Iran, and Iraq: How Peacemaking Changed* (Indiana University Press, 1994), 24–25. Hume reminds readers of the rationalization regarding the Iranian takeover of the formerly Emirati islands provided in the UN Security Council by the British permanent representative, Sir Colin Crowe, in which he explained: "It is a matter of great regret to the British Government that it was not possible to reach a negotiated settlement" regarding the disputed islands but encouraged Council members to remember the French expression *"le mieux est l'ennemi du bien"* [The best is the enemy of the good] and that "the overall-all outcome … represents a positive achievement and a contribution to peace." UN Security Council Official Record, 1610th meeting, December 9, 1971 (S_PV.1610), 20, paragraphs 228 and 230.
8   Martin S. Navias and E. R. Hooton, *Tanker Wars: Assault on Merchant Shipping During the Iran–Iraq Crisis, 1980–88* (I. B. Tauris, 1996), 21. Tom Cooper, Sirous Ebrahimi, and E. R. Hooton go on to write that London had an informal agreement with Tehran that, in exchange for Iran dropping its claims to Bahrain, the United Kingdom would effectively cede Abu Musa and the Tunbs to Iran as part of Britain's 1971 departure from the Gulf: "London then advised the British Ambassador to Iran to inform the Shah of the exact time the British would withdraw from the Persian Gulf; at 22.00hrs on 30 November 1971, the night the last British troops were to withdraw, the Ambassador relayed this information to the Iranian government, enabling Iranian Marines—supported by the IIN (Imperial Iranian Navy) and the USN (United States Navy)—to quickly secure both the Tunb Islands and Abu Musa" *Iran–Iraq Naval War, Volume 1: Opening Blows September–November 1980* (Helion, 2023), 11–12.
9   Alvandi, "Nixon, Kissinger, and the Shah," 338.
10 See discussion of how unusual and extensive this set of sales was—"henceforth, decisions on purchases of U.S. military equipment would be left primarily to the government of Iran," in Gary Sick, *All Fall Down: America's Tragic Encounter With Iran* (Reprinted by Author's Guild, 2001), 17–21.

11   Navias and Hooton, *Tanker Wars*, 24. The problem of sold weaponry being turned against the sellers is not unique to the United States. It turned out that Britain sold Argentina some £120 million worth of military equipment in the three years prior to Argentina invading the Falklands in 1982. In the event, the British-provided weaponry did not prove crucial, but the same might not be said regarding French assistance at around the same time which included sending French *Super Étendard* fighters to fight practice battles with British *Harriers*. Obituary of former RAF Minister Sir Geoffrey Pattie, *Daily Telegraph*, October 11, 2024.
12   Lt. Gen. Valeriy Kondratiuk, quoted in Adam Entous, "The Partnership: The Secret History of the War in Ukraine," *New York Times*, March 29, 2025.
13   The *New York Times* wrote that, in 1978, "There were 30,000 Americans in Iran, including 8,000 military advisers in every branch of the Iranian Army and Air Force." Youseff M. Ibrahim, "'We Used to Run This Country,' Said a Departing American Last Week," *New York Times*, February 25, 1979. 1978 numbers for the U.S. Military Mission with the Iranian Army and Military Advisory Group to Iran (ARMISH-MAAG) totaled 260 authorized, 218 actually assigned. Other DOD support elements totaled 971 authorized/858 actually assigned. Foreign Military Sales (FMS)-funded Mobile Training Teams, Contract Engineering Technical Services, Contract Management Services, and Technical Assistance Field Teams totaled 626 personnel. "Profiles of Military Assistance Advisory Groups in 15 Countries, IL-78–51; B-165731, September 1, 1978," *U.S. General Accounting Office* ID-78–51, September 1, 1978, 27–33.
14   Shah's comments at a January 29, 1972, press conference, quoted in Palmer, *Guardians of the Gulf*, 90. As Cooper et al. phrased the atmosphere of the early 1970s: "The Shah of Iran began an unprecedented military buildup—and announced in public that he did so in order to oppose the local basing of US armed forces." Cooper, *Iran–Iraq Naval War* 1, 13.
15   George K. Walker, "The Tanker War, 1980–1988: Law and Policy," *International Law Studies* 74 (2000): 41.
16   Vivian Nereim, "As Iran Seizes Tankers in Gulf, U.A.E. Pulls Back from U.S.-led Maritime Force," *Washington Post*, May 31, 2023.
17   Till, *Seapower*, 31.
18   Anthony Cordesman and Abraham Wagner, *The Lessons of Modern War, Volume II: The Iran–Iraq War* (Westview Press, 1990), 34.
19   Gaylord Shaw and William C. Rempel, "Billion-Dollar Iran Arms Search Spans U.S., Globe: Even Pentagon Penetrated by Massive Effort," *Los Angeles Times*, August 4, 1985.
20   Sardonically described by U.S. Middle East specialist Fred Hof as a "state within a non-state" when assessing Hezbollah's performance in comparison with other Lebanese political actors. Quoted by Jeffery Feltman, "Hezbollah: Revolutionary Iran's most successful export," *Brookings Institution*, January 17, 2019.
21   Caspar Weinberger, *Fighting for Peace: Seven Critical Years in the Pentagon* (Penguin, 1990) Weinberger, 100. Weinberger noted that both he and CJCS Vessey argued against uniformed U.S. military involvement but that President Reagan, concerned about the heavy civilian casualties, had strongly supported the Multi-National Force with American involvement.
22   *Report of the DOD Commission on Beirut International Airport Terrorist Act, October 23, 1983, 20 December 1983*, 7–8.
23   DOD Commission Report, 64. As the Report continued on page 66: "It is obviously not the intention of the United States to place its power and prestige at the disposal of one or more of Lebanon's sectarian-based political factions. It is undeniable, however, that the facts of political life in Lebanon make any attempt on the part of an outsider to appear nonpartisan virtually impossible."

24 Alexandra T. Evans and A. Bradley Potter, "When Do Leaders Change Course? Theories of Success and the American Withdrawal from Beirut, 1983–1984," *Texas National Security Review* 2, no. 2 (February 2019). For a review of the series of events following the Marine barracks bombing that led to the American withdrawal, see Jack Carr and James M. Scott, *Targeted: Beirut: The 1983 Marine Barracks Bombing and the Untold Origin Story of the War on Terror* (Simon and Schuster, 2024).

25 Jonathan C. Randal, "Hostages to Be Held Until at Least 1989, PLO Official Asserts; Captives Will Not Be Harmed, Aide Says," *Washington Post*, February 20, 1987.

26 See discussion about the counter-Soviet angle to Iran–Contra in Jeffrey J. Matthews *Generals and Admirals, Criminals and Crooks* (Notre Dame Press, 2023), 187–188, concerning National Security Advisor Robert McFarlane's eight-page memo—"a bold Cold War initiative recommending that the United States develop closer political relations with Iran." Matthews writes: "McFarlane reasoned that if Washington did not seize the initiative with Tehran, Moscow would."

27 Some have gone so far as to say that President Reagan, recognizing Iran's dependence on American military equipment, had indicated to the Iranians as early as 1980 that he was willing to resume arms shipments. See Stephen E. Ambrose and Douglas G. Brinkley, *Rise to Globalism: American Foreign Policy Since 1938*, 9th revised edition (Penguin Books, 2011), 312. Of note, the only American arms shipped appear to be the TOW and HAWK missiles; neither system ended up being used against American forces.

28 "The Iran–Contra scandal had broken, and its revelation harmed America's standing worldwide, especially among Arab nations, who bridled at the superpower's duplicity. Rear Admiral Harold J. Bernsen, USN, commander of Middle East naval forces, learned of the scandal during a meeting with a Lebanese defense official: 'When I walked in the door, I realized I was in trouble,' the admiral recalled. In the course of a severe dressing-down, the official told Bernsen, 'You can tell all of your buddies that they might as well not come around here anymore.'" Andrew Marvin, "OPERATION EARNEST WILL: The U.S. Foreign Policy behind U.S. Naval Operations in the Persian Gulf 1987–89; A Curious Case," *Naval War College Review* 73, no. 2 (Spring 2020), 89.

29 Weinberger, *Fighting for Peace*, 275.

30 Ibid.

31 Cordesman and Wagner, *Lessons of Modern War*, 27.

32 Ibid., 30.

33 Kenneth M. Pollack, *Arabs at War: Military Effectiveness, 1948–1991* (Council on Foreign Relations Book; University of Nebraska Press, 2002), 183. See also Sick, *All Fall Down*, xx.

34 Sick, *All Fall Down*, xxi.

35 The Gulf Cooperation Council (GCC) is comprised of Bahrain, Kuwait, Oman, Qatar, Saudi Arabia, and the United Arab Emirates. Formed in 1981, partly as a reaction to the Iran–Iraq War, the GCC has political, economic, and military components. The organization is headquartered in Riyadh; the military component—known as "Peninsula Shield"—was formed in 1984.

36 R. K. Ramazani, *The Gulf Cooperation Council: Record and Analysis* (University Press of Virginia, 1988), 119.

37 Ramazani, *Gulf Cooperation Council*, 119.

38 Cooper, *Iran–Iraq Naval War* 1, 13.

39 Tony Holmes, *US Navy F-14 Tomcat Units of Operation Iraqi Freedom* (Osprey Publishing, 2005), 16–17.

40 Tom Cooper and Farzad Bishop, *Iranian F-14 Tomcat Units in Combat* (Osprey Publishing, 2004), 85.

41 Tom Cooper, Sirous Ebrahimi, and E. R. Hooton, *Iran–Iraq Naval War, Volume 2: Convoy Battles, 1981–1984* (Helion, 2024), 5.
42 Palmer, *Guardians of the Gulf*, 121.
43 George K. Walker, "The Tanker War, 1980–1988: Law and Policy," *International Law Studies* 74 (2000): 74. Of note, the extraordinarily large oil tankers used in the 1980s skews the tonnage comparison—the ships in the Tanker War weigh in at hundreds of thousands of tons apiece. During World War II, individual freighters displaced between 5,000 and 10,000 tons; tankers displaced roughly 15,000 tons. By the time of the Tanker War, revolutions in ship construction and shipping patterns resulted in individual tankers displacing nearly 500,000 tons. Tom Cooper, Sirous Ebrahimi, and E. R. Hooton, *Iran–Iraq Naval War, Volume 1: Opening Blows September-November 1980* (Helion, 2023), 8–9. Additionally, the loss of merchant mariner lives in the two conflicts—432 in the Tanker War, 40,000 to 50,000 in World War II—speaks to an entire other level of measuring cost.
44 Martin S. Navias and E. R. Hooton, *Tanker Wars: The Assault on Merchant Shipping During the Iran–Iraq Conflict*, 1980–1988 (I.B. Tauris Publishers, 1996), 183.
45 Navias and Hooton, *Tanker Wars*, 183, 186.
46 Ronald Reagan, 1984, quoted in Navias and Hooton, *Tanker Wars*, 96.
47 Cordesman and Wagner, *Lessons of Modern War*, 212.
48 Ibid.
49 "Most of its crude was exported through oil terminals on Kharg Island, a perennial favorite for Iraqi air strikes. Iran offered steep discounts for companies willing to fuel up at Kharg, and even self-insured tankers for the period that they were loading." Andrew R. Marvin, "Operation Earnest Will—The U.S. Foreign Policy behind U.S. Naval Operations in the Persian Gulf 1987–89; A Curious Case," *Naval War College Review* 73, no. 2, 88.
50 Oil platform case, American Memorial, January 1993, 9, paragraph 1.08.
51 Ron O'Rourke, "Gulf Ops," *Proceedings* 115, no. 5/1035 (May 1989): Table 1.
52 Cordesman and Wagner, *Lessons of Modern War*, 213.
53 Ibid., 236.
54 Ibid., 246.
55 Nadia el-Shazly writes that the Kuwaitis in fact reached out to all five permanent members of the UN Security Council for possible reflagging, not simply the United States and the Soviet Union. Nadia El-Sayed El-Shazly, *The Gulf Tanker War: Iran and Iraq's Maritime Swordplay* (Palgrave Macmillan, 1998), 271–273, a point also made by Navias and Hooton, *Tanker Wars*, 138–139.
56 Cooper et. al, *Iran–Iraq Naval War, Vol 1*, 14, 19.
57 Cordesman and Wagner, *Lessons of Modern War*, 156–157.
58 Gwynne Dyer, *War: A Commentary* (Crown Publishers, 1985), 171–172. The phrase "it's a pity that both sides can't lose" is often attributed to former U.S. Secretary of State Henry Kissinger.
59 Michael A. Palmer, *On Course to Desert Storm: The United States Navy and the Persian Gulf*, Contributions to Naval History Number 5 (U.S. Navy Historical Center, 1992), 255.
60 Lee Allen Zatarain, *Tanker War: America's First Conflict with Iran, 1987–88* (Casemate Publishers, 2008), 158.
61 Quoted in Hume, *Iran, Iraq, and the United Nations*, 106.
62 An official U.S. history of the war suggests that any country could request to reflag its ships under the American flag at any time—ordinarily, this would be a business decision in which a company chose to meet exacting American maritime standards. The wrinkle for the Kuwaitis was that they would not be able to meet the standards in a timely fashion, prompting the need for an American waiver. See discussion in Palmer, *On Course to Desert Storm*, 176n46.

63 Palmer, *Guardians*, 123; Zatarain, *Tanker War*, 34.
64 Weinberger, *Fighting for Peace*, 273–274.
65 Secretary of Defense Caspar W. Weinberger, "A Report to the Congress on Security Arrangements in the Persian Gulf," June 15, 1987, 25.
66 "Statement by Assistant to the President for Press Relations Fitzwater on United States Policy in the Persian Gulf," June 30, 1987.
67 Fitzwater June 30, 1987, press statement.
68 Paul Stillwell and Harold Bernsen, U.S. Navy (Retired), *The Reminiscences of Rear Adm. Harold J. Bernsen* (U.S. Naval Institute Press, 2019), 21–22.
69 John H. Cushman Jr., "U.S. Fleet in Gulf: Mission Inscrutable," *New York Times*, May 19, 1987.
70 Palmer, *Guardians*, 149.
71 Examples of the quote being used can be found in interviews with former U.S. national security advisors—Brent Scrowcroft in a discussion with Nixon Library Director Tim Naftali on June 29, 2007, as well as Condoleezza Rice with Oprah Winfrey, *O, The Oprah Magazine*, February 2002.
72 Thomas J. Downey, "Let a U.N. Task Force Guard the Persian Gulf," *New York Times*, June 8, 1987.

Chapter 3

1 Commander Jeremy Robertson, USS *Carney* (DDG-64)'s commanding officer, on return to homeport of Jacksonville, Florida, after unexpectedly fighting the Houthis. News4JAX The Local Station, May 19, 2024.
2 U.S. Naval History and Heritage Command, "Bon Homme Richard (frigate)," *Dictionary of American Naval Fighting Ships*.
3 Of note, while a number of *Panay*'s sailors were wounded in the attack, it was not until 1952 that President Truman authorized the awarding of Purple Hearts—the U.S. military's medal for being wounded in action by the enemy. The delay was because—in 1937—the Japanese were not officially an enemy of the United States. Richard R. Slater, *Naval History Magazine*, December 2024, 5.
4 RADM Kemp Tolley recalled both incidents in reviewing American decision-making regarding the start of World War II: "There was some chat ["The War Council—Roosevelt, Hull, Secretaries of War and the Navy Stimson and Knox, Marshall, and Stark" meeting on November 28, 1941] about the USS *Panay* incident, and it may be assumed that the President's elephantine memory gave him total recall of the worldwide furor provoked when this tiny Yangtze gunboat was sunk by trigger-happy Japanese aviators on December 12, 1937. There was not much hope of inflaming American public opinion or Congress sufficiently to support a declaration of war, judging from their apathetic reactions to the Atlantic incidents." "On October 17, in response to the new doctrine, the U.S. destroyer Kearny attacked a U-boat west of Iceland and managed to survive a German torpedo. Germany did not declare war but countered off Iceland: on October 31 the U.S. destroyer Reuben James was sunk, with the loss of most of her crew. But to F.D.R.'s discomfiture these events apparently did little to stir the American public out of its lack of interest in Europe's war." Tolley believed his mission in taking over the schooner *Lanikai* on December 4, 1941, in Cavite Harbor with orders to sail to Indochina was to provide an incident with the Japanese Navy, but, "Following the unexpected outbreak of a very clearly expected war, *Lanikai* fell into a sort of limbo, her raison d'etre dissolved

by the 'incident' at Pearl Harbor." In one of his accounts of how he sailed *Lanikai* from the Philippines to Australia in the opening weeks of the Pacific War. Admiral Kemp Tolley, "The Strange Mission of the Lanikai," *American Heritage Magazine* 24, no. 6 (October 1973) in *Eagle Against the Sun*, comments that Tolley "has argued that Roosevelt was attempting to provoke an incident like that of the Panay in order to ensure US entry into war." Spector sides with Samuel Eliot Morrison and Stanley Falk in arguing against "such devious motives" on the part of Roosevelt and instead observes that FDR had a number of different methods to provoke a war with Japan—all unused—if that was real intention. Ronald Spector, *Eagle Against the Sun: The American War With Japan* (Free Press, 1984), 87–88. It's worth noting that even the *Panay* incident itself did not directly lead to war.

5   Michael A. Palmer, *Guardians of the Gulf: A History of America's Expanding Role in the Persian Gulf, 1833–1992* (Free Press, 1992), 9.

6   Office of the Chief of Naval Operations, *The United States Navy in "Desert Shield" / "Desert Storm,"* Ser OO/lU500179, May 15, 1991.

7   Peter W. DeForth, "U.S. Naval Presence in the PErsian Gulf: The Mideast Force Since World War II," *Naval War College Review* 28, no. 3 (Summer 1975), 30. A 1972 congressional review of MIDEASTFOR concluded: "A low-profile policy should be designed to promote great power restraint and insulate the Persian Gulf from great power politics and competition." Ibid., 32.

8   Michael A. Palmer, *On Course to Desert Storm: The United States Navy and the Persian Gulf*, Contributions to Naval History Number 5 (U.S. Navy Historical Center, Washington, D.C. 1992), 3. Palmer is using the phrase accurately, though tongue in cheek, and he derives it from a complaint made in 1879 by U.S. Navy Commodore Robert Wilson Shufeldt on completion of USS *Ticonderoga*'s visit to the Persian Gulf, which he described as an "English Lake." Perceiving that the inhabitants of the region were more than ready to entertain non-English challengers to the regional balance of power, Shufeldt proposed that that the United States take a more active role in the region and not "continue the role long ago assigned to us in China—of No. 2 Englishman," 6.

9   U.S. Navy Surface Warfare Officer School, Department Head Training, Engineering Training Module (Code 60), Assignment Sheet Number 64P7–101 (undated).

10 Michael Vlahos, "The Stark Report," *U.S. Naval Institute Proceedings*, May 1988.

11 "Lookouts on board *Stark* heard four loud explosions at 0915 on 19 October 1984, as Iranian missiles plunged into *Pacific Protector*, a 1,538 ton diving support ship. *Stark* dispatched her embarked *Seasprite* to investigate, and a short time later the aircrew sighted the ship ablaze, about 20 miles from the frigate. The helo hovered near the scene while *Stark* came about and made for the area at maximum speed. The *Seasprite* meanwhile spotted survivors gathered on the ship's fantail and returned to the frigate for a lift stretcher and to refuel. The helo then returned to *Pacific Protector* and in a two trip lift brought back two badly injured men. The first man succumbed to his injuries and was pronounced dead on arrival. The ship's medical team treated the second victim but he too died a short while later. *Stark* meanwhile reached the area of the attack, lowered her motor whaleboat, and the boat's sailors rescued all of the remaining 16 survivors and returned them to the ship in two trips. The frigate's hospital corpsman and his assistants treated the survivors and later that day the MEF's *Sea King* transported all of them to Bahrain for further medical treatment (and also flew the two dead mariners ashore)." *U.S. Naval History and Heritage Command* history of Admiral Stark and the USS Stark (FFG-31) 1982–1999, accessed 23 May 2024.

12 Naval History and Heritage Command Stark history, *MEF 2–87* (5 February–5 August 1987).

13 See discussion in Stephen Phillips, "A Poisoned Chalice: The U.S. Navy in the Persian Gulf, 1987–1988." PhD Dissertation for the Department of War Studies, King's College London, 76–77.

14　Jeffrey Levinson and Randy Edwards, *Missile Inbound: The Attack on the Stark in the Persian Gulf* (U.S. Naval Institute, 1997), 15.
15　*Exocets* were defeatable when facing an alerted enemy warship, despite the British experience in the Falklands (a 1982 MOD note to PM Thatcher argued: "It is nearly impossible to intercept [an *Exocet*] except straight down the targeted vessel's line of sight." Falklands: MOD letter to No.10 ("Exocet Attack, 25th May") [attack on the Atlantic Conveyor], June 2, 1982, Prime Ministerial Private Office files.) It was probably more accurate to say that it was impossible for Britain's Royal Navy, utilizing the equipment with which they have been provided, to intercept an *Exocet*. There is a 1982 account of the Iranian Vosper Mk 5 IRIS *Zaal* shooting down an Iraqi *Exocet* after firing chaff and engaging the target with gunfire, albeit downing the missile less than one mile from the ship. Cooper, Ebrahimi and Hoon, *Iran–Iraq Naval War: Volume 2: Convoy Battles, 1981–1984* (Helion, 2024), 36.
16　Robert Fisk, *The Great War for Civilisation: The Conquest of the Middle East* (Knopf, 2005), 218–219.
17　Fisk, *Great War*, 221.
18　Phillips, *Poisoned Chalice*, 77.
19　The ships Tactical Operations Officer (TAO) is the watch officer responsible for fighting the ship, particularly when the captain is elsewhere. Quote from Commander, Cruiser Destroyer Group TWO, *Formal Investigation into the Circumstances Surrounding the Attack on USS Stark (FFG-31) on 17 May 1987*," Report 5102 Ser00/S-0487, June 12, 1987, paragraph (4), 2; see also description in Phillips, *Poisoned Chalice*, 77–84.
20　*Stark* Investigation, 2, paragraph 4.
21　*Stark* Investigation, 2, paragraph 5.
22　*Stark* Investigation, 2–3, paragraph 6.
23　*Stark* Investigation, 3, paragraph 10. Emphasis in original.
24　Naval History and Heritage Command, *Dictionary of American Naval Fighting Ships*, Index, Stark (FFG-31) 1982–1999, retrieved May 24, 2024.
25　*Stark* Investigation, 22.
26　Lee Allen Zatarain, *Tanker War: America's First Conflict with Iran, 1987–1988* (Casemate Publishers, 2008), 18.
27　*Stark* Investigation, 43.
28　Admiral C. A. H. Trost, Chief of Naval Operations, *Third Endorsement on RADM Grant Sharp, USN, Letter 5102, Ser 00/S-0487 of June 12, 87*, 7. Emphasis in original.
29　Zatarain, *Tanker War*, 43; Navy and Marine Corps Awards Manual (SECNAV Instruction 1650.1H), 2–25.
30　Trevor Armbrister, *A Matter of Accountability: The True Story of the Pueblo Affair* (Lyons Press, 2004), 350.
31　Armbrister, *Matter of Accountability*, 385.
32　"Man in the News; No-Nonsense Admiral Ulysses Simpson Grant Sharp Jr." *New York Times*, February 28, 1964.
33　Commander, Cruiser Destroyer Group TWO, *Formal Investigation into the Circumstances Surrounding the Attack on USS Stark (FFG-31) on 17 May 1987*, Report 5102 Ser00/S-0487, June 12, 1987.
34　John H. Cushman Jr., "U.S. Fleet in Gulf: Mission Inscrutable," *New York Times*, May 19, 1987, 10.
35　Molly Moore, "Two Officers on USS Stark Are Allowed to Quit by Navy," *Washington Post*, July 28, 1987.
36　John H. Cushman Jr., "Navy Forgoes Courts-Martial for Officers of Stark," *New York Times*, July 28, 1987.

37 Glenn F. Bunting, "Promising Career Goes Down in Flames: Stark's Skipper, 2 Officers Relieved of Duties," *Los Angeles Times*, June 20, 1987.
38 Armbrister, *Matter of Accountability*, 386.
39 Herman Wouk, *The Caine Mutiny* (Dell, 1951), 563.
40 Zatarain, *Tanker War*, 53.
41 Ambrister, *Matter of Accountability*, 394.
42 Lou Cannon, "Reagan Pays Tribute to Victims, Says Iran Is 'The Real Villain,'" *Washington Post*, May 19, 1987.
43 President Ronald Reagan, *Remarks on United States Policy in the Persian Gulf*, White House, Washington, D.C. May 29, 1987.
44 Reagan, May 29, 1987 remarks.
45 Impromptu speech to embassy staffers, Embassy Baghdad, December 31, 2004, witnessed by the author. Armitage, a decorated U.S. Navy special operations officer in Vietnam, had also served as assistant secretary of defense for international security affairs during the Tanker War.
46 David Crist, *The Twilight War: The Secret History of America's Thirty-Year Conflict with Iran* (Penguin Press, 2012), 227.
47 Quoted in David Crist, *Twilight War*, 241–242.
48 Osama bin Ladin, "Declaration of Jihad Against the Americans Occupying the Land of the Two Holy Mosques," *Al-Islah* (London), September 2, 1996, Reference number AFGP-2002–003676, a document the U.S. Justice Department later described as "A Declaration of War" in its December 2001 indictment of accused 9/11 plotter Zacarias Moussani (paragraph 8). The fatwa went on to say, "You moved tens of thousands of international forces, including twenty-eight thousand American solders into Somalia. However, when dozens of your troops were killed in minor battles, and one American pilot was dragged in the streets of Mogadishu, you left the area defeated, carrying your dead in disappointment and humiliation." 13–14.
49 Clausewitz, *On War*, 259.
50 Clausewitz, *On War*, 259. He writes: "Armies, with their fortresses and prepared positions, came to form a state within a state, in which violence gradually faded away. All Europe rejoiced at this development. It was seen as a logical outcome of enlightenment. This was a misconception." 591. Reviewing the impact of Napoleon and the French Revolution, he continues, "War, untrammeled by any conventional restraints, had broken lose in all its elemental fury." 593.
51 Clausewitz, *On War*, 260. His condemnation could have been written today: "Governments and commanders have always tried to find ways of avoiding a decisive battle and of reaching their goal by other means or of quietly abandoning it. Historians and theorists have taken great pains, when describing such campaigns and conflicts, to point out that other means not only served the purpose as well as a battle what was never fought, but were indeed evidence of a higher skill. This line of thought had brought us almost to the point of regarding, in the economy of war, battle as a kind of evil brought about by mistake—a morbid manifestation to which an orthodox, correctly managed war should never have to resort." 259.
52 Ronald Reagan, "Remarks on United States Policy in the Persian Gulf," May 29, 1987.
53 Crist, *Twilight War*, 229.
54 Michael Vlahos, "The Stark Report," *Proceedings* 114, no. 5/1023, May 1988.
55 Zatarain, *Tanker War*, 44.
56 Michael A. Palmer, *On Course to Desert Storm*, 228.
57 Ibid.

58 Senate Committee on Armed Services, U.S. Military Forces to Protect Reflagged Kuwaiti Oil Tankers, S.Hrg. 100–269, 100th Cong., 1st sess., June 5, 11, 16, 1987, 29.
59 CIA Directorate of Intelligence, "The Iranian Mine Warfare Threat: An Intelligence Assessment," NESA 84–10292C, November 1984, originally classified Top Secret; redacted and unclassified July 30, 2009, 9.
60 Definition from Michael Howard, "Reassurance and Deterrence: Western Defense in the 1980s," *Foreign Affairs* 61, no. 2 (Winter 1982/83), 315, quoted as the definition of "the strategy of deterrence" in Janice Gross Stein, "The Wrong Strategy in the Right Place: The United States in the Persian Gulf," *International Security* 13, no. 3 (Winter 1988/89): 142.
61 Edward J. Marolda, "The Siege of Wonsan," *Naval History Magazine* 37, no. 4 (August 2023).
62 Crist, *Twilight War*, 235–237.
63 David B. Crist, "What Obama Should Learn From Reagan's War With Iran" *Politico*, May 3, 2015.
64 Crist, *Twilight War*, 342.
65 Crist, *Twilight War*, 240. MIDEASTFOR Commander Bernsen is very clear on this point in *Reminiscences*: "Presence of the escorts, the fact that we had the carrier battle group off the coast—all those things taken together were going to deter the Iranians from attacking the convoy. Did I believe in that? Yes, I believed in it; I really did, and I'll admit that. I really did not think the Iranians were going to lay mines on me." Bernsen, *Reminiscences*, 26.
66 As a *Time of London* article chose to phrase it: "U.S. Navy's Incompetence Blown Open by a Single Mine," quoted in Zatarain, *Tanker War*, 72–73.
67 Clausewitz, *On War*, 101.
68 Ibid.

Chapter 4

1 Clausewitz, *On War*, 119.
2 Quoted by Lieutenant Commander H. B. Hird, U.S. Navy & Lieutenant J. B. Heffernan, U.S. Navy, "Professional Notes," *Proceedings* 49, no. 11/249, November 1923.
3 Bernsen, *Reminiscences*, 27.
4 The pre-World War I era contact mine design proved to be remarkably durable: "The successful operational MCM efforts in World War II limited MCM development after the war. Despite rapid advances in influence mine development, the largest mine threat throughout the war remained the antique, World War I moored contact mine." Tamara Moser Melia. *"Damn the Torpedoes": A Short History of U.S. Naval Mine Countermeasures, 1777–1991* (Department of the Navy, Naval Historical Center, 1991), 67.
5 There is an interesting cultural point about the U.S. Navy and mine warfare—on the one hand, the small platforms allow for officer development and command opportunity at a very young age; on the other hand, the small, slow ships do not fit with the ethos of an at-sea force operating as far forward as possible. As a history of U.S. mine warfare observed: "For young officers and enlisted men in the late 1950s and early 1960s, assignment to the new MCM force provided an unusual experience in both seamanship and leadership. Command came early, and the career advancement possible with MCM ship command enticed some of the most promising graduates of the destroyer force schools into the new mine force for at least one command tour. Young lieutenants obtained command of MSCs; lieutenants and lieutenant commanders captained MSOs; ensigns served early tours as department heads; and lieutenants (junior grade) served as executive officers. Senior enlisted men who commanded

ENDNOTES • 195

MSBs and smaller vessels often advanced into the MCM officer community through such experience ... Everything that had to be done on a big ship also had to be done on a small one, and the expanded MCM force became a hands-on training school for a whole generation of naval officers who exercised command at an early age ... Minesweepers often operated in close sweep formation with other vessels of their units, and thus had requirements for precision navigation and seamanship that were well beyond those of most larger ships ... Because of the exacting navigation needs of minesweeping vessels, crews gained great experience in piloting. Few destroyer force officers who passed through the MCM force ever swept a real mine, but they gained early command experience and, perhaps more important, familiarity with the more practical aspects of mines and MCM ... The MSOs ... had only been designed for a top speed of fourteen knots, and slow-but-capable did not fit the needs of the faster, forward-deployed postwar Navy." Melia, *Damn the Torpedoes*, 88–90.

6   Melia, *Damn the Torpedoes*, 84.
7   "As a young lieutenant in November 1945, Zumwalt had witnessed Pacific minesweepers with inadequate intelligence and minehunting capabilities struggling to clear uncharted minefields at the mouth of the Yangtze River. He concluded at the time that surface minesweeping vessels were slow and uncertain. By 1970 he also considered them outdated. Within sixty days of becoming CNO, Zumwalt had developed Project 60, a comprehensive plan to revitalize the U.S. Navy during his tenure, and had decided to push through a complete helicopter MCM program. Believing that the aging surface MCM force was a financial drain on scarce Navy resources, Zumwalt scrapped the surface MCM fleet that was the product of the lessons learned at Wonsan 'to economize on and modernize minesweeping techniques.' He predicted huge savings in operating expenses and the development of a worldwide, quick-strike, cost-effective, and safe method of countering the Soviet mine threat. The only problem was that the systems for using the helicopter as the sole sweeping unit were still developmental." Melia, *Damn the Torpedoes*, 98. Later experience in clearing Haiphong Harbor in 1973 suggested problems ahead: "Helicopters did sweep three to six times faster than the MSOs but suffered high equipment stress, long downtime, lack of dedicated support ships, and difficult supply logistics. What the operation did prove was that AMCM vehicles could not clear mined waters without a complex support system of surface MCM vessels, amphibious mother ships, and a strong logistic chain. Air assets were as labor intensive as surface ships because AMCM required so much support." Melia, *Damn the Torpedoes*, 109–110.
8   Scott C. Truver, "Writing U.S. Naval Operational History 1980–2010: U.S. Navy Mine Countermeasures in Terror and War" in *Needs and Opportunities in the Modern History of the U.S. Navy*, edited by Michael J. Crawford (U.S. Naval History and Heritage Command, 2018), 47.
9   Captain James Martin, U.S. Naval Reserve (Retired), "We Still Haven't Learned," *Proceedings*, July 1991.
10 Melia, *Damn the Torpedoes*, 82. "The Vietnam War and Admiral Zumwalt's policy decisions were the death knell of the MCM surface fleet, and the number of ships on active service declined from sixty-four in 1970 to nine in 1974." Melia, *Damn the Torpedoes*, 113.
11 John B. Hattendorf and Peter M. Swartz, Peter M., "U.S. Naval Strategy in the 1980s", *Newport Papers*, no. 33 (Naval War College Press, 2008). DOCUMENT TWO: "The Maritime Strategy, 1984" (45–104) includes the following key passages: "The primary mine countermeasures campaign will be as far forward as possible, targeting delivery platforms to prevent mines from being sown at all. For those that get through and must be swept, envisioned U.S. and allied mine countermeasures responsibilities are depicted here [in the GLOBAL WAR MINE COUNTERMEASURES chart]. It is anticipated that the allies would bear the lion's share of

the task." 90. "Mine countermeasures form yet another important aspect of the [Maritime] strategy. The West must be ready to clear mines whenever and wherever necessary. Mine warfare provides a striking example of the importance of our allies to the Maritime Strategy. The Commander, Mine Warfare Command, executes a very aggressive cooperative program with our allies, traveling to roughly 40 nations every year to ensure that we integrate both allied mine-clearing and allied offensive mine-laying operations." 220. The Maritime Strategy itself had three distinct phases: "Phase I: Transition to War; Phase II: Seize the Initiative; Phase III: Carry the Fight to the enemy." 70. The end point of the Maritime Strategy: "The desired culmination of this strategy is *war termination on favorable terms*. This requires putting sufficient conventional pressure on the Soviets to convince them that they would have no gain in continuing aggression and in fact should retreat, while giving them no incentives to escalate to nuclear war. For the Navy, this means neutralization or destruction of the Soviet Navy and of ground and air forces on the Eurasian flanks; sea control; and intervention in the land battle. *What happens at sea* is important primarily as it can contribute to the *land battle ashore* or to a *favorable settlement* of the conflict." 92. Emphasis in original.

12 *Newport Papers*, 168.
13 Ibid., 179.
14 Phillips, *Poisoned Chalice*, 258.
15 "Unlike their steel-hulled predecessors that depended solely on degaussing to mask the magnetic parts of the ship, the open-ocean sweeping [*Aggressive*-class] MSOs were built with wooden hulls, few magnetic materials, and improved degaussing. They were powered by special nonmagnetic Packard or General Motors diesel engines and were also outfitted with controllable-pitch propellers for increased maneuverability in a minefield. Considered the Cadillacs of the international mine fleet of the 1950s, the MSOs were larger than most other wooden vessels and were considered sterling examples of craftsmanship and shipbuilding technology." Melia, *Damn the Torpedoes*, 83. While the *Aggressive*-class were designed in 1955 by famed naval architect Philip L. Rhodes, with the lessons of the recent mine-infested Korean War in mind, they still represented 1950s technology and the larger mine-warfare organization in the U.S. Navy had reverted to its usual backwater status. "MCM vessels simply never caught the hearts and minds of most Navy men. After 1958 additional MCM ship construction funds were regularly deleted from the tightening Navy budget, leaving programmed replacements for the MCM force in question for future generations." Melia, *Damn the Torpedoes*, 86.
16 Zatarain, *Tanker War*, 118.
17 Ibid., 126.
18 Lyons also believed the French carrier in the region would support the operation. Gregory L. Vistica, *Fall from Glory: The Men Who Sank the U.S. Navy* (Simon & Schuster, 1996), 260.
19 Vistica, *Fall from Glory*, 258–261. Vistica reports Lyons briefing Weinberger that "we're going to strike a blow for freedom. It may even bring down the Khomeini regime." 261. "We blew a golden opportunity to clobber the Iranians while the threat was manageable, perhaps even bring down the regime." Ace Lyons, quoted in Crist, *Twilight War*, 272. Lyon was a bona-fide maritime strategist, but it's not at all clear why a series of maritime raids would overthrow the Islamic Republic of Iran. A bit like Iranian mine-laying, this was operational level of war thinking untethered to a political "then what?"
20 Crist, *Twilight War*, 259.
21 Quoted in Crist, *Twilight War*, 258.
22 Crist, *Twilight War*, 262–263.
23 Palmer, *Guardians of the Gulf*, 131.

24 Loren Jenkins, "Explosion Rocks Saudi Plant on Persian Gulf; Ship Strikes Mine, Sinks Off Emirates." *Washington Post*, August 16, 1987.
25 Crist, *Twilight War*, 265.
26 Ibid., 241.
27 Michael Howard, "Men against Fire: The Doctrine of the Offensive in 1914," in *Makers of Modern Strategy from Machiavelli to the Nuclear Age*, ed. Peter Paret (Princeton University Press, 1986), 522.
28 Fisk, *Great War*, 254. The title of Fisk's book—*The Great War for Civilization*—comes from the inscription on the back of one his father's World War One campaign medals; Fisk's father "was a soldier of the Great War, fighting in the trenches of France because a shot fired in a city he'd never heard of called Sarajevo." Fisk, xvii.
29 Fisk, *Great War*, 356. Emphasis in original.
30 Zatarain, *Tanker War*, 95–96.
31 Crist, *Twilight War*, 293.
32 Crist, *Twilight War*, 295; Zatarain, *Tanker War*, 106–112.
33 Powell, in his memoirs—*My American Journey* (Random House, 2005), 207–208—perhaps anachronistically speaks of the influence Clausewitz had on him while studying at the U.S. National War College 1975–76 (the Howard/Paret translation—the *On War* version used for American Joint Professional Military Education—did not come out until late 1976). It's very clear that Powell understands the relationship between politics and war; indeed, he almost personifies it. Yet, in many ways, he also differs with Clausewitz, who wrote in *On War*'s opening page: "Kind-hearted people might of course think there was some ingenious way to disarm or defeat an enemy without too much bloodshed and might imagine this is the true goal of the art of war. Pleasant as it sounds, it is a fallacy that must be exposed; war is such a dangerous business that the mistakes which come from kindness are the very worst." 75.
34 Crist, *Twilight War*, 296.
35 Zatarain, *Tanker War*, 114.
36 Crist, *Twilight War*, 297.
37 Zatarain, *Tanker War*, 115.
38 Quoted in Sheldon M. Stern, *The Week the World Stood Still* (Stanford University Press, 2005), 157.
39 Phillips, *Poisoned Chalice*, 180.
40 Zatarain, *Tanker War*, 116.
41 Phillips, *Poisoned Chalice*, 183.
42 Zatarain, *Tanker War*, 120; Crist, *Twilight War*, 297.
43 In addition to releasing photographs of the captured *Iran Ajr* with mines on its deck, the United States also reported the incident to the UN Security Council (S/19149, September 22, 1987).
44 Don Oberdorfer, "Iranian President Threatens U.S.: Khamenei's Hard-Line U.N. Speech Ignores Cease-Fire Resolution" *Washington Post*, September 22, 1987.
45 Crist, *Twilight War*, 301–302.
46 Ibid., 303–304.
47 Ibid., 304–306.
48 The United States reported this event to the UN Security Council (S/19194, October 8, 1987) citing Article 51 of the UN Charter, stating "the United States has exercised its inherent right of self-defense under international law by taking defensive action," and cautioning,

"The United States Government had previously informed the Iranian Government that it would take appropriate defensive measures against such hostile actions."
49 Crist, *Twilight War*, 307.
50 Ibid., 309.
51 Ibid., 310.
52 David B. Ottaway and David Hoffman, "Iranian Missile Hits U.S.-Flagged Ship at Kuwaiti Port—U.S. Condemns Attack Reagan, Advisers Confer," *Washington Post*, October 17, 1987.
53 Ibid.
54 Quote credited to "senior government official here," Patrick E. Tyler, "Iranian Missile Hits U.S.-Flagged Ship at Kuwaiti Port; Ruling Family Reviewing 'Appropriate Response,'" *Washington Post*, October 17, 1987, datelined Kuwait.
55 Zatarain, *Tanker War*, 153; David B. Ottaway and Lou Cannon, "U.S. Sets Military Retaliation Against Iran for Ship Attack," *Washington Post*, October 18, 1987.
56 Joseph B. Treaster "2 U.S. Jets Downed by Syrian Gunfire; Navy Staged Raid," *New York Times*, December 4, 1983.

Chapter 5

1 Quoted in Wise, *Inside the Danger Zone*, 433. Strike planners are generally mid-level military officers—experienced enough to know what is going on, but insufficiently senior to actually affect policy.
2 Richard A. Mobley, "London and Washington Maintaining Naval Cooperation Despite Strategic Differences During Operation Earnest Will," *Naval War College Review* 74, no. 2 (Spring 2021), 139; Ron O'Rourke, "The Tanker War," *U.S. Naval Institute Proceedings* 114, no. 5/1,023 May 1988.
3 See, for example, the "Page-13" administrative remarks placed in the personnel files of the crew of the USS *Hoel* officially recognizing their participation in *Nimble Archer*: "THIS COORDINATED STRIKE WAS IN RETALIATION FOR IRAN'S MISSILE ATTACK AGAINST A U.S. FLAGGED KUWAITI TANKER." USS HOEL (DDG-13), Cruisebook 1987–88, 74.
4 "The Court indicates that it is not sufficiently convinced that the evidence available supports the contentions of the United States as to the significance of the military presence and activity on the Reshadat oil platforms; and it notes that no such evidence is offered in respect of the Salman and Nasr complexes. However, even accepting those contentions, for the purposes of discussion, the Court finds itself unable to hold that the attacks made on the platforms could have been justified as acts of self-defence. In the case both of the attack on the Sea Isle City and the mining of the USS Samuel B. Roberts, the Court is not satisfied that the attacks on the platforms were necessary to respond to these incidents.

As to the requirement of proportionality, the attack of 19 October 1987 might, had the Court found that it was necessary in response to the Sea Isle City incident as an armed attack committed by Iran, have been considered proportionate. In the case of the attacks of 18 April 1988, however, they were conceived and executed as part of a more extensive operation entitled 'Operation Praying Mantis.' As a response to the mining, by an unidentified agency, of a single United States warship, which was severely damaged but not sunk, and without loss of life, neither 'Operation Praying Mantis' as a whole, nor even that part of it that destroyed the Salman and Nasr platforms, can be regarded, in the circumstances of this case, as a proportionate use of force in self-defence."

Case concerning Oil Platforms (Islamic Republic of Iran v. United States of America), Summary of the Judgment of 6 November 2003, International Court of Justice, Available at https://www.icj-cij.org/sites/default/files/case-related/90/9745.pdf, see page 8.

5   Pieter H. F. Bekker, "The World Court Finds that U.S. Attacks on Iranian Oil Platforms in 1987–1988 Were Not Justifiable as Self-Defense, but the United States Did Not Violate the Applicable Treaty with Iran," *American Society of International Law Insights* 8, no. 25, November 11, 2003.
6   Richard A. Mobley, "Deterrence Without Escalation: Fresh Insights into U.S. Decisionmaking During Operation Earnest Will," *Joint Force Quarterly* 106 (July 2022): 71–81.
7   Quoted in Mobley, "Deterrence without Escalation."
8   Paul Stillwell, *Reminiscences of Rear Admiral Harold J. Bernsen* (Naval Institute Press, 2019), 94; also quoted in Mobley, "Deterrence without Escalation."
9   The quoted language is from the October 19, 1987, "Statement on the United States Reprisal Against Iran" by President Reagan. The statement also invokes Article 51 of the UN Charter, justifying U.S. actions as one of self-defense and goes on to call for "urgent implementation" of UNSCR 598.
10 Secretary of State message, "USG Proposal for Direct Official Channel with Iran," September 16, 1987, Digital National Security Archive (DNSA); U.S. diplomatic note, "U.S. Readiness to Meet with a Senior Iranian Official," November 8, 1987 (delivered by U.S. Embassy London to Foreign & Commonwealth Office [FCO] on November 12, 1987) (FCO 8/7251), The National Archives (United Kingdom) (TNA).
11 Bernsen, *Reminiscences*, 24.
12 USS *Kidd* was one of four ships originally constructed for Imperial Iranian service. While these non-AEGIS-equipped ships were decommissioned from the U.S. Navy in the late 1990s, they still had plenty of service-life left and, since 2005, have served in the Taiwanese Navy.
13 Zatarain, *Tanker War*, 156–157.
14 As it happens, the fact that the oil platforms were not being used to produce oil turned out to be a key factor in denying Iran's later ICJ claims.
15 Wise, *Inside the Danger Zone*, 346.
16 Patrick E. Tyler, "U.S. Warning Iraq to Control Planes or Risk Losing Them," *Washington Post*, February 22, 1988; Ron O'Rourke, "Gulf Ops," *U.S. Naval Institute Proceedings*, May 1989.
17 It's also a reminder that inaction is not necessarily indicative of balance. "Inaction cannot be explained by the concept of balance. The only explanation is that both are waiting for a better time to act … If the other state is ready to accept the situation, it should sue for peace. If not, if must do something: and if it thinks it will be better organized for action in four weeks' time it clearly has an adequate reason for not taking action at once." Clausewitz, *On War*, 82–83.
18 Gwynne Dyer, *War: A Commentary* (Crown Publishers, 1985), 156. Or as Michael Howard once put it: "If history shows any record of 'accidental' wars, I have yet to find them. Certainly statesmen have sometimes been surprised by the nature of the war they have unleased, and it is reasonable to assume that in at least 50 percent of the cases they got a result they did not expect. But that is not the same as a war begun by mistake and continued with no political

purpose." Michael Howard, "The Causes of Wars," in *The Causes of Wars* (2nd edition, enlarged) (Harvard University Press, 1984), 12.
19 Discussion of Roberts's forward-leaning approach is contained in detail in Philips, *Poisoned Chalice*, 228–231, including an interview with Captain Rinn.
20 Crist, *Twilight War*, 326–327.
21 Zatarain, *Tanker War*, 202; Wise, *Inside the Danger Zone*, 423; Phillips, *Poisoned Chalice*, 261, which quotes Rinn as saying tests showed that tests showed that the ship should have sunk even more quickly.
22 Naval History and Heritage Command, Navy History Matters, April 2024.
23 Cox, H-018–1. See also discussion in Phillips, *Poisoned Chalice*, 243, which reports Captain Rinn as getting on the bridge-to-bridge radio with the Iranian frigate and warning them away and also the possibility that the Iranian ship was the *Sahand* and not the *Sabalan*.
24 Crist, *Twilight War*, 336.
25 Palmer, *Guardians*, 139.
26 O'Rourke, Gulf Ops, 44; Duffy unpublished 1989 MA Thesis, 18.
27 Samuel J. Cox, "H-018–1: No Higher Honor—The Road to Operation Praying Mantis, 18 April 1988," *Naval History and Heritage Command*, April 2018.
28 Palmer, *Guardians*, 140.
29 Ibid., 141.
30 Cox, H-018–1.
31 Palmer, *Guardians* 141.
32 Cox, H-018–1.
33 Palmer, *Guardians* 142.
34 Cox, H-018.
35 Later versions of the SM-1—now launched out of high-capacity, vertical launch magazine, rather than the one or two at a time fired by ships in the 1980s—have continued to prove their utility. Some 155 SM-1s were fired by U.S. Navy ships against the Houthis over the course of nine months by ships of the USS *Eisenhower* strike group in 2023/2024. Carrier Strike Group Two (CSG-2) "Unprecedented: Dwight D. Eisenhower Carrier Strike Group Returns from Combat Deployment", U.S. Navy Press Office Story, July 15, 2024.
36 "To introduce the principle of moderation into the theory of war itself would always lead to logical absurdity … War is an act of force, and there is no logical limit to the application of that force. Each side, therefore, compels its opponent to follow suit; a reciprocal action is started which must lead, in theory, to extremes." Clausewitz, *On War*, 76–77.
37 *Janes Fighting Ships, 1988/89*, 140.
38 Cordesman assesses the post Praying Mantis Iranian naval OOB: "At this point in time, Iran still had three destroyers, but they were at best capable of limited service, if any. It had two frigates, two corvettes, eight fast attack craft, 10–12 Hovercraft, 1 minesweeper, 40–50 speed boats and 70 or more small fast motorcraft. The U.S. forces in the area had a total of 29 ships, with 21 in the Gulf and a carrier battle group outside it." Cordesman and Wagner, *Lessons of Modern War*, 212.
39 O'Rourke, Gulf Ops, *Proceedings* 115, no. 5/1,035, May 1989.
40 Patrick E. Tyler, "France Expands Role of Its Navy in Gulf: Neutral Ships under Attack to Be Aided," *Washington Post*, January 20, 1988.
41 Ibid.
42 George C. Wilson, "U.S. Role in Gulf Expands; President Orders Navy to Protect Neutral Shipping," *Washington Post*, April 29, 1988.

Chapter 6

1. "Khomeyni Message on Hajj, UN Resolution 598" LD2007173388 Tehran Domestic Service in Persian 1053 GMT, July 20, 1988, FBIS-NES-88–140.
2. Hume, *Iraq, Iran, and the United Nations*, 104.
3. Giandomenico Picco, *Man Without a Gun: One Diplomat's Secret Struggle to Free the Hostages, Fight Terrorism, and End a War* (Crown, 1999), 75.
4. See Picco's discussion on the use of UNSCR 598 Operative Paragraph 6 in *Man Without A Gun*, 150–151. OP6 requested the Secretary General to look into the responsibility for the Iran–Iraq War and issue a report. Picco notes: "At the time Resolution 598 was drafted, no one could have imagined the role its sixth paragraph was to play in freeing the hostages. The mullahs—indeed, the Iranian people—saw it as a way to obtain justice, which mattered so much to them after all their suffering in the war." 151. Picco notes that the eventual report "was academically solid and nonpolitical, and avoided the more inflammatory accusations the Iranians wanted. But it did accuse Iraq of entering Iran with ten armored divisions on September 22, 1980. Although there had been other border skirmishes, the academics judged the Iraqi tank attack had been a disproportionate reaction and a violation of international law." 235. The Secretary General's report (S/23373, December 9, 1991) found in paragraph 6 that "the attack of 22 September 1980 against Iran … cannot be justified under the Charter of the United Nations, any recognised rules and principles of international law or any principles of international morality and entails the responsibility for the conflict."
5. George P. Shultz, *Turmoil and Triumph: My Years as Secretary of State* (Scribners, 1993), 932.
6. Sir Geoffrey Howe, Remarks to the UN Security Council, S/PV.2750, July 20, 1987, 16.
7. Hume, *Iran, Iraq, and the United Nations*, 3.
8. Chapter VII also includes Article 51, the "self-defense" article of the UN Charter now almost routinely cited when any country takes military action.
9. Hume, *Iran, Iraq, and the United Nations*, 116.
10. See discussion of Iranian attitudes toward the Security Council and attempts to work through third parties in Hume, *Iran, Iraq, and the United Nations*, 112. As Hume summed up Iranian efforts to influence what became UNSCR 598: "Iran's effort to exert influence over the negotiations flopped."
11. Hume, *Iran, Iraq, and the United Nations*, 116.
12. CIA, "Iran–Iraq: Negotiating an End to the War," NESA Special Report 88–10033, May 1988, declassified August 22, 2012. It's one of history's ironies that that these turned out to be America's unlimited war aims in 2003.
13. Letter dated August 11, 1987, from the Permanent Representative of the Islamic Republic of Iran to the United Nations addressed to the Secretary-General, S/19031, paragraphs 2 and 6.
14. Cordesman, 9.8.
15. Hume, *Iran, Iraq, and the United Nations*, 137.
16. Given that 598's operative paragraph five was a direct lift from UNSCR 582's operative paragraph seven—a common-enough UNSC practice—and that 582 was passed on February 24, 1986, well prior to any intellectual conceptualization of what became *Earnest Will*, it's clear that 598's OP5 was not specifically directed at American efforts in 1987. Hume, *Iran, Iraq, and the United Nations*, 116.
17. Hume, *Iran, Iraq, and the United Nations*, 131.
18. Cyrus R. Vance and Elliot L. Richardson, "Let the U.N Reflag Gulf Vessels," *New York Times*, July 8, 1987.

19 Vance and Richardson, "Let the U.N. Reflag Gulf Vessels." Srebrenica was a massacre that occurred eight years later, when Dutch peacekeepers operating as part of the UN peacekeeping operation UNPROFOR were attacked and withdrew, leading to the killing of over 8,000 civilians.
20 Hume, *Iran, Iraq, and the United Nations*, 133.
21 "Following traditional UN practice, neither U.S. nor Soviet forces would directly participate in the peacekeeping operation," Hume, *Iran, Iraq, and the United Nations*, 133.
22 Norman Cigar, "The Soviet Navy in the Persian Gulf: Naval Diplomacy in a Combat Zone." *Naval War College Review* 42, no. 2 (Spring 1989), 74.
23 Cigar, "Soviet Navy in the Persian Gulf," 72.
24 Text of Soviet non-paper is in Hume, *Iran, Iraq, and the United Nations*, 229, as well as in Appendix 2.
25 Hume, *Iran, Iraq, and the United Nations*, 135–137.
26 Cigar, "Soviet Navy in the Persian Gulf," 74.
27 Hume, *Iran, Iraq, and the United Nations*, 160–161.
28 Cordesman and Wagner, *Lessons of Modern War*, 210.
29 Thomas McNaugher, "Walking Tightropes in the Gulf," in *The Iran–Iraq War: Impact and Implications*, ed. Efraim Karsh (Palgrave Macmillan, 1989), 190.
30 "Rafsanjani New Commander of Iran's Military" *Los Angeles Times*, June 3, 1988.
31 Youssef F. Ibrahim, "Ex-Premier Attacks Khomeini as Despot," *New York Times*, June 3, 1988.
32 Cordesman and Wagner, *Lessons of Modern War*, 208.
33 O'Rourke, "Gulf Ops," *Proceedings* 115, no. /5/1035, May 1989.
34 Office of the Chairman of the Joint Chiefs of Staff, "Second Endorsement on Rear Admiral Fogary's ltr of 28 July 1988 [the Fogarty Report], Subj: FORMAL INVESTIGATION INTO THE CIRCUMSTANCES SURROUNDING THE DOWNING OF IRAN AIR FLIGHT 655 on 3 JULY 1988," CM-1485-88, 18 August 1988, 7–8.
35 Quoted in Crist, *Twilight War*, 363.
36 Vincennes report, 8, paragraph 10.
37 Vincennes report, 7.
38 Quoted in Crist, *Twilight War*, 363–364; "Captain Rogers repeatedly lobbied the commander of the Joint Task Force Middle East, Rear Admiral Anthony 'Tony' Less, to permit *Vincennes* to take a more active role than just providing air defense coverage to the southern Arabian Gulf." Samuel Cox, Director U.S. Naval History and Heritage Command, "H-020–1: The Fog of War: USS *Vincennes* Tragedy—3 July 1988," July 2018; Rogers's Vietnam-era Navy Commendation Medal with Combat V and Combat Action Ribbon are described in his biography in the *1988 USS Vincennes Cruise Book* (United States Navy, 1988).
39 Neil Sheehan, *The Arnheiter Affair* (Random House, 1971), 194.
40 Sheehan, *Arnheiter Affair*, 205.
41 Lieutenant Colonel David Evans, U.S. Marine Corps (Retired), "Vincennes: A Case Study" *Proceedings* 199, no. 8/1,086, August 1993.
42 Commander David R. Carlson, U.S. Navy, "The Vincennes Incident," *Comment and Discussion* section, *Proceedings*, September 1989. Veteran intelligence analyst Richard Mobley takes on the issue of intelligence support in "Fighting Iran: Intelligence Support During Operation Earnest Will, 1987–88." *Studies in Intelligence* 60, no. 3 (Extracts, September 2016), though he does not address the *Vincennes* incident. Mobley found that "the CIA probably could not have done much better in assessing Iranian intent, given the limited available evidence and the probability that analysts were trying to anticipate decisions the Iranians themselves had yet to make." Mobley points out: "An internal CIA memo captured the problem as one of insufficient

evidence: 'No one has all the information and, based on the limited facts, a disagreement existed on the degree of threat.'" His points sum up the challenges and limitations intelligence to policy making. It should raise questions about whether the fidelity of information is sufficient for deterrence to work as a policy option.

43 Cox, H-020–1.
44 "Sea of Lies," *Newsweek*.
45 Vistica, *Fall from Grace*, 275.
46 "Under the rules of engagement in effect at the time, the *Vincennes*'s helicopter, piloted that morning by Lieutenant Mark Collier, should not have been flying close enough to be threatened by the light weapons on the Iranian small craft. If Lieutenant Collier was in danger, it was because he was not following the rules: to approach no closer than four miles. In a letter published last August [1992], in the wake of a *Newsweek* magazine cover story on the incident, Lieutenant Collier wrote that he was never closer than four miles from the Iranian craft. However, that letter is at variance with Lieutenant Collier's sworn testimony to the investigators, in which he conceded that he had closed to within two to three miles of the Iranian craft. In fact, when the investigating officer asked Lieutenant Collier, "You were actually inside the CPA [closest point of approach] that you were told not to go inside, is that correct?" Lieutenant Collier replied, "Yes, sir." David Evans, "Vincennes: A Case Study," *Proceedings* 199, no. 8/1,086, August 1993.
47 "When this question [of why *Vincennes* headed north at 30 knots] was posed in a telephone interview with Captain Rogers, he replied, "I wanted to get him [my helicopter] back under my air defense umbrella. That's why I was heading north." This rationale raises questions. The *Vincennes*'s helicopter could dash away from danger at 90 knots, three times the speed of the advancing mothership and, in addition, Captain Rogers already had control of the airspace his helicopter was occupying, some 19 miles distant given the extended range of his anti-air warfare weapons. In fact, in the August 3, 1992, *Navy Times*, Captain Rogers offered a different explanation for his decision to press north. "Because of the bad atmospherics, any time the helo was farther than 15 miles, we lost contact," he said. Captain Carlson recounted that "Rogers then started asking for permission to shoot at the boats. We already knew the helicopter was okay, and if the boats were a threat, you didn't need permission to fire." Evans, "Vincennes: A Case Study."
48 *Vincennes*'s chief enlisted navigator announced that the ship had crossed the 12 nautical mile limit demarcating Iranian territorial waters; Captain Rogers made no reply—as one critical account put it: "Rogers paid no attention. He was in hot pursuit." When the IRGCN boats turned around and started heading toward *Vincennes*—which they were legally permitted to do—Rogers asked Bahrain for permission to engage. JTFME was operating without a clear operating picture and, protective of its ships, granted permission. The officers of the nearby USS *Sides*, listening to the exchange on the radio, wondered "Why doesn't he just push his rudder over and get his ass out of there?" Vistica, *Fall from Grace*, 276.
49 See, for example, the text of President Reagan's letter to Congress in accordance with the War Powers Act: "At about 1010 local Gulf time (2:10 a.m. EDT), when the helicopter had approached to within only four nautical miles, it was fired on by Iranian small boats (the *Vincennes* was ten nautical miles from the scene at this time). The LAMPS helicopter was not damaged and returned immediately to the *Vincennes*. As the *Vincennes* and *Montgomery* were approaching the group of Iranian small boats at approximately 1042 local time, at least four of the small boats turned toward and began closing in on the American warships. At this time, both American ships opened fire on the small craft, sinking two and damaging a third. Regrettably, in the course of the U.S. response to the Iranian attack, an Iranian civilian

airliner was shot down by the *Vincennes*, which was firing in self-defense at what it believed to be a hostile Iranian military aircraft. We deeply regret the tragic loss of life that occurred. The Defense Department will conduct a full investigation. The actions of U.S. forces in response to being attacked by Iranian small boats were taken in accordance with our inherent right of self-defense, as recognized in Article 51 of the United Nations Charter, and pursuant to my constitutional authority with respect to the conduct of foreign relations and as Commander in Chief." 1988–89 PPPUS 920–921 (Public Papers of the Presidents of the United States: Ronald Reagan, 1988–89 (Book 2). The U.S. position in the ICJ case brought by the Iranians makes a similar, if highly original, argument: "Since the USS *Vincennes* was under armed attack by Iranian small boats, it was clearly entitled to maneuver as necessary (including entry into Iranian territorial waters) as a matter of self-defense. Moreover, under the Treaty of Amity between the United States and Iran … a U.S. warship in distress is entitled to enter territorial waters claimed by Iran."

50 "Tab A to Appendix B to Annex C to COMIDEASTFOR OPORD 4000-85 amplifying the ROE provided in paragraph 9," cited in "Rear Admiral William Fogarty, USN, Subj: FORMAL INVESTIGATION INTO THE CIRCUMSTANCES SURROUNDING THE DOWNING OF IRAN AIR FLIGHT 655 on 3 JULY 1988," Serial number 1320, 28 July 88, 21.

51 Zatarain, *Tanker War*, 301.

52 National Research Council, *Improving the Continued Airworthiness of Civil Aircraft: A Strategy for the FAA's Aircraft Certification Service* (The National Academies Press, 1998), 23.

53 "In July 1988, a U.S. warship, USS *Vincennes*, under a disastrously gung-ho commander, sailed into Iranian territorial waters in pursuit of some Iranian gunboats and after a series of bungles shot down an Iranian civilian airliner with a pair of surface-to-air missiles, killing 290. The Reagan administration gave explanations that contained more misleading inaccuracies and self-justifications than contrition, and later awarded the commander of Vincennes a campaign medal. Many Iranians still believe that the destruction of the airliner was not an accident but a deliberate act." Michael Axworthy, *A History of Iran: Empire of the Mind* (Basic Books, 2008), 269–270. Axworthy was a former British diplomat and academic Iran specialist who served in Tehran from 1998 to 2000.

54 "Destruction of Iran Airbus A300 in the Vicinity of Qeshm Island, Islamic Republic of Iran on 3 July 1988: Report of ICAO Fact-Finding Investigation, November 1988" ICAO Document, C-WP/8708, paragraph 2.1.1, p. 10.

55 Zatarin, *Tanker War*, 302; ICAO report, paragraph 2.5.1.

56 ICAO report, paragraph 2.10.3, p. 15.

57 ICAO report paragraphs 2.9.2, 2.9.4, pp. 14–15.

58 ICAO report, paragraph 2.10.19, p. 17.

59 ICAO report, paragraph 3.1.22.

60 Norman Friedman, "The Vincennes Incident" *Proceedings* 115, no. 5/1,035, May 1989.

61 John Barry and Roger Charles, "Sea of Lies," *Newsweek*, July 12, 1992.

62 Zatarain, *Tanker War*, 309; Captain Keith F. Amacker, U.S. Navy, Letter in "Comment and Discussion," *Proceedings*, December 1999.

63 Vincennes Investigation Report, 6, paragraph 5.

64 CJCS William Crowe, 3, cover letter to Fogarty investigation.

65 Details on *Vincennes*'s movements included in Crist, *Twilight War*, 365–366 and footnote 14.

66 John Barry and Roger Charles, "Sea of Lies," *Newsweek*, July 12, 1992.

67 Molly Moore, "2 Vincennes Officers Get Medals; Citations Do Not Mention Downing of Iranian Airliner That Killed 290," *Washington Post*, April 22, 1990. Roger's citation contained the standard Navy award language: "Captain Rogers's dynamic leadership, logical judgment

and unexcelled devotion to duty reflected great credit upon himself and were in keeping with the highest traditions of the U.S. Naval Service."

68   One of the most notable is an unusual letter sent to *Proceedings* by Captain David Carlson, the commanding officer of USS *Sides* when the frigate was operating closely with Vincennes in June and July 1988: "I cannot bear to read yet another apologia for the Vincennes (CG-49) incident without commenting ... The Vincennes was never under attack by Iranian aircraft ... Captain Will Rogers III, no doubt, did what he thought he had to do, but he was wrong ... All of us were done grave disservice by an intelligence system that covered its six by forecasting every possible worst-case scenario. Combined with heightened safety concerns (and not a few career concerns as well) in the wake of the *Stark*'s and *Samuel B. Roberts*'s, experiences, this aided in creating an undercurrent of tension and a sense of imminent danger." Letter in response to Norman Friedman's 1989 article on the *Vincennes* Incident, Comment and Discussion Section, *Proceedings*, September 1989. Writing some 10 years later, *Sides*'s Executive Officer commented in his own letter to *Proceedings*, then Captain Keith F. Amacker, U.S. Navy wrote: "I have followed this story until the bitter end, when he closed out his 30-year naval career, dejected and saddened because the Navy made no effort to learn from the mistakes that were made in both ships [*Sides* and *Vincennes*] that day, or take corrective action. It chose instead to attack Captain Carlson's credibility and shift blame to the Iranians."

69   Hume, *Iran, Iraq, and the United Nations*, 162–63.
70   Ibid., 163.
71   Ibid.
72   Michael Axworthy, *Revolutionary Iran: A history of the Islamic Republic* (Oxford University Press, 2013), 277.
73   Remarks to the UN Security Council, document S/PV.2818, July 14, 1988, 21.
74   S/PV.2818, 22.
75   S/PV.2818, 31.
76   Rafsanjani is quoted in his memoirs as saying, "What made Emam Khomeini accept this was the chemical bombing of Halabja and Sardasht. It was predicted that in the future we would see the use of Weapons of Mass Destruction by Saddam (with a green light from the superpowers) against cities like Tabriz, Esfahan, Qom, and Tehran, with the launch of chemical missiles." Axworthy, *Revolution* 279.
77   Axworthy, *Revolution*, 279.
78   Hume, *Iran, Iraq, and the United Nations*, 168.
79   Ibid.
80   Fox Butterfield, "Iran, in Reversal, Accepts U.N. Plan for a Cease-Fire; A Surprise to Diplomats," *New York Times*, July 19, 1988, A-1.
81   "The fire of the war which was started by the Iraqi regime on 22 September 1980 through an aggression against the territorial integrity of the Islamic Republic of Iran has now gained unprecedented dimensions, bringing other countries into the war and even engulfing innocent civilians. The killing of 290 innocent human beings, caused by the shooting down of an Airbus aircraft of the Islamic Republic of Iran by one of American warships in the Persian Gulf is a clear manifestation of this contention ... In this context, we have decided to officially declare that the Islamic Republic of Iran—because of the importance it attaches to saving the lives of human beings and the establishment of justice and regional and international peace and security—accepts Security Council Resolution 598." "Text of Iranian Letter to U.N.," *New York Times*, July 19, 1988, A-9.
82   Quoted in Robert Pear, "U.S. Says Teheran Will Honor Truce," *New York Times*, July 20, 1988, A-6.

83 *The Caine Mutiny*, 7, opening page. Janice Gross Stein wrote of Rafanjani and Khomeini's explanations that "their evidence cannot be taken at value," but it's also true that she did not provide any evidence as to why that should be the case; "Wrong Strategy in the Right Place," 166n74.
84 Axworth, *Revolution*, 280.
85 FBIS-NES-88–140, "Khomenyni Message on Hajj, UN Resolution 598," 49. This is the famous speech in which Khomeini goes on shortly thereafter to say that he had "drunk the poisonous chalice of accepting the resolution." 49.
86 Axworthy, *Revolution*, 289.
87 Quoted in Axworthy, *Revolution*, 281.
88 Axworthy, *Revolution*, 292–293.

Chapter 7

1 See discussion in "The British Withdrawal," in David Winkler, *Amirs, Admirals, and Desert Sailors: Bahrain, the US Navy, and the Arabian Gulf* (Naval Institute Press, 2007), 47–51.
2 "But by this time [end of 1980] we have put in the Armilla Patrol to protect our ships." Thatcher memoirs, 91.
3 "Jane's Defense Weekly," May 2, 1987, 824. *Christian Science Monitor*, January 21, 1987, 1; *Washington Post*, January 28, 1987, A-1. Cordesman and Wagner, *Lessons of Modern War*, 198.
4 Richard A. Mobley, "London and Washington—Maintaining Naval Cooperation despite Strategic Differences during Operation EARNEST WILL," *Naval War College Review* 74, no. 2 (Spring 2021), 140.
5 U.S. Committee on Armed Services, *Interim Report of the Defense Burden Sharing Panel*, U.S. House of Representatives, 100th Congress, Second Session, Committee Report no. 23, Washington, D.C. U.S. Government Printing Office, 1988.
6 List of likely British "cons" from Mobley, 143–147.
7 "Weinberger Asks for Help in Gulf: Calls for NATO Allies to Join U.S. in Protecting Tankers," *New York Times*, May 26, 1987.
8 In writing about the thinking behind *Earnest Will*, Weinberger writes: "In an attempt to respond pre-emptively to what I knew would be Congressional and other demands for our allies to do more and that we should not carry the whole burden, I suggested that we sound out Britain and other Naval members of NATO to see if they would be prepared to assist in the convoying operations." Weinberger, *Fighting for Peace*, 280.
9 "At this meeting [May 1982 NATO defense ministerial] I also resumed my plea with NATO on "out of area actions'. I had long urged NATO to recognize that events outside its borders could affect its mission and its ability to defend Europe. The British requirements in the Falklands made it necessary for the UK to detach part of the forces they had committed to NATO and I made the point that, while this was only a 'temporary displacement' and not a loss, it did underline the fact that NATO had to be concerned with events outside its borders, including events in the Middle East that could disrupt vital oil supplies, and that there should be some contingency planning for such events." Caspar Weinberger, *Fighting for Peace: Seven Critical Years in the Pentagon* (Penguin, 1990), 211–212.
10 "Allies Turn Down Weinberger on Helping in Gulf," *New York Times*, May 28, 1987.
11 *New York Times*, May 27, 1987. It would appear some of those discussions happened on the margins of the May 26–27 NATO Defense Ministerial; in his May 27 concluding remarks to reports, Weinberger ended with a tantalizing coda to his "satchel" remark: "And we aren't

going to leave here empty-handed," with *The Times* interpreting as meaning that the Defense Secretary was satisfied with the NATO talks.
12   Tyler Marshall, "U.S. Asks Britain to Help Sweep Persian Gulf Mines," *Los Angeles Times*, July 31, 1987.
13   Tyler Marshall, "U.S. Asks."
14   "The Italian Navy in the Gulf," 149.
15   Quoted language from Weinberger letter to Shulz, July 27, 1987, contained in Crist, *Twilight War*, 249.
16   *Deutsche Presseagentur*, July 29, 1987; *Silddeutsche Zeitung*, July 30, 1987.
17   Foreign Office spokesman David Mellor went on to somewhat obviously observe: "It would take several weeks for them to get there," and, "It's much easier to sow a mine than to clear it," appearing not to realize that such factors applied even more to the obsolescent U.S. minesweepers going to the Gulf in their stead. Francis X. Clines, "Britain Rebuffs a Request by U.S. for Minesweepers," *New York Times*, August 1, 1987.
18   *The Persian Gulf and the U.S. Naval Presence: Issues for Congress* (Congressional Research Service, August 3, 1987), 10.
19   Crist, *Twilight War*, 236. In looking at the international response to Red Sea mining in 1984, noted Navy analyst Scott Truver wrote: "Later, in 'private conversations,' senior French and Italian diplomats in Cairo revealed that their governments' reluctance to become institutionally linked to the ECC [Egyptian Coordinating Committee (ECC)] stemmed from their perception that they were not sufficiently consulted about U.S. policies in Lebanon, which made their forces 'assigned' to the Multinational Peacekeeping Force targets for rebel attacks. One French diplomat said: 'We still have quite a bad memory of what happened in the multinational force in Lebanon. We want absolutely no confusion about what we're doing here. We are helping the Egyptian government to make the Red Sea safe for shipping. Our actions here are not, repeat not, directed against any country. Whatever our friendship with the Americans is, we do not want to be associated with any American crusade in the Red Sea.'" Quoted in Dr. Scott C. Truver, "Mines of August: An International Whodunit," *Proceedings*, 111, no. 5/987, May 1985. Bitter memories remained from the recent debacle in Beirut, and the Italians and French refused to participate in any military arrangement with the United States. Paris had no desire to work with the American navy, publicly stating that it wanted no part of an American "crusade" in the Red Sea. Crist, 236.
20   There was also a report that, when the United States objected to a 1985 West German contract signed with Iran for six type-209 submarines, the Germans responded by suggesting the United States instead buy the submarines. Kenneth R. Timmerman, *Fanning the Flames: Guns, Greed & Geopolitics in the Gulf War*, syndicated by New York Times Syndication Sales, 1987, published in book form as "Öl ins Feuer Internationale Waffengeschäfte im Golfkrieg" Orell Füssli Verlag Zürich and Wiesbaden 1988, Chapter 7.
21   Crist, *Twilight War*, 249.
22   Tamara Melia, *Damn the Torpedoes: A Short History of U.S. Naval Mine Countermeasures, 1777–1991*, Contributions to Naval History number 4 (Washington, D.C. U.S. Naval Historical Center, 1991). As retired four-star Admiral Wes McDonald, who had been NATO supreme allied commander Atlantic at the time of his retirement in 1985 put it: "The answer lay in a combination of fiscal constraints and expectation of allied naval support. The U.S. Navy built types of ships that it was in position to afford—aircraft carriers. Aegis cruisers, and long-range nuclear submarines. At the same time, the United States invested modestly in areas such as mine warfare and mine countermeasures, in which our allies were strongest." Admiral Wesley L. McDonald, U.S. Navy (Retired), "The Convoy Mission," *Proceedings* 144, no. 5/1,023, May 1988; see also "During the Cold War, the U.S. Navy viewed MCM forces as small-scale specialty forces. Thus, conscious

policy dictated reliance on NATO allies for MCM forces in the event of conflict with the Soviet Bloc."—ascribed to the Office of the Chief of Naval Operations, *Mine Warfare Plan: Meeting the Challenges of an Uncertain World* (Washington, D.C. Department of the Navy, January 29, 1992), "The Paradigm of Naval Mine Countermeasures: A Study in Stagnation," LCDR Joel T. Griner Jr., USN, thesis for USMC Command and Staff School, 1997, 36.

23 Tamara Melia, *Damn the Torpedoes: A Short History of U.S. Naval Mine Countermeasures, 1777–1991*, Contributions to Naval History number 4 (Washington, D.C. U.S. Naval Historical Center, 1991), 116. There is a complementary relationship regarding helicopter and surface assets when it comes to dealing with mines: "Helicopters provide the capabilities for high-visibility, worldwide, quick-reaction operations, and are ideally suited for large-area mine hunting and sweeping. Their limitations are compensated by the capabilities of mine countermeasures vessels: long endurance, the ability to stop and scrutinize a single contact, and the ability to carry out operations in narrow and confined sea areas, at night, and in weather that would ground helicopters." Dr. Scott C. Truver, "Mines of August: An International Whodunit," *Proceedings* 111, no. 5/987, May 1985.

24 USS *Avenger* (MCM-1) Command Histories for 1987, 1988, 1989 and 1990; "In presenting its FY78 budget request, the U.S. Navy set out a 19-ship procurement objective for a new mine countermeasure vessel (MCM). The tentative program called for US$60 million in FY79 for the lead ship, followed by six vessels each in the following three fiscal years. The projected total program cost for 19 ships was US$1.16 billion, excluding outfitting and post delivery costs. The FY79 budget request did not ask for any vessels, but the Five Year Shipbuilding Plan for FY79 through FY83 called for one vessel in FY80 and two in FY81, two in FY82 and two in FY83. Again, in the FY80 budget request, the service did not ask for funding, but the FY80 Five Year Shipbuilding Plan had one vessel in FY81 and two each in FY83 and 1984." Defense Secretary Brown told Congress that "MCM shipbuilding plans have been delayed for a year while mine hunting hardware is developed and ship design is modified." Forecast International, *MCM-1 Avenger Class—Archived 9/97* (September 1996), https://www.*forecastinternational.com/archive/disp_old_pdf.cfm?ARC_ID=1758*.

25 Forecast International, *MHC-51 Osprey Class—Archived 5/2002 (May 2001)*, https://www.forecastinternational.com/archive/disp_old_pdf.cfm?ARC_ID=1761.

26 John H. Cushman Jr., "U.S. Has Fallen Years Behind on a Fleet for Clearing Mines," *New York Times*, July 29, 1987.

27 Zatarain describes these moves as uncoordinated—which may literally be true—but it is also clear the British believed they led the Continent in a change of policy. Zatarain, *Tanker War*, 93–94.

28 Dr. Werner Funk, Dr. Romain Leick and Hans Hielscher, Interview for *Der Spiegel* with Margaret Thatcher, September 8, 1987.

29 Margaret Thatcher, Interview for *Woman's Own*, September 23, 1987.

30 Mobley, 148–149. It is also possible that her post-election trip to Washington, D.C. on July 19, 1987 influenced her views. While she was riding high after her successful campaign, "By contrast, my old friend and his Administration were reeling under the continuing 'Irangate' revelations. I found the President hurt and bemused by what was happening … I was determined to do what I could to help President Reagan ride out the storm." Thatcher memoirs, 770.

31 Quoted in Francis X. Clines, "British, in Switch, Add Minesweepers for Gulf Patrol; Growing Dangers Cited; France Also Is to Send Ships to Protect Its Tankers off the Arabian Peninsula." *New York Times*, August 12, 1987.

32 Ibid.

33 Ibid.

34 Anselm J. van der Peet, *Out-of-area. De Koninklijke Marine en multinationale vlootoperaties 1945* (Out of Area. The RNLN and Multinational Fleet Operations 1945), PhD Thesis Utrecht University (Van Wijnen, Franeker 2016), 292.
35 Edward Cody, "Chain of Events," *Washington Post*, September 20, 1987.
36 Dutch Ministry of Defense website, "Historical Missions," "The Iran–Iraq war: The Dutch contribution to ensuring the security of maritime traffic," retrieved August 12, 2024; Zatarain, *Tanker War*, 95.
37 Cordesman and Wagner, *Lessons of Modern War*, Chapter 9.
38 Anselm J. van der Peet, *Out-of-area. De Koninklijke Marine en multinationale vlootoperaties 1945* (Out of Area. The RNLN and Multinational Fleet Operations 1945), PhD Thesis Utrecht University (Van Wijnen, Franeker 2016), 530.
39 Zatarain, *Tanker War*, 94.
40 Harrison, Michael M. "The Italian Navy in the Gulf." *Italian Politics* 3 (1989): 149.
41 Harrison, *Italian Navy*, 150.
42 Harrison, Michael M. "The Italian Navy in the Gulf." *Italian Politics* 3 (1989): 153.
43 "Italy to Take Warships Out of the Persian Gulf," *New York Times*, November 10, 1988.
44 Philips, *Poisoned Chalice*, 258.
45 Ibid.
46 Quoted in Francis X. Clines, "British, in Switch, Add Minesweepers for Gulf Patrol; Growing Dangers Cited; France Also Is to Send Ships to Protect Its Tankers off the Arabian Peninsula." *New York Times*, August 12, 1987.
47 U.S. General Accounting Office, *BURDEN SHARING: Allied Protection of Ships in the Persian Gulf in 1987 and 1988*, (U.S. General Accounting Office, Washington, D.C.; September 1990) GAO/NSIAD-90-282BR The Persian Gulf, 13.
48 U.S. General Accounting Office, "BURDEN SHARING: Allied Protection of Ships in the Persian Gulf in 1987 and 1988," (U.S. General Accounting Office, Washington, D.C.; September 1990) GAO/NSIAD-90-282BR The Persian Gulf, 12.
49 Peter W. DeForth, "U.S. Naval Presence in the Persian Gulf: The Mideast Force Since World War II", *Naval War College Review* 28, no. 4 (Summer 1975), 30; Palmer, *Guardians*, 86.
50 Palmer, *Guardians*, 281.
51 *Soviet Military Power*, 4th edition (U.S. Department of Defense, 1985), 106.
52 Ralph A. Cossa, *Iran: Soviet Interests, U.S. Concerns*, McNair Paper no. 11 (Institute for National Strategic Studies, 1990), 55–56; Cigar, "Soviet Navy in the Persian Gulf," 67.
53 Cigar, "Soviet Navy in the Persian Gulf," 68.
54 Norman Cigar, "The Soviet Navy in the Persian Gulf: Naval Diplomacy in a Combat Zone", *Naval War College Review* 42, no. 2 (Spring 1989), 56; Cordesman, 9.1: "As a result, both Soviet and Western naval forces began to take action. The USSR reacted in mid-January [1987] by sending a Krivak-class missile frigate to escort four Soviet ships carrying arms to Iraq from the Straits to Kuwait. This was the second Soviet warship to enter the Gulf since 1982—the first had been sent when Iran detained two Soviet ships in September, 1986—and was clearly intended as a signal to Iran, Iraq, and the southern Gulf states that the USSR would protect its ships."
55 Cigar, "Soviet Navy in the Persian Gulf," 59.
56 Crist, *Twilight War*, 215.
57 Cigar, "Soviet Navy in the Persian Gulf," 66.
58 Ibid., 62.
59 Ibid., 63.
60 Joseph Alexander and Merrill Bartlett in *Sea Soldiers in the Cold War*, quoted in Alexey D. Muraviev, "The Russian Pacific Fleet: From the Crimean War to Perestroika," *Papers in Australian Maritime Affairs Number 20* (Seapower Centre Australia, 2007), 39.

61. Alexey D. Muraviev, "The Russian Pacific Fleet: From the Crimean War to Perestroika," *Papers in Australian Maritime Affairs Number 20* (Seapower Centre Australia, 2007), 39.
62. Cigar, "The Soviet Navy in the Persian Gulf," 66.
63. "A Cobra helo crew, our closest air asset, evaluated a 25-knot contact closing from the northeast as a warship. This quickly took shape as a 'possible Iranian *Saam* FFG,' and the *Merrill* made preparations to launch a Harpoon attack. We then asked for further descriptive information and ultimately for a hull number. The contact turned out to be a Soviet *Sovremennyy*-class DDG. The skipper, when asked his intention, replied with a heavy accent, "I vant to take peectures for heestory." We breathed easier."—Captain J. B. Perkins III, U.S. Navy, "The Surface View: Operation Praying Mantis," *Proceedings,* May 1989.
64. Cigar, "The Soviet Navy in the Persian Gulf," 70.
65. For example, the Japanese Maritime Self-Defense Force has deployed ships and commanded Combined Task Force 151, an international collection of ships focused on counter-piracy operations off the Somalia coast, four separate times since 2013. Germany is also a prominent participant in the Combined Maritime Forces, having commanded CTF 150—an at-sea organization focused on Maritime Security Operations in the wider Indian Ocean area—5 times since February 2002, including as its inaugural commander.
66. Quoted in 1987 U.S. burden-sharing report.
67. Norman Friedman, "West European and NATO Navies," *Proceedings* 114, no. 3/1,021, March 1988.
68. U.S. General Accounting Office, "*BURDEN SHARING: Allied Protection of Ships in the Persian Gulf in 1987 and 1988*" (U.S. General Accounting Office, Washington, D.C.; September 1990), GAO/NSIAD-90-282BR The Persian Gulf, 8.
69. Webb, USMC Oral History, 245.
70. Osama bin Ladin, "Declaration of Jihad Against the Americans Occupying the Land of the Two Holy Mosques," *Al-Islah* (London), September 2, 1996, Reference number AFGP-2002-003676.
71. James Gerstenzang and David Lauter, "Saudis to Sweep Gulf for Iranian Mines Off Kuwait," *Los Angeles Times,* June 24, 1987.
72. "In June, Weinberger convinced the Saudis to let the EARNEST WILL JTF connect the radar feeds from the ELF-1 surveillance aircraft to its naval ships, giving the United States better situational awareness." Andrew Marvin, "Operation Earnest Will—The U.S. Foreign Policy behind U.S. Naval Operations in the Persian Gulf 1987–89; A Curious Case," 92.
73. CJCS Crowe reportedly "had little regard for the Saudis' training and little faith in any real cooperation." Crist, *Twilight War,* 248.
74. CIA Directorate of Intelligence, "The Iranian Mine Warfare Threat: An Intelligence Assessment," NESA 84-10292C, November 1984, originally classified Top Secret; redated and unclassified July 30, 2009, 7.
75. Loren Jenkins, "Explosion Rocks Saudi Plant on Persian Gulf," *Washington Post,* August 16, 1987.

Chapter 8

1. Weinberger, *Fighting for Peace,* 272–301.
2. Clausewitz, *On War,* 80.
3. Arthur Wellesley, First Duke of Wellington, *The Dispatches of Field Marshal the Duke of Wellington, K.G.: France and the Low Countries, 1814–1815* (John Murray, 1838), 590.

4　Phillips, *Poisoned Chalice*, 42.
5　Hew Strachan, "Strategy in Theory; Strategy in Practice," *Journal of Strategic Studies* 42, no. 2 (2019), 173, 185.
6　*The New Makers of Modern Strategy: From the Ancient World to the Digital Age*, edited by Hal Brands (Princeton University Press, 2023), 1. To be fair, neither of the two earlier *Makers of Modern Strategy* volumes (Edward Mead Earle's edition of 1943 or Peter Paret's of 1986) had chapters on Corbett either. The phrase "the next generation of the definitive work on strategy" comes from the Amazon.com advertising description but is also an accurate assessment of how the security studies community of the 2020s views the book.
7　And evidently a conscious choice on the part of the editor of the 2023 version. Peter Paret's 1986 edition begins by citing Clausewitz and emphasizes, "Strategy is the use of armed force to achieve the military objectives and, by extension, the political purpose of the war." *Makers of Modern Strategy: From Machiavelli to the Nuclear Age* (Princeton University Press, 1986), 3. Similarly, Edward Mead Earle's introduction to the 1943 edition flatly states "Strategy deals with war preparation for war, and the waging of war." *Makers of Modern Strategy: Military thought from Machiavelli to Hitler* (Princeton University Press, 1943), viii. There is palpable shift in tone in how Brands sets the stage for the third edition of this series.
8　Strachan, "Strategy in Theory," 175. See also Strachan's consideration on page 174 on post–World War II thinking and the Charter of the United Nations, as well as the advent of nuclear weapons, changing the focus of strategy toward preventing war rather than fighting it.
9　Bernsen, *Reminiscences*, 24.
10　Captain Sam Tangredi, U.S. Navy (Retired), Professor of Strategic and Operational Warfare, Center for Naval Warfare Studies, U.S. Naval War College, Review of Steve Wills (2022) "Strategy Shelved: The Collapse of Cold War Naval Strategic Planning," *Naval War College Review* 75, no. 1, Article 22.
11　Bruce Stubbs, "I Blame the Navy's Strategic Woes on the Chiefs of Naval Operations" *War on the Rocks,* November 13, 2024.
12　Admiral James D. Watkins, U.S. Navy, "The Maritime Strategy," *Proceedings* 112, no. 1/995, January 1986, Supplement. This lengthy article provides a good overview of the highlights of the Maritime Strategy.
13　Ronald O'Rourke, "The Maritime Strategy and the Next Decade," *Proceedings* 114, no. 4/1022, April 1988.
14　John Mearsheimer. "A Strategic Misstep: The Maritime Strategy and Deterrence in Europe," *International Security* 11, no. 2 (Fall 1986): 55. Mearsheimer may have been onto something, given the Maritime Strategy's focus on attacking Russian ballistic missile submarines. In 2024, British newspapers reported seeing secret Russian planning files dating between 2008 and 2014 that included "a separate training presentation for naval officers [that] outlines broader criteria for a potential nuclear strike, including … destruction of 20 per cent of Russia's strategic ballistic missile submarines, 30 per cent of its nuclear-powered attack submarines, three or more cruisers." Max Seddon and Chris Cook, "Leaked Russian Military Files Reveal Criteria for Nuclear Strike," *Financial Times*, February 28, 2024.
15　Description of phases can be found in Watkins, 1986.
16　Janice Gross Stein, "The Wrong Strategy in the Right Place: The United States in the Gulf," *International Security* (Winter 1988/89): 142. Dr. Stein, a professor of political science, meticulously examined the events of *Earnest Will* through the lens of the concept of "extended deterrence." By any standards of deterrence—extended or otherwise—it's hard to argue that U.S. military efforts were a success—but as she also pointed out: "The Gulf is the right place: unlike Lebanon in 1982, important American and Western interests are at stake." 165.

17 Stephen Andrew Kelley, "Better Lucky Than Good: Operation Earnest Will as Gunboat Diplomacy" Naval Postgraduate School, Monterey, California, Thesis, June 2007.
18 Thomas McNaugher, "Walking Tightropes in the Gulf." In Efraim Karsh, *The Iran–Iraq War: Impact and Implications* (Palgrave Macmillan, 1989), 194.
19 U.S. General Accounting Office, "*BURDEN SHARING: Allied Protection of Ships in the Persian Gulf in 1987 and 1988*" (U.S. General Accounting Office, Washington, D.C.; September 1990) GAO/NSIAD-90-282BR The Persian Gulf, 14.
20 GAO Report, 18.
21 Caspar Weinberger, *Fighting for Peace: Seven Critical Years in the Pentagon* (Penguin, 1990), 298.
22 Weinberger, *Fighting for Peace*, 298.
23 Ibid.
24 Ibid.
25 "The Uses of Military Power," Remarks prepared for delivery by the Hon. Caspar W. Weinberger, secretary of defense, to the National Press Club, Washington, D.C., November 28, 1984, archived at https://www.pbs.org/wgbh/pages/frontline/shows/military/force/weinberger.html.
26 Colin Powell, in his memoirs, writes that Weinberger "was put off by fancy phrases like 'interpositional forces' … that turned out to mean putting U.S. troops in harm's way [comment: yet another invocation of that John Paul Jones phrase] without a clear mission." Colin Powell with Jospeph Persico *My American Journey* (Random House, 1995), 303.
27 Note here that Weinberger is speaking of limited force in terms of means, not political ends. He does not go on to discuss whether the "small combat force" would have only retaken the Rhineland or whether it was supposed to depose Hitler.
28 Clausewitz, *On War*, 579.
29 Powell, *American Journey*, 302.
30 Ibid., 303.
31 Hew Strachan, "The Case for Clausewitz: reading On War today." *The Direction of War: Contemporary Strategy in Historical Perspective* (Cambridge University Press, 2013), 55.
32 The phrase comes from former Defense Secretary James Schlesinger in a February 1985 congressional testimony and is quoted on page 313 of then-Colonel David Petraeus's 1987 PhD dissertation.
33 Strachan, "Case for Clausewitz," 62.
34 In actual fact, Roosevelt at the time reportedly took an extended fishing trip to avoid reporters' questions regarding the Rhineland. Arnold Offner, "The United States and National Socialist Germany," *The Fascist Challenge and the Policy of Appeasement*, edited by Wolfgang Mommsen and Lothar Kettenacker (George Allen & Unwin, 1983), 415.
35 Paul Dickson, *The Rise of the G. I. Army, 1940–1941: The Forgotten Story of How America Forged a Powerful Army Before Pearl Harbor* (Atlantic Monthly Press, 2020), i.
36 Frederick R. Barkley, "Army Bill is Adopted by One Vote," *New York Times*, August 13, 1941. Part of the same headline reported "Petain Yields, Pledging to Work with Hitler."
37 Weinberger, *Fighting for Peace*, 299.
38 Hew Strachan, "Strategy in the Twenty-First Century," in *The Changing Character of War*, eds Hew Strachan and Sibylle Scheipers (Oxford University Press, 2011), 507.
39 John H. Cushman, "James Webb's New 'Fields of Fire,'" *New York Times*, February 28, 1988.
40 Oral History Transcript, Captain James H. Webb Jr. U.S. Marine Corps (Retired), (Quantico, VA: History Division, U.S. Marine Corps, 2021), 245.

41 Crist, *Twilight War*, 251.
42 John M. Broder, "Gulf Role Open-Ended, Navy Chief Says," *Los Angeles Times*, September 17, 1987.
43 Ibid.
44 John H. Cushman Jr., "Gulf Doubts Over, Naval Chief Says," *New York Times*, September 9, 1987.
45 Crist, *Twilight War*, 251.
46 See discussion in Thomas M. Duffy, *U.S. Naval Actions in the Persian Gulf 1987–88: An Effective Use of Force?* unpublished Extended Essay for the M.A. in War Studies, King's College London, September 8, 1989, 29.
47 Which is not to say that Weinberger always gambled correctly. While as secretary of defense, he consistently internally opposed the policies that lead to Iran–Contra; his lack of candor with Congress on the matter led to federal indictments in 1992 on two counts of perjury and one count of obstruction of justice. President George H. W. Bush issued pardons on all three counts shortly before leaving office. David Johnston, "Bush Pardons 6 in Iran Affair, Aborting a Weinberger Trial; Prosecutor Assails 'Cover-Up,'" *New York Times*, December 24, 1992.
48 See Gwynne Dyer's opening argument: "Wars are not an interminable series of historic accidents, nor the product of evil men, nor yet the result of some simple single cause like capitalism or overpopulation. Neither is warfare merely the heritage of our evolutionary past, an outlet for our "natural aggressiveness." War is a central institution in human civilization, and it has a history precisely as long as civilization" Dyer, *War*, xi.
49 Robin Wright, *In the Name of God: The Khomeini Decade* (Touchstone Publications, 1990), 186–191.
50 It's worth noting that France—a strong critic of the 2003 invasion—participated in Operation *Southern Watch*, enforcing the southern no-fly zone over Iraq what they called "Operation *Alysse*," until 1998. Arnaud DeLalande, "Warning-Mig25!," *War is Boring*, August 15, 2016.

Chapter 9

1 Ambrister, *Matter of Accountability*, 385. Bergner, a 1940 U.S. Naval Academy graduate, was aboard a U.S. ship attacked at Pearl Harbor, saw extensive submarine wartime service in World War II and in addition to several combat awards, was a 1944 recipient of "the Navy and Marine Corps Medal for accomplishing the transfer, in a small rubber boat in heavily patrolled enemy waters, of an injured crewman to another submarine returning to port." Naval History and Heritage Command biographical file, Allen Alfred Bergner, 29 May 1916–22, March 2010.
2 Clausewitz, *On War*. 363. Clausewitz continues that "strategic success lies in the exploitation of a victory won." Michael Howard takes up this overall point in "When Are Wars Decisive?" *Survival* 41, no. 1 (Spring 199): 126–135.
3 Till, *Seapower A*: *Guide for the 21st Century, 4th Edition* (Routledge, 2018), 1.
4 Navias and Hooton, *Tanker Wars*, 184.
5 Michael Howard, "The Use and Abuse of Military History," in *The Causes of War*, 2nd edition, 195–210, Harvard University Press, 1984, 194.
6 Stephen R. Covey, *The 7 Habits of Highly Effective People* (Simon and Schuster, 2020), Habit 2.
7 Clausewitz, *On War*, 577.
8 Hew Strachan, "Michael Howard and the Dimensions of Military History," Annual Liddell Hart Centre for Military Archives Lecture, King's College London, December 3, 2002;

Andrew Lambert, *The British Way of War: Julian Corbett and the Battle for a National Strategy* (Yale University Press, 2021).
9   Till, *Seapower*, 81.
10 Ibid., 23.
11 Michael Howard, "The British Way in Warfare: A Reappraisal." In *The Causes of War* (Harvard University Press, 1984), 180. Emphasis in original.
12 Of the GCC countries, Kuwait had maintained diplomatic relations with the USSR since 1963. The UAE and Oman established relations only in 1986. Saudi Arabia had not hosted a Soviet ambassador since the 1930s, and neither Qatar nor Bahrain had diplomatic relations. Central Intelligence Agency Research Paper "Soviet Policy toward the Middle East," SOV 86–10048X, December 1986, 93, Declassified in Part—Sanitized copy approved for release 29 December, 2011.
13 "Ten years of aggressive forward naval operations had convinced the Soviet leadership that they could not defend their strategic assets and their homeland without impossibly large increases in spending. That fact had removed the political power of the Soviet military and created the political opportunity for strong leaders like Yeltsin and Gorbachev to pursue perestroika and glasnost and to seize the opportunity to negotiate an end to the Cold War." John Lehman, *Oceans Ventured: Winning the Cold War at Sea* (W. W. Norton, 2018), 274.
14 Clausewitz, *On War*, 86. Nicholas A. A. Murray goes on to argue "Clausewitz's 'greatest wisdom' is the courage to act in uncertainty." "Geniuses Dare to Ride Their Luck: Clausewitz's Card Game Analogies," *Parameters* 53, no. 2 (2023), 88. Murray contrasts Clausewitz with "Maurice, count de Saxe [who] argues that battles are too risky and should be avoided and contends it is possible to make war 'without trusting anything to accident.' Applying pure reason can help avoid hasty or fear-based decisions, and accurate calculability could permit armies to make war without trusting to accident." 91.
15 Nate Silver, "Doing Nothing About Biden Is the Riskiest Plan of All," *New York Times*, July 3, 2024.
16 U.S. National Archives, National Personnel Records Center, "Veterans Preference" and "Wartime Service" https://www.archives.gov/personnel-records-center/vso/veterans-preference-and-wartime-service.
17 The phrase is from the opening page of Clausewitz's *On War*: "*War is thus an act of force to compel our enemy to do our will.*" Clausewitz, *On War*, 75. Emphasis in original.
18 On December 8, 2004, in response to an American national guardsman complaining about having to use unarmored vehicles in Iraq, Rumsfeld responded: "As you know, you go war with the Army you have—not the Army you might want or wish to have at a later time." Rumsfeld contextualized and defended the statement in his memoirs: "My statement carefully laid out the reality of the armed forces that existed when President Bush took office. Any president or any secretary of defense has available the military their predecessors bequeath to them … The number of up-armored vehicles available in 2004 were the consequences of decisions made years before President Bush or I took office in 2001." Donald Rumsfeld, *Known and Unknown: A Memoir* (Sentinel, 2011), 646–647.
19 Corbett, *Some Principles*, 57.
20 Chief of Naval Operations, *Navigation Plan for America's Warfighting Navy, 2024* (Department of the Navy, 2024), 6.
21 Ibid.
22 The "Big Five" were the U.S. Army's newest weapons systems developed during the 1970s and 1980s, originally for use against Soviet forces: the Apache AH-64 Helicopter, UH-60 Black

Hawk Helicopter, M1 Abrams Tank, Bradley Fighting Vehicle, and Patriot Missile System. All of these systems have seen subsequent extensive use.
23 See, for example, the work of USAF Colonel John Warden and the idea of "The Enemy as a System." *Airpower Journal* 9, no. 2 (Spring 1995).
24 See, for example, "in Desert Storm the United States raised the execution of joint warfare to an unprecedented level of competence." Brigadier General Robert H. Scales Jr. Director Desert Storm Study Project, *Certain Victory* (Office of the Chief of Staff United States Army, 1993), 370.
25 As Steve Wills observes, "In the Gulf War, the Army and Air Force ultimately validated many of the operational concepts that they had developed for Cold War combat." Wills, *Strategy Shelved*, 142.
26 Wills, *Strategy Shelved*, 141.
27 It's worth considering that, conversely, AirLand Battle wasn't applicable to the Tanker War and would not have received any "validation" from that conflict.
28 This situation may be endemic to all Washington-based war fighting efforts. Writing of his efforts to oversee the wars in Iraq and Afghanistan, former Secretary of Defense Robert Gates concluded: "The Department of Defense is structured to plan and prepare for war, but not to fight one." *Duty: Memoirs of a Secretary at War* (Knopf, 2014), 245.
29 Details can be found in Gregory L. Vistica, *Fall from Glory: The Men Who Sank the U.S. Navy* (Simon & Schuster, 1997).
30 Wills, *Strategy Shelved*, 228–229.
31 The phrase is from Steve Wills, who argues "The idea of a defense marketplace of ideas seems to fly in the face of the Goldwater–Nichols' concept of efficiency through centralization, but thirty-four years of what has been in effect 'defense socialism' does not seem to have solved the budgetary or strategy issues as desired." Wills, *Strategy Shelved*, 224–225.
32 Captain Sam Tangredi, U.S. Navy (Retired), "Jointness Versus Strategy: How Joint Ideology Distorts U.S. National Security." *Proceedings*, June 2022. When viewed with Tangredi's questions in mind, a 2016 CRS assessment on jointness can be read in a completely different light: "The changes that the Goldwater–Nichols legislation made to the Department of Defense, and in particular, the way that DOD conducts military operations, are in many ways central to how the Department conducts military operations today. Indeed, many organization design decisions that were taken—in particular, clarifying the chain of command for more effective prosecution of joint operations and improving the quality of military advice provided to senior leaders—are so fundamental to the way DOD does business today that it is difficult to recall that it once conducted its operations quite differently." Congressional Research Service "Goldwater–Nichols at 30: Defense Reform and Issues for Congress," June 2, 2016, Report Number R44474, 2.
33 Corbett, *Some Principles*, 41.
34 Ibid., 54.
35 Ibid., 74.
36 General Douglas MacArthur Farewell Address to Congress delivered April 19, 1951, Washington, D.C. This speech—where MacArthur ends with the observation that old soldiers never die, they just fade away—is also an example of where MacArthur speaks in terms reminiscent of Halford Mackinder: "This is the direction of Asian progress and it may not be stopped. It is a corollary to the shift of the world economic frontiers as the whole epicenter of world affairs rotates back toward the area whence it started." As well as a classic Continentalist view of how oceans work that could well come from a PLA General: "The

western strategic frontier of the United States lay on the littoral line of the Americas, with an exposed island salient extending out through Hawaii, Midway, and Guam to the Philippines. That salient proved not an outpost of strength but an avenue of weakness along which the enemy could and did attack." The speech, which also stressed the importance of control of the Pacific Island chains, goes on to warn "under no circumstances must Formosa [Taiwan] fall under Communist control. Such an eventuality would at once threaten the freedom of the Philippines and the loss of Japan and might well force our western frontier back to the coast of California, Oregon and Washington."

37 See, for example, Basil Henry Liddell Hart, *The British Way in Warfare* (Faber and Faber, 1932) and the discussion in Lambert *21st Century Corbett*, 15–16.
38 Congressional Research Service, "Goldwater–Nichols at 30: Defense Reform and Issues for Congress" June 2, 2016, Report Number R44474, 13.
39 U.S. Department of State, Office of the Spokesman, Press Release, "Secretary Antony J. Blinken, National Security Advisor Jake Sullivan, Director Yang and State Councilor Wang at the Top of Their Meeting," Anchorage, Alaska, March 18, 2021.
40 John Pomfret, "U.S. takes a tougher tone with China," *Washington Post*, July 30, 2010.
41 Sullivan's use of the "secret sauce" term is another example of business strategy creeping in matters of classical strategy; the term originates from an American hamburger company and is now frequently used in American business literature.
42 Sullivan himself has been consistent since leaving office in 2025—in response to a question from a reporter regarding the Biden Administration's "biggest accomplishment," the response was: "He says he is proud to have helped create a situation where the "core engines of American power are humming." Demetri Sevastopulo, "Former national security adviser Jake Sullivan: 'The core engines of American power are humming,'" *Financial Times*, January 30, 2025.
43 "The Elements of the China Challenge," State Department Policy Planning Staff, December 2020 revised version, 1. The document goes on to argue: "Meeting the China challenge requires the United States to return to the fundamentals. To secure freedom, America must refashion its foreign policy in light of ten tasks," and outlines in 74 pages the steps needed to secure freedom as the preferred method to deal with China.
44 "HMS *Java* Battle," USS *Constitution* museum website, accessed July 26, 2024. U.S. Navy History and Heritage Command, "USS *Constitution* vs HMS *Java*."
45 Patrick O'Brian, *The Fortune of War* (W. W. Norton and Company, 1991), 98.
46 Julian Corbett, *Successors of Drake* (1900), quoted in Kevin McCranie, *Mahan, Corbett, and the Foundations of Naval Strategic Thought* (Naval Institute Press, 2021), 28.
47 Julian Corbett, *England in the Seven Years War, Volume 1* (Longmans, Green, 1907), 6.
48 Sir Julian Corbett, *Some Principles of Maritime Strategy* (Naval Institute Press, 1988), 8.
49 Detail of these operations can be found at Ralph Wetterhahn, *The Last Battle: The Mayaguez Incident and the End of the Vietnam War* (Carroll and Graf, 2001). "Admiral George P. Steele, 7th Fleet commander, recounted his view on command and control [of the unnecessary attack on Koh Tang island, in which 41 servicemen died in attempt to rescue 40 captured civilian crewman located in a separate, unknown location]: "This complicated, jury-rigged arrangement and detailed management from the Joint Chiefs of staff level endangered and nearly destroyed the forces on [Koh Tang] island," 214; James L. Holloway, "Special Operations Review of Iranian Hostage Rescue Mission," Joint Chiefs of Staff, Washington, D.C., August 23, 1980, 60–61; Stephen E. Anno and William E. Einspahr, "The Grenada Invasion," in Stephen E. Anno and William E. Einspahr, *Command and Control Lessons Learned: Iranian Rescue, Falklands Conflict, Grenada Invasion, Libya Raid* (Air University Press, 1988), 36–45.

50 National Commission on Terrorist Attacks Upon the United States. *The 9/11 Commission Report: Final Report of the National Commission on Terrorist Attacks Upon the United States* (W. W. Norton and Company, 2004), 344.
51 Hew Strachan, "Maritime Strategy and National Policy." In *The Direction of War: Contemporary Strategy in Historical Perspective* (Cambridge University Press, 2013), 155.

Appendix 1

1 https://en.wikisource.org/wiki/United_Nations_Security_Council_Resolution_598.
2 Hume, *Iraq, Iran, and the United Nations,* 227. The additions from the non-permanent members are an example of how a UNSCR makes its way through the legislative process. While one can debate the substance of the changes, what is undebatable is the need to modify UNSCR text to secure voting buy-in from all members.

Appendix 2

1 Hume, *Iraq, Iran, and the United Nations*, 229. In diplomatic parlance, a "non-paper" is a useful tool in that it is not an official document attributed to a particular government, even if all participants know who authored the paper. Non-papers allow negotiators to float ideas or sensitive topics in a more informal manner, meaning that rejections or major modifications carry a different weight than objecting to a formal, national proposal.

Bibliography

Alvandi, Roham. "Nixon, Kissinger, and the Shah: The Origins of Iranian Primacy in the Persian Gulf." *Diplomatic History* 36, no. 2 (April 2012): 337–372.
Amacker, Captain Keith F., U.S. Navy. Letter in "Comment and Discussion," *Proceedings*, December 1999.
Ambrose, Stephen E., and Douglas G. Brinkley. *Rise to Globalism: American Foreign Policy Since 1938*. 9th revised edition. Penguin Books, 2011.
Armbrister, Trevor. *A Matter of Accountability: The True Story of the Pueblo Affair*. Lyons Press, 2004.
Axworthy, Michael. *A History of Iran: Empire of the Mind*. Basic Books, 2008.
Axworthy, Michael. *Revolutionary Iran: A History of the Islamic Republic*. Oxford University Press, 2013.
Barry, John, and Roger Charles. "Sea of Lies," *Newsweek* (July 12, 1992): 28–39.
Bernsen, Harold, and Paul Stillwell. *The Reminiscences of Rear Adm. Harold J. Bernsen, U.S. Navy (Retired)*. U.S. Naval Institute Press, 2019.
Bin Ladin, Osama. "Declaration of Jihad Against the Americans Occupying the Land of the Two Holy Mosques." *Al Islah*, September 2, 1996. Reference Number: AFGP-2002-003676.
Brands, Hal, ed. *The New Makers of Modern Strategy: From the Ancient World to the Digital Age*. Princeton University Press, 2023.
Carlson, David R., Commander, U.S. Navy. "The *Vincennes* Incident," Comment and Discussion section, *Proceedings* (September 1989): 87–92.
Carter, Jimmy. "Address by President Carter on the State of the Union Before a Joint Session of Congress." Washington, January 23, 1980.
Cigar, Norman. "The Soviet Navy in the Persian Gulf: Naval Diplomacy in a Combat Zone." *Naval War College Review* 42, no. 2 (Spring 1989): 56–88.
Coll, Steve. *The Achilles Trap: Saddam Hussein, the CIA, and the Origins of America's Invasion of Iraq*. Penguin Press, 2024.
Commander, Cruiser Destroyer Group TWO. *Formal Investigation into the Circumstances Surrounding the Attack on USS Stark (FFG-31) on 17 May 1987*. U.S. Navy, 1987.
Cooper, Tom, Sirous Ebrahimi, and E. R. Hooten. *Iran–Iraq Naval War, Volume 1: Opening Blows September–November 1980*. Helion, 2023.
Cooper, Tom, Sirous Ebrahimi, and E. R. Hooten. *Iran–Iraq Naval War, Volume 2: Convoy Battles, 1981–1984*. Helion, 2024.
Corbett, Julian. *England in the Seven Years War, Volume 1*. Longmans, Green, 1907.
Corbett, Julian. *Some Principles of Maritime Strategy*. Naval Institute Press, 1988.
Cordesman, Anthony H., and Abraham R. Wagner. *The Lessons of Modern War, Volume II: The Iran–Iraq War*. Westview Press, 1990.
Cox, Samuel J. "H-018-1: No Higher Honor—The Road to Operation Praying Mantis, 18 April 1988," *Naval History and Heritage Command*, April 2018.

Cox, Samuel J. "H-020-1: The Fog of War: USS *Vincennes* Tragedy—3 July 1988," *Naval History and Heritage Command*, July 2018.
Crist, David B. "Gulf of Conflict A History of U.S.-Iranian Confrontation at Sea." *Policy Focus* no. 95. Washington Institute for Near East Policy, June 2009.
Crist, David B. "Joint Special Operations in Support of Earnest Will," *Joint Force Quarterly* no. 29 (Autumn–Winter 2001–2002): 19.
Crist, David, B. *The Twilight War: The Secret History of America's Thirty-Year Conflict with Iran.* Penguin Press, 2012.
DeForth, Peter W. "U.S. Naval Presence in the Persian Gulf: The Mideast Force since World War II", *Naval War College Review* 28, no. 4 (Summer 1975): 45–62.
Department of Defense. *Report of the DOD Commission on Beirut International Airport Terrorist Act, October 23, 1983.* Department of Defense, December 20, 1983.
Duffy, Thomas M. "US Naval Actions in the Persian Gulf: An Effective Use of Force?" Unpublished extended essay for MA in War Studies, King's College London, September 1989.
Dunn, Michael. "Hiding Our Gulf Success?" *Washington Times*, September 23, 1988.
Dyer, Gwynne. *War: A Commentary.* Crown Publishers, 1985.
Elkeus, Adam. "Abandon All Hope, Ye Who Enter Here: You Cannot Save the Gray Zone Concept." *War on the Rocks*, December 30, 2015.
Evans, David, Lieutenant Colonel, U.S. Marine Corps (Retired). "Vincennes: A Case Study." *Proceedings* 199, no. 8/1,086, August 1993.
Fisk, Robert. *The Great War for Civilisation: The Conquest of the Middle East.* Knopf, 2005.
Fogarty, William M. Rear Admiral. U.S. Navy. *Formal Investigation into the Circumstances Surrounding the Downing of a Commercial Airliner by the USS Vincennes (CG 49) on 3 July 1988.* U.S. Navy, 1988.
Freedman, Lawrence. *Strategy: A History.* Oxford University Press, 2013.
Friedman, Norman. "The Vincennes Incident." *Proceedings* 115, no. 5/1,035, May 1989.
Friedman, Norman. "West European and NATO Navies." *Proceedings* 114, no. 3/1,021, March 1988.
Gates, Robert. *Duty: Memoirs of a Secretary at War.* Knopf, 2014.
Gross Stein, Janice. "The Wrong Strategy in the Right Place: The United States in the Gulf." *International Security* 13, no. 3 (Winter 1988/89): 142–167.
Handel, Michael. "Corbett, Clausewitz, and Sun Tzu." *Naval War College Review* 53, no. 4, (Autumn 2000): 106–124.
Hattendorf, John B., and Peter M. Swartz. "U.S. Naval Strategy in the 1980s." *Newport Papers*, no. 33. Naval War College Press, 2008.
Helfont, Samuel. "The Gulf War's Afterlife: Dilemmas, Missed Opportunities, and the Post-Cold War Order Undone." *Texas National Security Review* 4, no. 2 (Spring 2021): 82–97.
Heuser, Beatrice. *The Evolution of Strategy.* Cambridge University Press, 2012.
Hoagland, Jim. "How CIA Secret War on Saddam Collapsed." *Washington Post*, June 26, 1997.
Howard, Michael. "The British Way in Warfare: A Reappraisal." In *The Causes of War*. Harvard University Press, 1984.
Howard, Michael. *Captain Professor: A Life in War and Peace.* Continuum, 2006.
Howard, Michael. "The Classical Strategists." In *Studies in War and Peace*. Viking Press, 1971.
Howard, Michael. *Clausewitz: A Very Short Introduction.* Oxford University Press, 2002.
Howard, Michael. "Men against Fire: The Doctrine of the Offensive in 1914." In *Makers of Modern Strategy from Machiavelli to the Nuclear Age*, edited by Peter Paret. Princeton University Press, 1986.
Howard, Michael. "Mistake to Declare This a War." *Royal United Services Institute Journal* 146, no. 6 (December 2001): 1–4.

Howard, Michael. "Reassurance and Deterrence: Western Defense in the 1980s," *Foreign Affairs* 61, no. 2 (Winter 1982/83): 309–324.
Howard, Michael. "The Strategic Approach to International Relations," *British Journal of International Studies* 2, no. 1 (April 1976): 21–30.
Howard, Michael. "The Use and Abuse of Military History." In *The Causes of Wars and Other Essays*, 2nd edition, 188–198. Harvard University Press, 1984.
Howard, Michael. "When Are Wars Decisive?" *Survival* 41, no. 1 (Spring 1999): 126–135.
Hume, Cameron. *The United Nations, Iran, and Iraq: How Peacemaking Changed*. Indiana University Press, 1994.
International Civil Aviation Organization. *Destruction of Iran Airbus A300 in the Vicinity of Qeshm Island, Islamic Republic of Iran on 3 July 1988*: Report of *ICAO Fact-Finding Investigation*. ICAO Document, C-WP/8708, November 1988.
International Court of Justice. *Case Concerning Oil Platforms (Islamic Republic of Iran v. United States of America): Summary of the Judgment of 6 November 2003*.
Khomeini, Ruhollah al-Musavi. "Khomeyni Message on Hajj, UN Resolution 598." LD200716488, read by announcer and signed Ruhollah al-Musavi al-Khomenyni, July 20, 1988 (29/4/67).
Kornbluh, Peter, and Malcom Byrne. *The Iran–Contra Scandal: The Declassified History*. New Press, 1993.
Lambert, Andrew. *The British Way of War: Julian Corbett and the Battle for a National Strategy*. Yale University Press, 2021.
Lehman, John. *Oceans Ventured: Winning the Cold War at Sea*. W. W. Norton, 2018.
Levinson, Jeffrey, and Randy Edwards. *Missile Inbound: The Attack on the Stark in the Persian Gulf*. U.S. Naval Institute, 1997.
Liddell Hart, Basil Henry. *The British Way in Warfare*. Faber and Faber, 1932.
Marolda, Edward J. "The Siege of Wonson," *Naval History Magazine* 37, no. 4 (August 2023): 28–35.
Marolda, Edward J., and Robert Schneller. *Shield and Sword: The United States Navy and the Persian Gulf War*. U.S. Government Reprints Press, 1991.
Marvin, Andrew. "Operation Earnest Will: The U.S. Foreign Policy behind U.S. Naval Operations in the Persian Gulf 1987–89; A Curious Case," *Naval War College Review* 73, no. 2 (Spring 2020): 81–103.
Matthews, Jeffrey J. *Generals and Admirals, Criminals and Crooks*. Notre Dame Press, 2023.
McCranie, Kevin D. *Mahan, Corbett, and the Foundations of Naval Strategic Thought*. Naval Institute Press, 2021.
McNaugher, Thomas. "Walking Tightropes in the Gulf." In *The Iran–Iraq War: Impact and Implications*, edited by Efraim Karsh. Palgrave Macmillan, 1989.
Mearsheimer, John. "A Strategic Misstep: The Maritime Strategy and Deterrence in Europe." *International Security* 11, no. 2 (Fall 1986): 3–57.
Melia, Tamara Moser. *"Damn the Torpedoes": A Short History of U.S. Naval Mine Countermeasures, 1777–1991*. Department of the Navy, Naval Historical Center, 1991.
Mobley, Richard A. "Fighting Iran: Intelligence Support During Operation Earnest Will, 1987–88." *Studies in Intelligence* 60, no. 3 (September 2016).
Mobley, Richard A. "Deterrence Without Escalation: Fresh Insights into U.S. Decision-making During Operation Earnest Will," *Joint Force Quarterly* 106 (July 2022).
Mobley, Richard A. "London and Washington Maintaining Naval Cooperation Despite Strategic Differences During Operation Earnest Will," *Naval War College Review* 74, no. 2 (Spring 2021). https://digital-commons.usnwc.edu/nwc-review/vol74/iss2/9.
Morris, James. *Farewell the Trumpets: An Imperial Retreat*. Harvest/HBJ, 1978.

National Commission on Terrorist Attacks Upon the United States. *The 9/11 Commission Report: Final Report of the National Commission on Terrorist Attacks Upon the United States.* 2004.

National Security Council. *National Security Decision-54: Responding to Iraqi Aggression in the Gulf.* January 15, 1991.

Naval Postgraduate School Weekly Media Report, February, 9–15, 2021.

Navias, Martin S. and E. R. Hooton. *Iran–Iraq Naval War, Volume 1: Opening Blows September–November 1980.* Helion, 2023.

Navias, Martin S., and E. R. Hooton. *Tanker Wars: Assault on Merchant Shipping During the Iran–Iraq Crisis, 1980–88.* I.B. Tauris, 1996.

Office of the Chief of Naval Operations, *The United States Navy in "Desert Shield"/ "Desert Storm."* Ser OO/lU500179. Washington, D.C. May 15, 1991.

O'Brian, Patrick. *The Fortune of War.* W. W. Norton and Company, 1991.

O'Rourke, Ronald. "Gulf Ops," *Proceedings* 115, no. 5/1,035, May 1989.

O'Rourke, Ronald. "The Maritime Strategy and the Next Decade," *Proceedings* 114, no. 4/1,022, April 1988.

O'Rourke, Ronald. "The Tanker War," *Proceedings* 114, no. 5/1,023, May 1988.

Palmer, Michael A. *Guardians of the Gulf.* Free Press, 1992.

Palmer, Michael A. *On Course to Desert Storm: The United States Navy and the Persian Gulf.* Contributions to Naval History, no. 5. U.S. Navy Historical Center, 1992.

van der Peet, Anselm J. *De Koninklijke Marine en multinationale vlootoperaties 1945 (Out of Area. The RNLN and Multinational Fleet Operations 1945).* PhD Thesis, Utrecht University, Franeker, Van Wijnen, 2016.

Perkins III, J. B., Captain., U.S. Navy. "The Surface View: Operation Praying Mantis," *Proceedings* 115, no. 5/1,035, May 1989.

Phillips, Stephen. "A Poisoned Chalice: The U.S. Navy in the Persian Gulf, 1987–1988." PhD Dissertation for the Department of War Studies, King's College London.

Picco, Giandomenico. *Man Without a Gun: One Diplomat's Secret Struggle to Free the Hostages, Fight Terrorism, and End a War.* Crown, 1999.

Pollack, Kenneth M. *Arabs at War: Military Effectiveness, 1948–1991.* Council on Foreign Relations Book. University of Nebraska Press, 2002.

Porter, M. E. "What Is Strategy?" *Harvard Business Review* 74, no. 6 (1996): 61–78.

Powell, Colin, with Josphe Persico. *My American Journey.* Random House, 1995.

Ramazani, R. K. *The Gulf Cooperation Council: Record and Analysis.* University Press of Virginia, 1988.

Rayburn, Joel D., Colonel, and Colonel Frank K. Sobchak. *The US Army in the Iraq War, Volume 2: Surge and Withdrawal 2007–2011.* Strategic Studies Institute and U.S. Army War College Press, 2019.

Reagan, Ronald. "Address to the Nation on the Venice Economic Summit, Arms Control, and the Deficit." June 15, 1987.

Rumsfeld, Donald. *Known and Unknown: A Memoir.* Sentinel, 2011.

Scales, Robert H., Jr., Brigadier General, Director Desert Storm Study Project. *Certain Victory.* Washington, D.C. Office of the Chief of Staff, United States Army, 1993.

Schurman D. M. *The Education of a Navy: The Development of British Naval Strategic Thought, 1867–1914.* Cassell, 1965.

Senate Committee on Armed Services, U.S. Military Forces to Protect Reflagged Kuwait Oil Tankers. S.Hrg. 100–269, 100th Cong., 1st sess., June 5, 11, 16, 1987.

Sharp, RADM Grant, U.S. Navy. *Formal Investigation into the Circumstances Surrounding the Attack on USS Stark (FFG-31) on 17 May 1987.* Report 5102 Ser00/S-0487, June 12, 1987.

Shultz, George P. *Turmoil and Triumph: My Years as Secretary of State.* Scribners, 1993.

El-Shazly, Nadia El-Sayed. *The Gulf Tanker War: Iran and Iraq's Maritime Swordplay*. Palgrave Macmillan, 1998.
Sheehan, Neil. *The Arnheiter Affair*. Random House, 1971.
Sick, Gary. *All Fall Down: America's Tragic Encounter with Iran*. Authors Guild, 2001.
Stoker, Donald. "Everything You Think You Know About Limited War is Wrong." *War on the Rocks*, December 22, 2016.
Stoker, Donald. *Why America Loses Wars*. Cambridge University Press, 2022.
Stoker, Donald and Craig Whiteside. "Blurred Lines: Gray-Zone Conflict and Hybrid War—Two Failures of American Strategic Thinking," *Naval War College Review* 73, no. 1 (2020): 12–48.
Strachan, Hew. *The Direction of War: Contemporary Strategy in Historical Perspective*. Cambridge University Press, 2013.
Strachan, Hew. "The Lost Meaning of Strategy," *Survival* 47, no. 3, 2005: 33–54.
Strachan, Hew. "Michael Howard and the Dimensions of Military History." Annual Liddell Hart Centre for Military Archives Lecture, King's College London, December 3, 2002.
Strachan, Hew. "Strategy in Theory; Strategy in Practice," *Journal of Strategic Studies* 42, no. 2 (2019): 171–190.
Strachan, Hew. "Strategy in the Twenty-First Century." In *The Changing Character of War*, edited by Hew Strachan and Sibylle Scheipers. Oxford University Press, 2011.
Takeyh, Ray. "The Iran–Iraq War: A Reassessment," *Middle East Journal* (Summer 2010): 365–383.
Tangredi, Sam, Captain, U.S. Navy, Retired. "Jointness Versus Strategy: How Joint Ideology Distorts U.S. National Security." *Proceedings* 148, no. 6/1,432, June 2022.
Thatcher, Margaret. *The Downing Street Years*. HarperCollins, 1993.
Till, Geoffrey. *Seapower: A Guide for the Twenty-First Century*. 4th edition. Routledge, 2018.
Truver, Scott C. "Mines of Aug.t: An International Whodunit," *Proceedings* 111, no. 5/987, May 1985.
Truver, Scott C. "Writing U.S. Naval Operational History 1980–2010: U.S. Navy Mine Countermeasures in Terror and War." In *Needs and Opportunities in the Modern History of the U.S. Navy*, edited by Michael J. Crawford. U.S. Naval History and Heritage Command, 2018.
UN Security Council. Further report of the Secretary-General on the implementation of Security Council resolution 598 (1987), December 9, 1991. S/23373.
UN Security Council. Letter dated 11 August 1987 from the Permanent Representative of the Islamic Republic of Iran to the United Nations addressed to the Secretary-General, August 11, 1987. S/19031.
UN Security Council. Letter dated 22 September 1987 from the Acting Permanent Representative of the United States of America to the United Nations addressed to the President of the Security Council. September 22, 1987. S/19149.
UN Security Council. Letter dated 9 October 1987 from the Permanent Representative of the United States of America to the United Nations addressed to the President of the Security Council. October 8, 1987. S/19194.
UN Security Council. Official Record, 1610th meeting, December 9, 1971. S_PV.1610.
UN Security Council. Provisional verbatim record of the 2750th meeting, held at Headquarters, New York, July 20, 1987. S/PV.2750.
UN Security Council. Provisional verbatim record of the 2818th meeting, held at Headquarters, New York, July 14, 1988. S/PV.2818.
UN Security Council. UNSCR 598 (1987).
U.S. Congress. *Iraq Liberation Act of 1988*. H.R. 4655, 105th Congress (1997–1998).
U.S. Naval History and Heritage *Command history of Admiral Stark and the USS Stark* (FFG-31) 1982-1999.

Vistica, Gregory L. *Fall from Glory: The Men Who Sank the U.S. Navy.* Simon & Schuster, 1996.
Vlahos, Michael. "The Stark Report," *Proceedings* 114, no. 5/1023, May 1988.
Walker, George K. "The Tanker War, 1980–1988: Law and Policy," *International Law Studies* 74 (2000): 33–105.
Warden, John, Colonel. "The Enemy as a System." *Airpower Journal* 9, no. 2 (Spring 1995): 40–55.
Watkins, James D. Admiral, U.S. Navy. "The Maritime Strategy," *Proceedings* 112, no. 1/995 (January 1986): Supplement.
Webb Jr., James H., Captain., U.S. Marine Corps (Retired). Oral History Transcript. Quantico, VA: History Division, U.S. Marine Corps, 2021.
Weinberger, Caspar. *Fighting for Peace: Seven Critical Years in the Pentagon.* Penguin, 1990.
Weinberger, Caspar. "The Uses of Military Power." Remarks prepared for delivery by the Hon. Caspar W. Weinberger, Secretary of Defense to the National Press Club, Washington, D.C., November 28, 1984.
Weinberger, Secretary of Defense Caspar W. "A Report to the Congress on Security Arrangements in the Persian Gulf," June 15, 1987.
Wellesley, Arthur, First Duke of Wellington. *The Dispatches of Field Marshal the Duke of Wellington, K.G.: France and the Low Countries, 1814–1815.* John Murray, 1838.
Wills, Steve. *Strategy Shelved: The Collapse of Cold War Naval Strategic Planning.* Naval Institute Press, 2021.
Winkler, David. *Amirs, Admirals, and Desert Sailors: Bahrain, the US Navy, and the Arabian Gulf.* Naval Institute Press, 2007.
Woods, Kevin. IDA Paper P-4217 Iraqi Perspectives Project Phase II Um Al-Ma'arik (The Mother of All Battles): *Operational and Strategic Insights from an Iraqi Perspective Volume 1.* Revised May 2008.
Wouk, Herman. *The Caine Mutiny.* Dell, 1951.
Wright, Robin. *In the Name of God: The Khomeini Decade.* Touchstone Publications, 1990.
Zatarain, Lee Allen. *Tanker War: America's First Conflict with Iran, 1987–88.* Casemate Publishers, 2008.

Index

Italicized page numbers indicate maps, tables, or texts; **bolded** page numbers indicate photographs.

Abu Musa Island, 18, 33, 60, 66, *79*, 87, **88**, 90, 94, 105, 107
AEGIS Weapons System, 107, 108, 112, 114, 117
Afghanistan, 9, 10, 11, 13, 30, 36, 60, 124, 131, 134, 154, 161, 163, 167
AH-6 helicopter, 61, 67
Albright, Madeleine, 9
Algiers Accord, 19
Airborne Mine Counter-Measures (AMCM), 60
AN/SPG-51C/D shipborne fire control radar, 90
AN/SPG-55 shipborne fire control radar, 56
Anita (offshore supply vessel), 65, 129
Armacost, Michael, 50
Armilla Patrol, 34, 124, 129
Armitage, Richard, 47
Arnheiter, Marcus Aurelius, 109
auxiliary propulsion unit (APU), 83, 84

Bacon, Francis, 157
Bahrain, 20, 30, 35, 37, 39, 42–44, 66, 68, 69, 71, 83, 86, 10, 111, 115, 123, 137, 158
Baker, James, 9
Bandar Abbas, *38*, 54, *55*, 64, 76, *79*, 86, **88**, 91, 92, 94, 95, 108, 113, *116*
Beirut, 17–18, 30, 47, 48, 65, 124, 148, 149, 153, 155, 157
Bernsen, Harold, 29, 57, 67, 76, 76, 77, 144, 194
bin Ladin, Osama, 47, 138

Black Monday, 80
Blinken, Antony 163, 164
Boghammar (Iranian speedboat), 56, 71, 72, 90, 91, 96
Bridgeton (tanker), 53, 54, 57, 60, 65, 66, 81, 126
Brodie, Bernard, 5
burden sharing, 58, 59, 124, 125, 127, 128, *133*, 137
Bush, George H. W., 8, 9, 30, 68, 117
Bush, George W., 31

Caine Mutiny, The, 46, 119
Carlucci, Frank, 27, 68, 86, 94, 97
Carrington, NATO Secretary General Lord, 125
Carter, Jimmy, 13, 30
Carter Doctrine, 13, 134
China, 4, 11, 15, 19, 24, 26, 33, 100, 159, 161, 164, 165
choke points, 13, 53, 72
Clausewitz, Carl von, 4, 5, 6, 7, 19, 48, 52, 53, 68, 94, 141, 146, 148, 155, 156, 158, 160, 161, 164
Cold War, 1, 2, 3, 4, 13, 15, 27, 28, 46, 58, 60, 99, 100, 101, 103, 125, 137, 139, 145, 157, 160, 161
command of the sea, 7, 157, 159
Congress, United States, 9, 18, 31, 46, 62, 132, 142, 149, 150, 152
Continentalist, 16, 160, 162
Corbett, Julian, **4**, 5, 7, 19, 57, 144, 146, 156, 159, 160, 161, 162, 164, 166
Crist, David, 16, 52
Crist, George, 76, 86, 155
Crowe, William, 86, 94, 108, 111, 115, 117, 127, 135, 155

Davos, 1
deterrence, 29, 48, 57, 58, 63, 76, 77, 86, 104, 112, 132, 144, 145, 146, 153
Doctrine of the Offensive, 66
Downey, Congressman Thomas, 31
Dual Containment, 154
Duke of Wellington, 141, 142, 146
Dyer, Gwynne, 27, 87, 213

East of Suez, 14, 35, 123, 134, 186
Eekelen, W. F. van, 123, 130
Explosive Ordnance Disposal (EOD), 60, 68, 80, 131, 139
Exocet (missile), 23, 24, 27, 30, 39, 40, 41, 42, 91, 113

Farsi Island, 57, 71
FFG-7, 36–37, 54, 56, 67, 72, 77, 82, 84, 90, 91, 95, 108
Fisher, Jackie, 53, 156
Fisk, Robert, 39, 66
Fitzwater, Marlin, 73
Freedman, Lawrence, 2
Friedman, Norman, 114

Gas Prince (tanker), 53, 63
Goldwater-Nichols, 62, 159, 161, 162, 163, 166
Gorbachev, Mikhail, 105
gray zone, 5, 6
Gulf Cooperation Council (GCC), 20, 137, 138, 139
Gulf of Oman, 29, 49, 53, 65, 74, 128, 130, 135

Handel, Michael, 7
Harpoon (missile), 15, 41, 91, **93**, 94, 95
Harvard Business Review, 2
Hercules (barge), 61, 71, 72
Heuser, Beatrice, 2
Hezbollah, 16, 17, 154
High Level Week, UNGA, 69
Howard, Michael, 2–5, 58, 156
Houthis, 73, 154
Hume, Cameron, 102, 105, 119
Hussein, Saddam, 8, 9, 19, 20, 21, 23, 25, 47, 100, 101, 103, 107, 137, 139
hybrid warfare, 6

Identify-Friend-or-Foe (IFF), 110
International Civil Aeronautics Organization (ICAO), 113, 114
International Court of Justice (ICJ), 75, 76
Indian Ocean, 13, 14, 34, 123, 134
Iran
  as a continental power, 7, 8, 155
  as a potential land target, 10, 63, 76, 86, 153, 155
  as target of Operation *Staunch*, 16, 18
  Iranian Revolution, 13, 15, 16, 19–21, 49, 50, 66, 77, 82, 119, 120, 137, 153, 158
  U.S. relations with, 13, 15, 16, 35, 36, 50, 60, 74, 76, 77, 96, 101–3, 117–19 125, 132, 144, 147, 154, 155
  views on control of the Persian Gulf, 15–16, 123, 158
  war aims of, 20, 23, 25, 57, 65, 66, 70–71, 75, 82, 103, 142, 150, 157–59
Iran Air Flight 655, 109, 111, 113–15, *116*, 117, 118, 119, **120**
Iran Ajr (Iranian Navy ship), 66–70, **67**, **70**, 103, 131
Iran-Contra, 10, 18, 21, 31, 100, 101, 142
Iran–Iraq War, 1, 11, 13, 16, 18–21, 26–29, 31, 36, 46, 60, 63, 65, 70, 99, 100, 104, 117, 121, 124, 131, 140, 142, 146, 147, 153, 156, 157
Iranian Revolutionary Guard Corp Navy (IRGCN), 51, 87, 89, 92, 93, 107, 108, 117, 127
Iraq, 7–9, 11, 14, 16, 21–25, 30, 35, 39, 46, 47, 81, 96, 106, 107
Iraq Liberation Act, 9

joint approach/force/strategy, 36, 62, 63, 67, 159, 160, 161, 162, 166
Joint Chiefs of Staff (CJCS), 68, 86, 149
Joint Task Force Middle East (JTFME), 62, 83, 86, 90, 109, 110, 111, 112, 114, 115, 155
Jones, John Paul, 33, 109
Joshan (Iranian Navy ship), 91, 92, 83, 95

Kelso, Frank, 1, 2, 45, 108
Khamenei, Ali, 67, 69, 74, 75, 119
Kharg Island, 23

Khomeini, Ruhollah, 10, 19, 20, 52, 56, 99, 107, 119, 120, 121, 141, 147
Khor Fakkan, 64, 65, 66, 82, 128
Kuwait, 8, 9, 20, 22, 25–30, 47, 52, 57, 61, 71–73, 100, 104, 105, 127, 135, 137, 157

Larak Island, 23
Lebanon, 16, 17, 18, 74, 100, 112, 114, 126, 154
Lehman, John, 157
Less, Anthony, 83, 86, 91, 109, 155
Liddell Hart, Basil Henry, 156
limited and unlimited wars, 4, 6–10, 17, 19–21, 23, 29, 47, 48, 63, 76, 86, 154, 159–64
limited liability, 61, 62, 138, 139, 156, 162, 163
Little Bird (MH-6 helicopter), 61, 67, 72
Locarno, 150
Lyons, James, 62, 63, 155

MacArthur, Douglas 150, 162, 215–16
Mahan, Alfred Thayer, 144, 167
Manavi, Abdollah 51, 82, 94
maritime strategy, 1, 4, 6, 7, 10, 53, 144–46, 155, 156, 161, 166
Maritime Strategy, The, 59, 145, 146, 155, 160
Matter of Accountability, A, 45
McCranie, Kevin, 7
Mine Counter Measures (MCM), 58–60, 127, 135
Middle Shoals buoy, 71, 72, *143*
MIDEASTFOR (Middle East Force), 29, 34, 35, 43, 49, 57, 61, 67, 71, 135
mines, 50–53, **52**, 57, 59–61, 64–68, **70**, 82–84, 86, 103, 129, 131, 132, 147, 157, 159
minesweepers, 58–61, 63, 65, 68, 105, 123, 124, 126–31, 133, 135, 138, 139, 142, 154
Mirage (fighter jet), 27, 39, 142
Mk III patrol boats, 27, 39, 142

NATO, 13, 58–60, 125–28, 130, 131, 134, 136, 137, 155
Naval Gunfire Support, 17

Nicaragua, 10
Nixon Doctrine, 14
North Arabian Sea, 34, 36, 49, 54, 64, 78, 89

Oakley, Phyllis, 73
O'Brian, Patrick, 165
On War, 4, 5
Operation *Calendar II*, 130
Operation *Desert Storm*, 8, 9, 20, 31, 34, 49, 61, 63, 68, 138, 154, 160, 161, 162
Operation *Eagle Claw*, 36
Operation *Enduring Freedom*, 9
Operation *Iraqi Freedom*, 9, 63, 154
Operation *Nimble Archer*, 73–76, 78, *79*, 80, 86, 89, 111, 141, 142
Operation *Octopus*, 130
Operation *Praying Mantis*, 75, 87, *88*, 90, 91, **94**, 95, 96, 97, 106, 111, 136, 141, 152
Operation *Prime Chance*, 61, 71
Operation *Private Jewels*, 29
Operation *Window of Opportunity*, 63
operational level of war, 3, 6, 8, 64, 99, 160–63, 166, 167

Palestinine Liberation Organization (PLO), 17
Palmer, Michael, 30, 35, 87
Passchendaele, 66
Pax Britannica, 162
peace dividend, 2, 160
Perez de Cuellar, Javier, 100, 119
Phoenix (AIM-54 missile), 16, 21
Picco, Giandomenico, 100
Pompeo, Michael, 164
Powell, Colin, 68, 108, 149, 153, 162

Qasr-e-Shirin, 19

Rafsanjani, Hashemi, 105, 107, 119
Rakhish Oil Platform, 90
Rashadat Oil Platform, 74, 76, 78, 80, 90
Reagan, Ronald, 10, 13, 22, 27, 30, 31, 46, 48, 50, 63, 69, 74, 76, 78, 87, 96, 100, 117, 145, 148, 153, 154, 158
retaliation, 18, 22, 23, 40, 50, 73, 75–76, 81, 97, 112, 132, 146
Revolutionary Guard, 15, 24, 47, 50, 52, 56
Rhineland, 148, 150

Richardson, Elliot, 104
Rinn, Paul, 82–86
Rules of Engagement (ROE), 21, 48, 82, 92, 110–12, 136, 157
Rogers, William, 108–12, 114–17
Rostam Oil Platform, 71, 76, 78
Royal Navy, 5, 35, 53, 124, 125, 129, 130, 132, 142

Sabalan (Iranian Navy ship), 51, 82, 86, **87**, 89, 91–95
Sahand (Iranian Navy ship), 82, 93, **94**, 95
Sandinistas, 10
Sassan Oil Platform, 86–90
Saudi Arabia, 14, 20, 22, 25, 35, 39, 61–64, 71, 72, 89, 97, 100, 106, 123, 137–39, 154, 158
Sea Isle City (tanker), 66, 72, **73**, 74, 76, 78, 80, 81, 86, 95
seapower, 4, 11, 62, 144, 155, 161, 166, 167
Shatt al-Arab, 19, 20, 23, **35**
Shultz, George, 27, 101, **102**, 104, 126, 127
Sick, Gary, 16
Silkworm (missile), 24, 25, **26**, 27, 50, 52, 53, 56, 64, 72, 73–75, 81, 86, 94, 95, 107, 108, 142, 153
Sirri Oil Platform, 86, 87
SM-1, 40, 41, 56, 86, 90, 91, **92**, 95
SM-2, 56, 92, 114, **115**
Special Operations Forces (SOF), 61, 67, 71, 95
Somalia, 47, 69, 131
Somme, 66
Special Boat Units (SBUs), 61
Special Operations Executive (SOE), 61
Stinger (missile), 71, 72, 130
Strachan, Hew, 2, 6, 144, 149, 150
Strait of Hormuz, 14, 18, 23, 29, 50, 53, 54, 56, 64, 74, 78, 86, 87, **88**, 91, 95, 97, 107, 124, 128, 134
strategic level of war, 6, 8, 64, 161, 166
Suez (1956 intervention), 14
Sullivan, Jake, 163, 164
Super Étendard (aircraft), 14, 17
Syria, 22, 74

Taiwan, 161–63
Taliban, 10, 159

Tangredi, Sam, 161
terrorism, 9
Texaco Caribbean (tanker), 65, 128
Thatcher, Margaret, 117, 128, 129, 142
Thucydides, 47
Till, Geoffrey, 16, 155, 156
Total Quality Leadership (TQL), 2
Tunb, 14
Turkey, 22
Twin Pillars policy, 14, 35, 154

United Arab Emirates (UAE), 14, 63, 65, 90, 97, 137
Ukraine, 1, 3, 4
United Nations, 69, 99, 101, 102, 103, 104, 105, 123, 129, 164, 166
UNSCR 598, 29, 69, 99–106, 107, 118, 19, 120, 121, 136, 141, 142, 146, 147, 153, *175–77*, 201
UN Secretary General, 14, 100, 119
UN Security Council, 26, 29, 31, 69, 76, 99, 100, 101, **102**, 103, 104, 105, 107, 117, **118**, 119, 130, 139
United Nations Security Council Resolution (UNSCR), 16, 28, 31, 99, 100, 105
U.S. Coast Guard, 27
USS *Bon Homme Richard*, 33
USS *Cole*, 34
USS *Constellation*, 54
USS *Guadalcanal*, **54**, 60, 68, 69
USS *La Salle*, 35, 36, 37, **43**, 67, 68
USS *Maine*, 33
USS *Panay*, 33
USS *Pueblo*, 43, 44, 45, 46, 155
USS *Reuban James*, 33
USS *Samuel B. Roberts*, 82–85, **84**, **85**, 86, 106, 110, 131, 142
USS *Stark*, 27, 28, 30, 34, 36–45, *38*, **42**, **43**, **44**, 46–50, 52, 54, 56, 58, 65, 78, 85, 91, 100, 110, 112, 113, 115, 135, 142, 152, 165
USS *Thach*, 72, 78, 80
USS *Vincennes*, 96, 97, 106, 107, 108–16, **109**, **115**, *116*, 119, 120, 132, 142, 153

Vance, Cyrus, 104
Velayati, Ali Akbar, 117, **118**, 119
Versailles, 150

Viet Cong, 159
Vietnam, 14, 17, 47, 59, 65, 81, 87, 109, 126, 134, 151, 153, 159
visit/board/search/seizure, 23, 24, 25, 97, 110

War Powers Act, 30, 31, 142
ways and means, 6, 8, 10, 58, 72
Weapons of Mass Destruction, 9
Webb, James, 66, 126, 138, 147, **151**, 152, 153, 156, 157

Weinberger, Caspar, 18, 28, 65, 68, 86, 125, 127, 129, 141, 147, **151**, 152, 153, 156, 158
Weinberger Doctrine, 147–50
Wills, Steve, 160, 161
Wimbrown VII (barge), 61
Wonsan, 51
World Economic Forum, 1
World War I, 3, 5, 7, 19, 20, 51, 66, 156, 162, 166